SURVIVAL
&
GROWTH
Management Strategies for the Small Firm

SURVIVAL & GROWTH

Management Strategies for the Small Firm

THEODORE COHN
ROY A. LINDBERG

amacom
A Division of American Management Associations

Library of Congress Cataloging in Publication Data

Cohn, Theodore.
  Survival & growth.

  1. Small business—Management.   I. Lindberg, Roy A.,
joint author.   II. Title.
HD69.S6C65   658'.022   73-92163
ISBN 0-8144-5359-7

© 1974 AMACOM

A division of American Management Associations, New York.
All rights reserved. Printed in the United States of America.

First printing

PREFACE

THIS IS A BOOK for managers in companies with annual sales below $25 million who wish to improve the performance of their firms or to keep them healthy as they grow. At present it does not strain a firm's resources to stay alive, though launching a firm can be a considerable strain. Industrial society is quite tolerant of mediocrity and seldom drives out of business a firm that does not strive to excel. But to improve the performance of a small firm without making it larger, or to keep it alive while it is growing, is another matter. Those are significant accomplishments. Attainment of them requires much understanding of the conditions, advantages, and limitations of being small as well as the relevance of those factors to company size.

Small firms are not infantile versions of large ones, even though the two have much in common. True, both have to provide products or services that customers want, face competition, meet payrolls, observe laws, and so on. But a close look reveals differences other than the scale of their activities that tie back to their size. In other words, size differences occasion features or conditions unique to each size of company. As a company gets bigger it takes on new problems and brings some established problems to an end.

If it is true that small and large firms have different problems, then what managers in small companies should spend their time on differs from what managers in large companies should spend it on. A leading aim of this book is to provide guidelines for the use of managerial time in small firms. It is probable that no single excellence is more closely tied to superior performance in business than that of executive time usage, and in one way or another the whole of this book is a guide to what managers in small firms should spend their time on.

Few views are more widely held in American business than that there will always be a place for small business and that small businesses have natural advantages. Though probably true, these views tend to create a false sense of security in managers of small businesses and obscure the fact that small firms are getting a declining share of the gross national income. Managers in small firms need to be periodically reminded that being small offers no special protection against corporate failure.

That smaller companies are finding it increasingly difficult to maintain consistent profits and even survive as the technological and competitive pace intensifies is shown by the fact that since World War II the rise in sales volume of small firms has trailed far behind the rise in volume of the biggest firms and the profit margins of small firms have been lower than those of larger firms. Those are only two pieces of evidence in a picture of markets being dominated increasingly by large companies and competition intensifying between small companies for what's left. The automotive, beer, and appliance industries are examples of what has happened to markets that once were dominated by small firms. Of the thousands of firms that built cars or brewed beer or made appliances only a small fraction remain, and most of those are now large companies.

Thus the world of small business has changed markedly in recent years. But even greater changes are in the offing. Identifying and dealing positively with change are basic to the survival and profitability of small companies. This book is an effort to contribute to an understanding of the nature of the changes, of ways to cope with them, and of ways to turn them to the small firm's advantage. Perhaps such an understanding will help reduce the turnover among small firms, which now is significantly higher than among large businesses.

There are two prerequisites to achieving that understanding: one is to become disentangled from the many misconceptions that exist about small business, and the second is to learn the constraints and advantages of being small. Neither will be easily accomplished. Each reader comes to the book quite thoroughly conditioned, and it is likely that some of the statements made in this book about the differences between large and small firms will go contrary to these closely held opinions or sensibilities. But perhaps these pages will stimulate in each reader a new idea or two about the role and place of small business.

The chances of that happening will be best if, in going through the book, the reader makes a special effort to put aside whatever he thinks he knows about advantages or disadvantages of being small. Many such opinions are more attitudinal than factual and are not essential to the inquiry at hand. Essential to the inquiry are agreements on the characteristics of small firms realistic enough to provide a basis for comparison with the characteristics of large firms. Not that the differences are of great interest in themselves; they are of interest primarily because they cast light on how a small firm should be managed.

As is inevitable in books on small business, the question of what constitutes a small company must be settled. There are many definitions. For our purposes the small firm is defined as having $1 million to $25 million in annual sales volume whereas large companies are defined as being at least ten times bigger than the largest small firm—that is, having $250 million and more in sales. The observations made of small firms in the text will be most applicable to those between $5 million and $10 million in size. Firms below $1 million in sales but moving to that level should find some guidelines to help them in handling the new problems they will face.

Some authorities, such as Drucker, point to the shortcomings of defining a business as small or large on the basis of dollar volume alone. They have every justification in the interest of precision for doing so. But in a general treatise, such as this, it is impractical to define smallness in any way other than annual sales volume. Most firms that are truly small will be swept within the classification. Inclusion of the few firms doing a hundred million or more that are directed by a single top-level decision maker or that in other ways meet the standards of small business set down by authorities on the subject would not materially change the authors' findings. The authors have worked with such companies, and do not feel that the definition they have adopted in this case strains the conclusions they have reached.

The decision to concentrate on firms in the $1 million to $25 million range is based on the authors' experience. We feel that below $1 million in sales, companies require operating skills but not a great deal of management skill. The number of employees is usually so small that pronounced organizational differentiation is rare.

Above $1 million, differentiation begins to be clear and the need for a separate, distinctive administration emerges. At the $5 million level the differentiations have become almost universal and the need has become very clear indeed. The next threshold of organizational change is somewhere around $25 million, and—because it entails the next generation of management practices—that marks the point at which a company moves out of the small firm category.

The foregoing definition of small size does not, of course, accord with common understanding. Most of the concerns in the country have fewer than 100 employees, and people tend to think of a company as small that has less than this number. The companies that would be classed as small according to the authors' standards would include many with more than 100 employees. It is the authors' choice, however, and our definition places no great strain on any available size-related information.

In the interest of clarification, the book is not greatly concerned with the forces at work in the general business environment and their differential impact on companies. These forces—economic, technological, social, legislative—are generally well known. Features of businesses not much affected by variations in size, such as accounting and financial reporting, are not discussed either. Instead, the book deals as specifically as possible with what we see to be the major *differences* between the way small and large businesses are run or should be run.

Another point worth noting is that the book doesn't adhere to standard administrative analysis. For one thing, the functional approach to management is scarcely honored in these pages. Planning, for example, is not kept intact, but is spread under a number of headings. For another, several activities usually dealt with as unitary fields, such as marketing, are partitioned among several chapters with entirely different thrusts. The breakdowns chosen by the authors are not damaging to any essential condition of understanding. Externalization and rationalization, to pick two terms of the classification employed in this book, seem to be as useful in building understanding of the management process (in small business at least) as the traditional planning, organizing, directing, coordinating, and controlling approach.

As in all similar works, what follows is a mixture of facts and assumptions. The assumptions, given in the form of propositions, are these:

1. To survive and prosper, small companies must differ from large companies in their behavioral patterns.
2. The critical difference lies in rigorously exploiting the advantages available to small companies alone.

3. The leading advantage in being small is the capacity to achieve levels of productivity beyond the reach of large companies.
4. Attaining those levels requires that small firms operate differently from large firms and serve different markets. To do so with success requires a degree of integration far beyond the powers of large firms.
5. Achieving a high level of integration requires an individual with company-centered motivation, a flair for the unusual, and organizational skill.
6. Such a person can operate with greater effect in a small firm than in a large one.

In addition to the foregoing, there are several premises that relate to all businesses that bear on the perspectives of this book:

1. Managing is an enormously complex and demanding job.
2. Corporate performance hangs on the quality of the decisions made, particularly as they impinge on marketing, worker performance, and costs.
3. The quality of decision making depends upon the knowledge and motives of the decision makers.

We are indebted to a number of friends and business associates for their assistance in producing the book. Among them we are especially grateful to Jerry Farmer of J. K. Lasser & Company; Frank Goodman of Tappins Inc.; Arthur L. Hammond, formerly of C. R. Daniels Inc.; William A. Hoffman Jr. of Hoffman International, Inc.; George Kaye of the Felsway Corporation; Gerald LeBoff of Acme Rivett Machine Corporation; Alfred W. Roberts III of Arthur Young & Company; Alfred Ronald of the Erlee Manufacturing Corporation; and Samuel Shapiro of the Linen Supply Association of America.

For her constant enthusiasm and perceptive watching over of the manuscript, we are particularly grateful to Irene Graf.

—Theodore Cohn
Roy A. Lindberg

CONTENTS

I

THE SPECIAL CHARACTER
OF SMALL FIRMS

THERE ARE SUBSTANTIVE differences between small and large firms that
are not confined to differences in scale. Needless to say, small firms
have fewer vendors, employees, and customers as well as smaller production runs and sales territories. But there are also size-related differences that, in turn, cause differences in the way things are accomplished.

We know of few studies in the business field that are related particularly to the question of size-related differences.* But there are two
schools of thought on the subject. One is made up of those who take
the view that anyone who can manage one kind of company can manage any other kind. The other is made up of those who deny that
there can be a universal management discipline.

The view taken here lies somewhere in between. The *language
and concepts* of management are regarded as universal; without them,
communication and understanding in the field would be impossible.
But management *practices* cannot be the same in enterprises that are
radically different in size. This view is supported by the experience of a
financially distressed manufacturing company that had merged with a
much larger company. A vice president tells what happened when
personnel were brought in from the larger company to help straighten
things out. "Organization, systems, and procedures," he said, "were radically changed to conform with those of our new partner, but things

* See Theodore Cohn and Roy A. Lindberg, *How Management Is Different
in Small Companies.* New York: AMA, 1972.

1

went from bad to worse and had to be changed back. Something of the new survived, to be sure, but most was thrown out. Those people were great in their big company, but they didn't know how to do business in a smaller company."

For years people have been saying that if you know management, you can manage anything. But the fact is that management is universal only as a class name, not as it is applied. Specifically, if success in small business consists in powerful exploitation of the advantages of being small, it is in the exploitation of *differences,* and differences cannot be treated in a common fashion. Thus, in order to offset the competitive advantages of largeness, small firms must manage their activities with different emphasis and toward different results than large firms.

To talk meaningfully about how managerial activities should differ in large and small firms requires some knowledge about the general characteristics of each. The characteristics that generally distinguish small firms from large are:

> Greater identification of employees with the firm.
> Shortened distance between topmost and lowest levels.
> Greater centralization of decision making.
> Shorter cycles.
> Shortened feedback time.
> Greater difficulty in attracting funds for expansion.
> More reluctance about risk taking.
> Higher labor/investment ratio.
> Greater concern with financial matters.
> Greater owner influence.
> More product-dedicated.
> More one-person domination.
> Lower employee turnover.
> Longer tenure at all levels of employment.
> Less sharing of decision making.
> Decisions tend to be more reactive than innovative.
> Decisions are more subjective (less based on analysis).
> Less organizational differentiation.
> Commitments are narrower in scope.

It should be noted that a number of familiar small business descriptions are missing from the list, such as faster pace of decision making and greater flexibility and responsiveness. These descriptions have been omitted because they are at variance with experience and are part of the mythology that burdens American business.

Some of the listed items are self-evident and need little discussion. But all of them have important implications for the management of small firms, and all should be carefully examined to see what they offer as guides.

The item "more reluctance about risk taking" seems to be factual. The nature of most small firms' origins—arising as they often do out of the gamble of one or two men—militates against the taking of risks again. There is something about the fear-wracked period of seeing whether a venture will survive that turns the mind against a repetition of the experience. That is why most small firms become conservative about risk after they become successfully established.

The item "more product-dedicated" is intended to show that small firms are likely to be dominated by the things they make or the services they render. Of course, small firms are not altogether product-dedicated, but they do tend to be more so than large businesses, as evidenced by the fact that small firms usually find it less easy to shift from what they now produce to something radically different. For example, if they turn out screw machine products, they do not easily go into casting, assembly, cutting, or shearing activities. Small firms are usually product-intensive in the sense that we speak of conglomerates as being sensitive to the use of capital. Small companies stick more with the product that launched them, while conglomerates change more often and more radically because they are more conscious of return on investment.

Being product-intensive, small firms tie their objectives much more closely to the product line than to other matters, such as the use of capital. A strategy for using capital to achieve a desired rate of return is unusual in small companies. More commonly, investment decisions are based on a product-related factor.

As to cycles, nearly every one is shorter in small firms. The product development or R&D cycle, for example, has to be considerably shorter in small firms. A possible exception is collections; we suspect that the average age of accounts receivable is greater in small companies.

As a result of the shorter cycle span, small companies usually do not conceptualize their situation in life from the viewpoint of their opportunities, expertise, or strengths. The longer cycles of large firms have probably made it possible and even necessary to use models unknown to small firms. The absence of models in turn is probably a significant reason for the deficiencies in planning that prevail in small firms.

Equity in smaller firms is usually distributed over a much smaller base than in large companies. Because ownership and top management are often held by one individual or a small group, executive job occupancy generally and tenure in the top position particularly tend to be much longer than in large firms.

Small firms have minimal organization. They achieve the output and push the product out the door with a minimum of differentiation in job content. If Jack can't check the invoices, John does it; if the clerk does not have the inventory data, the controller finds it. And if Harry is busy with something other than what he normally handles, Bill will cover for Harry. This informality permits the handling of minor disruptions in normal routine with speed and efficiency, but it may be a factor in the failure of small firms to make significant strides in areas such as planning. Further, under such informality, performance standards become almost impossible to establish and enforce. Employee-employer relationships tend to be more difficult, especially when it comes to recognizing and correcting inefficiencies.

2

THE FOUNDATIONS
OF SUCCESS

THE FOLLOWING FACTORS bear critically on survival and growth in small business:

A cautious attitude toward growth.

A concern for liquidity.

A focus on providing wanted products or services and satisfying work while keeping costs lean.

Establishment and maintenance of an open system of communication and decision making.

Creation of a rational organization.

Control over certain functions.

Economical use of time.

Control of owner-manager subjectivity.

The concepts involved in each point are stated briefly and then developed throughout the rest of the book.

RELATIONSHIP OF GROWTH AND SURVIVAL

Small business has special problems with respect to growth in corporate size. The limited resources and financial vulnerability of small firms usually increase rather than diminish the risks. Growth also involves special vulnerability. Converting from a small firm to a larger one is almost always fatal when the firm is unaware of the new dangers.

5

That survival and growth decisions are related has long been recognized. But the concept has been oversimplified, as evidenced by the old saw "Grow or die." The relation between the two is complex. The symbiosis is poorly described by the easy generalizations applied to it. When managerial action is based on such generalizations, it can be dangerous to survival.

Among managerial aims, survival of the firm should be placed before all others, even before profitability and growth. The three often can be pursued at the same time—and, in the healthy firm, usually will be. But there are periods when a choice must be made between them, and it is at such times that survival must be preserved at the expense of profitability and growth.

Of course, relations between the elements are not such that one should always be put before the other. There are conditions under which one of the subordinate states, such as growth, should be made a leading objective. Such conditions arise, however, only when the precedent requirements have been met.

Take the famous case of Montgomery Ward and Sears, Roebuck. That case shows what happens when emphasis upon liquidity blinds a firm to its growth opportunities. Montgomery Ward placed a premium on liquidity when its profits were not in danger. Sears, sure of its survival and profitability, put its chips on growth and beat Ward badly in the marketplace. Ward's emphasis on liquidity was dictated not by the need to survive or secure profits but by a bad guess as to the future course of the American economy.

Thus, while it is recognized that growth in sales volume does not insure survival and profitability, and can in fact be a negative factor, the price of neglecting opportunities to grow that do not involve erosion of liquidity and profitability can be very high indeed. What may be at stake is a firm's market position, and if an opportunity to improve that position is unnecessarily forgone, there can eventually be serious consequences.

Following are five propositions that bear on the relationships between survival and growth:

1. The performance of any business can be improved by men determined to improve it.
2. Every business decision affects a firm's capacity to survive.
3. Survival and growth are both served by decisions that promote growth for sound business reasons, whereas decisions that promote growth for its own sake reduce the ability to survive.
4. Every firm should strive to increase its survival capacity.

5. Sound growth is the richest source of improvement in a firm's survival capacity.

If these propositions are realistic descriptions of relationships between survival and growth, their acceptance requires major changes in the customary way of looking at business. First, it requires a shift from being preoccupied with a firm's internal affairs to being occupied with all factors, external as well as internal, that bear on performance (call that externalization). Second, it requires a shift in thinking from the subjective and personal to a company-oriented and integrated basis for action (call that rationalization). Third, it requires a shift in seeking to achieve desired business results, from operating in a fluid, interactive way to operating in a more structured, coordinated way (call that institutionalization).

CORPORATE PERFORMANCE CAN BE IMPROVED

The first proposition—that the performance of any business can be improved by men determined to improve it—highlights a number of considerations that have special relevance to survival and growth.

1. Ordinary management skill ingredients such as interest, common sense, hard work, and patience are more important than brilliance, way-out technology, or formal education. Any manager can improve his own and his company's performance by working at it with an open and investigative mind.

2. Business institutions have a resilience that allows them to tolerate any number of mistakes stemming from honest efforts to improve their performance. It is hard to kill a firm by really trying to help it do better.

3. Decision making that is knowledge-based and company-oriented is relatively rare. More often, business decisions are uninspired, conventional, self-serving, and safe. The secret of business success is to identify and do the things that others lack the courage to do. (Model T, Diesel, nylon, DC-3, Univac, Xerox, laser are products of such action; all swiftly killed or are about to kill the markets for long-established products.)

Given these statements, it then follows that determined men exercising common sense and making adventurous, unconventional decisions can benefit their firms dramatically. There is little chance that the small firm manager can significantly improve his firm's results until he starts making decisions that are unusual in his industry. The op-

portunities to make unusual decisions fall more often to the manager ·
in a small business than in a large one for the same reason that a rab-
bit can turn more often than an elephant. The mass of one allows frequent shifts in directions whereas the mass of the other does not.

THE FIRST ORDER OF BUSINESS IS SURVIVAL

The second proposition, that every business decision affects a firm's
survival by strengthening or reducing its capacity to survive, makes
it clear that the first order of business in any firm should be survival.
No decisions, not even those with a high assurance of improving
some segment of the business, should be allowed to impair a firm's
capacity to survive (with the exception, of course, of the decision to
terminate a business).

Liquidity holds the key here, as it does in all states of a business.
The essential constant in business is maintenance of resources at levels
and in conditions of readiness needed for exploiting a firm's opportunities. The formula can be turned around for another guideline to corporate survival: Make no commitments that can overtax the firm's
resources.

Note that the formula does not speak of conserving resources except in proportion to opportunity. It cannot be expected that resources
will have constant value as measured by units of currency or purchasing power. Therefore, in a declining market it is not to be marked
against a firm that it fails to keep its sales up or growing or that its
resources are not maintained at a constant dollar value. The Great
Depression and many recessions have demonstrated the futility of
that. But every firm that wants to stay in business must be able to
seize and exploit its opportunities. On *that*, survival and growth both
hang.

With a small firm's limited resources of time, money, and management, everything is probably being used to the straining point, and the
manager may consider it academic to discuss finding the means to exploit opportunities. But the small firm does not fall outside the rules of
business survival. Since the small firm cannot rely as much on outside financial sources, it must be especially vigilant against buildups
of inventory or finished products that are not easily converted into
cash. It should try constantly to prune the unprofitable product, service,
or customer and maintain vigilance in cost controls.

That every business decision either adds to or reduces a firm's ability to survive may seem to some to be made more of theory than of fact. But a moment's reflection may show this to be an extension of the most basic of principles. Action of any kind adds to or takes away from a current state.

Take eating and drinking; either one raises the body's vital capacity or (in the case of "empty" or excess calories) lowers it. Similarly, business decisions either feed survival and growth or damage the firm's capacity to survive (and, therefore, grow).

HOW GROWTH DECISIONS BEAR ON SURVIVAL

The third proposition derives from the second. If every business decision affects a firm's capacity to meet its commitments, then a decision that does not sustain or add to a firm's survival capacity is dangerous —whatever its momentary virtues. And probably no decisions impinge more heavily on survival than those intended to produce growth.

Growth in sales, plant, or personnel may not be a necessary or even desirable consequence of good management, or a sign that a business is well managed. This is not to say growth should be decried when it is a consequence of business health. Nothing remains static through time in an enterprise; for example, sales volume is always rising or falling. Therefore, to achieve business success and keep it the wise manager consistently tries to secure improvement in all key activity areas, and that certainly means trying to win over more customers or secure bigger orders from existing customers. But corporate growth, *as a goal in itself,* often poorly serves a firm's need to survive.

As a general rule, small firms do not often look beyond the immediate effects of impending decisions to see what the consequences of growth decisions may be. This is mainly because of the generally unchallenged acceptance of the virtue of growth and the informality of decision making in small firms.

THE NATURE OF TRUE GROWTH

Thus, the only acceptable measures of productive growth are those that also meet the firm's survival requirements. Small firms should allow no move that does not favor their capacities to stay in business. Every risk—and business decisions necessarily entail risk—should be examined from that point of view. A risk that could jeopardize a firm's survival should not be taken *unless survival itself is at stake.*

Decisions that go beyond helping a firm meet its survival requirements cannot be couched solely in terms of getting bigger. This point is underscored by the fact that getting smaller can often produce an increase in corporate worth (for example, closing an inefficient plant or dropping an unprofitable line, product, or customer). Increased sales volume, venerated and touted though it has been, can be the cause of corporate death when it is bought at the expense of liquidity.

Most managers cannot see how anything can rank higher than profitability. Profits produce liquidity, they say, and profits spent wisely can buy growth. That view ignores economic reality. Profits do not necessarily produce liquidity. Assets are usually needed to bring in profits from increased sales volume, and the result may be a reduction of liquidity. Growth should not be bought without careful attention to the ability of the organization to digest it financially and organizationally.

So, when pushed against the wall of logic, it seems that the only true form of corporate growth is that which, whatever else it appears to do, results in an increase in survivability and profitability (our fourth proposition). That view of growth hardly squares with the one prevailing among businessmen. But it has great acceptance among managers at the top of companies that have stayed alive a long time.

GROWTH AS A SOURCE OF SURVIVAL CAPACITY

The fifth proposition, that sound growth is the richest source of improvement in a firm's survival capacity, practically implies that a firm *should* seek to grow. And so it should—whenever it can do so without impairing the qualities of survivability (at any point in time) or profitability (through time).

However, achieving this kind of growth is very different and requires a change in traditional business perspectives. The traditional view lays emphasis on choosing "safe" risks, rather than on the unconventional or the unusual as the safest avenue to growth. The idea is paradoxical in the context of prevailing attitudes in small businesses, which tend to grow by imitation and proliferation of existing products and procedures. But it is not paradoxical when viewed against the total picture.

Justification for the idea that there is value in unusual decisions rests on two propositions:

1. Most businessmen exhibit exceptional uniformity in their orientation to such basics as equity, manpower utilization, economic priorities, and so on.
2. Outstanding corporate performance is rare; probably no more than 5 percent of all small firms are well managed.

Taken together, the two propositions strongly imply that outstanding corporate performance is closely connected with unusual managerial viewpoints.

Unusual viewpoints, in the volume and quality necessary to support survival, profits, and growth, are most commonly found in companies that show themselves to be unusually well aware of what's going on in their larger world, that reconcile what they've learned with what they can do, and that organize properly to do it. These features we sum up in states we call externalization, rationalization, and institutionalization of management. Let's look at the states in some detail.

1. *Externalization* means shifting the focus of decision making from the perspective of owners to that of actual and potential customers and to the environment. We hear a lot about consumerism. But years before the word became popular, companies that enjoyed outstanding success paid attention to the outside world, particularly to customer needs, market segmentation, social changes, and competitor behavior.

In contrast, consider three cases:

1. The great locomotive companies that died because they couldn't see the diesel coming.
2. Univac, which almost perished because it was more interested in what its computers could do than in what business wanted them to do.
3. Packard, which perished because it was more concerned with its engineering designs than with what made drivers happy.

No company, regardless of its size, can safely shut itself off from the outside world. That world is changing too fast. Consider the effects of the laws being enacted to deal with ecology, pollution, consumers, imports, and pornography. Consider also the impact on cultural patterns of such developments as the three-day weekend, the pill, and loosening attitudes toward work, careers, and dress. These influences are in the outside world, and business managers must be aware of them in order to satisfy customer needs in a unique way. And, because small firms tend to have narrower spans of contact with the outside world, managers in them need to make special efforts to become aware.

2. By *rationalization* we mean applying the capacities and resources of the firm to the opportunities and threats arising in the outside world that were brought to light by externalization. This can be accomplished only if managers in small businesses shift from managerial primitivisms, such as thinking the key to success is to pay as little as possible for everything, to the recognition that business is a complex affair with high intellectual content. It is no accident that phrases like game plan, tradeoffs, and management by objectives have come into the language of business. Seat-of-the-pants management, management by impulse, and reactive management must give way to deliberate, informed, reasoned, and "long-haul" management.

If a firm takes a serious view of reconciling knowledge of the world beyond its corporate walls with the resources within them, it should move without much difficulty from the ad hoc, laissez-faire, elitist management that characterizes many small firms to management by plan, control, and adjustment, none of which is possible without structuring and formalizing

3. *Institutionalization,* therefore, refers to the process of building a long-range basis for the work of reconciling externalization and rationalization. In other words, a firm institutionalizes (and soundly) when it seeks to put a permanent foundation under its efforts to bring the demands of the real world and corporate existence in line with each other.

The main problem can be expressed simply: Small businesses suffer greatly from managerial imperialism, the fallacy that ownership is a sufficient guarantee that a business will be properly run. This is nonsense; ownership and managerial competence are not necessarily related. Particularly as a small company grows and begins requiring different managerial skills does this relationship become suspect.

In our view, human willfulness is the primary barrier to top-notch corporate performance. Therefore, we urge each small business manager to attempt a difficult but most rewarding act: honest self-appraisal. This requires taking a good look at his decisions, his motives, his attitudes, his values. There is room for improvement if his concepts are inimical to the generally held view of a business enterprise as a system that survives profitably by consistently providing the right product for the right price at the right time. Because self-appraisal is so difficult, the next chapter contains a section that describes practical techniques that have worked in many small firms.

3

EXTERNALIZATION

In the spring of 1973 there was a worldwide shortage of cotton. Foreign goods, a long-time source for U.S. manufacturers, were no longer available. The President had opened the trade gates with Russia and China, and cotton was one of the basic materials with which the new economic relationship was bound. Previously, U.S. cotton exports to the Far East had returned in the form of low-cost fabrics. But, because of the relaxation of trade barriers and rising demand, Russia and China consumed the cotton instead of putting it back into the Western economy. The problem was compounded by the long-term effects of President Kennedy's lowering of tariffs and cotton subsidies. And the last straw was devaluation of the dollar.

Soon afterward a shortage developed in a substitute fiber derived from petroleum. The pressures put on the consuming countries by the oil-producing consortium caused a shift from the production of benzine, the key ingredient in the fiber, toward more profitable products. Thousands of companies were deeply affected by the shortages, including three small firms known to us that were almost put out of business.

The experience of the three firms underlines two points. First, the events that threatened the survival of the three firms were beyond their control or the control of any company, regardless of size. Second, dealing with the consequences of the shortages was not beyond their control; the events could have been anticipated and planned for.

Admittedly, to discern the possible effects upon a given industry of events in the economic and political environment is not a simple task. To pick out those likely to affect a particular class of firms—large

13

or small, well or poorly financed, old or new—is harder yet. And to form
a strategy for dealing with the effects that fall within the financial and
manpower limits of a small company borders on crystal-ball gazing.
Nevertheless, to survive and grow a company must do all these things,
whatever its size.

Because small firms generally engage in a narrower range of activities, use a narrower range of materials, employ fewer skills, and serve
single markets or fragments of markets, it is probably even more important for them to anticipate changes in the factors impinging on
their welfare than it is for large firms. A great change in one factor is
likely to have far more effect on a small company.

This chapter focuses on some of the means by which small firms
can minimize the number of surprises they experience and the work
involved in adjusting to the changes imposed upon them. Specifically,
it deals with methods by which small firms can improve their knowledge of the outside world and their performance in that world.

THE NEED FOR A NEW ORIENTATION

The tale of the cotton shortage highlights the increasing dependence
of companies on the world outside. In the past, the primary competences and interests of a firm could in many respects be focused in-
ward without great damage. That orientation is no longer sufficient to
any company's need to exist. It is particularly damaging to small firms,
among which it is most prevalent because of the high incidence of
owner-managership.

The dangers of corporate self-centeredness have yet to be fully
appreciated by small business managers. At several trade association
conferences, small businessmen were asked, "What are your major
problems?" The answers tended to be similar regardless of the industry: taxes, unions, shortage of management personnel, employee indifference, credit, imports, dollar devaluation, and government regulations on pollution, safety, and the rest. The next questions were, "Do
these problems originate inside the firm or outside?" and "Can the individual business control these factors, or can it only be aware of them
and prepare to deal with them?" The answers generally agreed that
most of the problems originate in the outside environment and that
the forces that cause them are beyond the control of individual firms.
The answers agreed, also, that the outside forces bore more significantly on the firm's performance than many internal factors.

What was most significant about the exchange is that it did not make the businessmen resolve to go back and deal with the outside factors in a more direct and forceful way. As determined in private conversations late in the meetings, the businessmen were unshaken in their belief that they are defenseless in their world.

The feeling is unjustified. Small firms can do much in dealing with external events that bear on their fortunes. Though the forces in themselves are uncontrollable, businessmen who wish their firms and careers to survive must work hard in anticipating and dealing with the events and the forces. And no small firm is without recourse in respect to these matters.

To go back to the cotton shortage, the managers of the three small firms mentioned earlier certainly knew of their firms' dependence upon cotton and were not without experience in life's surprises and discontinuities. Thus they had sufficient time to make long-term cotton cloth commitments or to arrange for alternative synthetic materials before or even after the widely publicized announcements of the Russian and Chinese trade agreements. At least *one* of the firms did so. This particular small manufacturer ($1.5 million in annual sales) was a supplier for a giant textile firm that produced or bought and marketed a great variety of fabrics and finished goods. The small firm made a deal before the pinch came to use the economic power of its giant (and largest) customer to obtain cloth. It also tied its production to the long-range marketing plans of the large firm, thus eliminating speculative inventory investments. Without these arrangements the small firm would undoubtedly have been forced to close its doors.

Nothing rare about this, you may say; most companies anticipate strikes and other supplier interruptions by having several vendors. But to go beyond the obvious and take into consideration the life support factors is rare. It is as though General Motors or Ford were to ask, "What would we do if personal vehicles were to become outmoded?" and were then to lay plans in anticipation of each of the leading alternatives. The likelihood is far greater that even those dominant companies will wait until impelled by outside forces to plan substantively for different markets, products, and methods. Witness the furious scrambling of the automobile manufacturers to convert their production to smaller cars after they were surprised by the gasoline shortage. More surprising than the energy crunch was their total unpreparedness for it. How could a General Motors have been so blind, when the coming of fuel shortages has been predicted by authorities for so long?

Besides identifying and preparing for events that may have a
bearing on its fortunes, a business institution has other protections.
One of them lies in the character of its service. Every enterprise serves
needs external to itself and can stay in business as long as it continues
to do so. A company healthy in the truest sense knows a good deal
about those needs and about how well it is filling them.

Identifying and defining the needs to be filled, and anticipating
and preparing for impending changes, are most efficiently accomplished through a process of organizing, funding, and proceduralizing
contact with and responses to the outside world. This is the process
of externalization.

Externalization amounts to a new orientation, because maintaining
meaningful contact with the outside world calls for the redisposition
of the firm's resources. Probing the markets served, evaluating service
to the markets, and ascertaining the nature of emerging markets is not
light work. It takes a fair toll of a firm's resources.

Externalization is a rare phenomenon among small firms. This
orientation is incompatible with the centripetal character of small
firms, which causes resources to be applied almost exclusively to existing products, problems, and profitabilities. It is obvious to the informed observer that most small firms know too much about what's
going on inside and too little about what's going on outside. If it is
true that more factors affecting survival and growth are found outside
the firm than inside it, then most small firms have a marked imbalance
in their knowledge of the two.

In progressive firms the concept of externalization goes far beyond
tokenism. It goes beyond the traditional approaches to the external
world as represented by outside board members, stockholder meetings,
market research, magazine subscriptions, association memberships,
and periodic attendance at conventions, conferences, and seminars.
Because it is crucial to business survival that there be keen awareness
of the occurrence and meaning of developments in the external world,
all progressive firms, whatever their size, apply their most important
resources in well-organized efforts to find out what's happening in that
world and the relevance of those events to the fortunes of the firm.
Without such efforts a firm's survival is a matter of luck, as the following example shows:

EXAMPLE:

A manufacturer of school equipment with $2.5 million in annual
sales found his sales dropping during the 1960s as the school expansion
brought on by the post-World War II baby boom slowed down. By
chance he was asked to bid on tennis court installations and on recrea-

tional facilities for schools, camps, motels, and playgrounds. He was successful in his bid and quickly developed expertise in both fields. More than 75 percent of his current business, and the basis of his survival, is now in these new and growing fields.

He was lucky. True, the decline in the school equipment market and the rise in the recreational and tennis markets were beyond his ability to influence. But he had failed to keep track of changes in the market for educational equipment, on which his company was clearly dependent. Being asked to bid on recreational facilities was a stroke of fortune of the kind that sometimes comes along to save a firm. Management had been lucky, not smart.*

THE BARRIERS IN SMALL FIRMS

Although firms of every size should be suitably externalized, detecting rising threats and seeing how well needs in the marketplace are being met pose greater problems for small than large firms. The problems are largely caused by the fragmented markets, the staff deficiencies, and the monopoly on key decision making usually exercised by the owners of small firms.

Even with their staffs of specialists, large firms find it difficult to respond to external changes. They have to overcome the difficulties that go with the lengthened lines of communication and decision making as well as the inertia of large-scale investments, the orientation of masses of employees not easily reached, and so forth. Consider how slow the automobile makers and utilities have been to respond to the public outcry about air pollution. The products of both groups had been polluting the atmosphere for years with little complaint. Then, in an astonishingly short time, automobile and utility managers were faced with broad opposition to their long-accepted practices, and both were unprepared for the public's unwillingness to tolerate further pollution.

Even in respect to the size of cars the public wants, auto company plans lack precision, as the following makes clear:

> The Ford Motor Company is pushing hard this fall with the only genuinely new design of the 1974 models, the subcompact Mustang II. The advertising theme Ford will be trumpeting is "The right car

---

* School equipment and educational supply firms that do not want to wait for strokes of fortune should be preparing for the inevitable change to the metric system. Lessons in marketing opportunities are probably available from British firms that have lived through the change.

at the right time," and Ford's timing does indeed seem precise. But there's a little more to it than that and more than a little bit of luck. Lee A. Iacocca, president of Ford, concedes that the timing of the Mustang II was a case of being "more lucky than smart." "We didn't know two years ago that small cars would be heading toward 45 or 50 percent of the market." *

The failure of companies to keep a watchful eye on the environment in which they operate and to act in accordance with the intelligence so derived is often traceable to managerial naïveté which equates the success of a business with the president's efforts. Owner-managers in small firms are particularly prone to this view. One of the most difficult steps for the manager to take, particularly if he is an owner and entrepreneur as well as manager, is to stop looking on the business as an extension of himself. Louis XIV is supposed to have said, "I am the law." It is not hard to find parallels among small businessmen whose words and actions say, "I am the business." They are so at the firm's peril.

If each business exists by filling the needs of its customers, the firm's manager is one factor—when his behavior is company-oriented—in the need satisfaction process. His business can survive only as long as the decisions he makes or allows do not impair customer need fulfillment. Unless the rights of ownership or management are distinctly secondary, the organization is doomed, even though the end be a long time off.

Because so many small firms had to focus on controlling costs, pinching pennies, and developing an intimate knowledge of the internal organization in order to stay alive in their early years, their managers later find it difficult to keep in touch with the outside world. The techniques that sustain a company when it is small and undercapitalized may later make its manager turn his back on the need to invest in the firm's future. Such investments have little appeal because they are lacking in apparent short-term payoffs.

MEASURING PERFORMANCE

The starting place in a program of externalization is to build a basis for realistic performance measurement. The firm with a bright future does not spare itself self-evaluation and criticism. Choosing a firm's

* *The New York Times,* September 2, 1973.

destiny is no more important or difficult than knowing how well the firm is doing in trying to reach it. Such knowledge begins with rigorous, realistic performance appraisal.

The traditional measures of how a company is doing are its income statements and balance sheets. Most small firms continue to rely on them exclusively because finding meaningful alternatives is hard work. But financial statements do little more than describe a firm's economic condition in the recent past as a function of its performance in the more distant past. The statements tell little, even by implication, about how well customer needs are being met today or will be met tomorrow. Needs often change so fast that financial statements cannot even contain a hint that changes are taking place. Therefore, the best way to know whether the needs that can keep a firm alive are being fulfilled on a continuing basis is to diminish reliance on financial statements and turn to other means of keeping the firm attuned to the world.

There are nonfinancial measures which, though less precise than those rooted in accounting, nonetheless are excellent indicators of company health and lie more across than within corporate lines. Discussion of a number of measures well suited to use in small business follows.

The first group of performance measures deals with the market and calls for three kinds of information: the firm's share of the market, comparison of competitive products and services, and planned flow of new products and services. Since the need for the three types of information is evident, we will concentrate on the sources and uses of the data.

1. *Share of the market* provides a means of appraising a company's market posture through comparisons based on the market served rather than the company's own history. The quality of the data varies, depending on the sophistication and energy levels of the sources (such as trade or professional associations and government agencies). Many of the 4,500 trade and professional associations in the United States accumulate and publish data and abstract useful information from governmental sources. There is, simply speaking, a flood of information at hand, and not to make use of it is an open invitation to business risk.

EXAMPLE:

A manufacturer of specialty luxury goods turned a deaf ear to all pleas to change his management procedures, mainly because his company's annual sales growth over the preceding ten years had been averaging 6 percent and profits had been good. Information on the specific markets to which he was selling was obtained from the trade associations he was a member of. The information showed that in the same ten years the market had increased by 10 percent a year, revealing that his share had declined steadily. Spurred by the findings, the manufacturer investigated and found that new manufacturers, eager to break into a high-profit market, were creating new distribution and advertising techniques to reach his customers. He then acted upon the requests for changed methods.

When little or no information is available in the public domain, small firms can benefit greatly by developing cooperative relationships within their industry and sharing whatever they feel comfortable in disclosing. There is a growing trend in that direction. If they compete more or less directly, they may be inclined to share only changes in sales, using percentages of a base year instead of dollar amounts. On the other hand, if the group is not in direct competition they generally are inclined to share more, and the benefits can be proportionately greater.

2. *Comparison of competitive products and services.* It is an old saying that the first two Chevrolets sold in any model year are bought by Ford and Chrysler, which immediately compare the cars with their own. They are not alone. Large retailers also check competitors' quality and prices. Some firms consider it so important to find out what others in an industry are doing that they cross the lines of legal and moral propriety to ferret out closely held information. But not many of them are small. Small firms live more on a day-to-day basis, and tend to lose sight of the burnished teeth of their competitors.

What should a small firm do? Certainly, what competitors are doing is one of the factors in the external world likely to have an impact on profitability and survival, and managers of small firms must learn to provide the resources (time, people, money) needed to stay abreast of competitors. Much of the relevant information about competitors is readily available through trade journals, association meetings, advertisements, catalogs, price lists, distributors who handle competing lines, customers who buy from more than one source, and even competitors' ex-employees who are legally free to reveal information. (Many employment contracts prohibit disclosure of trade secrets for several years after an employee who has had access to sensitive information leaves a company.) Lost customers or lost bids can be useful sources of information because they can test the reasons for a customer's choice and the differences between competitors.

However, post-mortems on lost customers or lost bids are of little value unless they are undertaken regularly. Therefore, the small firm that wants to know how it is performing will establish procedures to insure regular analysis of feedback and dissemination of findings for future guidance.

Debriefing salesmen, sales representatives, or other personnel who deal directly with customers or clients can often provide useful information on competitors, particularly when the sales people have been asked to be alert to opportunities to obtain the information. Salespeople are rarely alert unless asked—and even then they must be reminded often in order to keep the information coming in.

3. *Flow of new products and services.* Development of sensitivity to the possible need for changes in products and services entails becoming familiar with those that have already taken place.

Firms that have been in business for more than five years have much to learn from investigating changes in the sales patterns of products or services, comparing the customers gained and lost year by year within the last five years, and so forth. It would be unusual to conduct such an inquiry and find that the products or services remained in the same proportion or relative profit contribution over a five-year period. Similarly, the contribution by class of customers to both sales and marginal (gross profit) income will probably have changed over the period. The fact is, analysis of past changes can tell a lot about changes to come.

Whatever its size, a firm alert to the dangers and opportunities of corporate existence will not fail to identify and monitor the trends affecting it that can be made explicit and meaningful. To act on the results is another matter; it requires tough-mindedness and freedom from the emotional involvements of customer relationships, products, or services. But the firm that has the fortitude to suffer the trials of informing itself about its world will have no trouble putting the information to work.

From that point of view, managers of small firms must realize that their size is against them. Large firms find it relatively easy to act on the results; they are usually less bound to individual customers. Small firms, which have just as great a need to act, find it harder to do so. They must push themselves to do the research and to act on their findings.

EXAMPLE 1:

A distributor of construction equipment conducted a steady, modestly profitable business for 20 years. A general contractor brought to his attention a unique tool whose European manufacturer was seeking North American distribution and suggested that the two set up a company to handle the tool. Because of hard, smart work, within three years the new company's sales were greater than those of either of the original firms. Though the general contractor could read the message and began to spend the bulk of his time on the new company, the construction equipment distributor continued to devote half his time to his original company, referring to the bread-and-butter aspect of the old firm and the fact that it had been the source of his living for so many years.

Under pressure from one of his advisers, the distributor agreed to compare figures for each firm's performance and sales projections. After considerable head-scratching and refusal to face facts, the distributor finally acknowledged the value of giving up day-to-day control of his original company. He then upgraded two employees in his original firm to handle sales and administration, installed simple budgetary controls, and set up a profit participation plan. Results? The old business maintained itself and the new firm showed a great increase in sales and profits.

EXAMPLE 2:

The son of the chief stockholder of a wholesale house owned by two families was introduced to the business by being turned loose on accounts receivable and customer service. The young man, fresh from business school, started with two analyses: comparison of aged accounts receivable for each of the preceding 12 quarters and the gross profit in dollars produced by each of the 100 largest customers, who represented 15 percent of the total customers and 75 percent of the sales dollars. He then computed the ratio of the annual gross profit for each of these customers to their average receivable balance for each of the three years. The result was a schedule of the approximate return on the company's investment in receivables from its major customers. The schedule is illustrated by Table 1, which gives a sample of six customers.

The return numbers are meaningful in comparing customers and in detecting trends. Note the declining return of five of the six, which indicates reduced profitability and increased investment in receivables. The young man knew that companies A, B, E, and F were old customers run by long-standing friends of his father. When the son pointed out that the company's return was declining on its receivables invested in these customers and was less than the average return for

Table 1

Customer	Gross Profit (P) in Year . . .			Average Accounts Receivable (R)* in Year . . .			Return (P/R) in Year . . .		
	1	2	3	1	2	3	1	2	3
A	$100	$120	$125	$50	$60	$70	2.0	2.0	1.8
B	90	90	80	50	60	60	1.8	1.5	1.3
C	80	85	90	40	45	50	2.0	1.9	1.8
D	95	110	120	45	40	40	2.1	2.8	3.0
E	120	100	80	50	40	40	2.4	2.5	2.0
F	50	75	100	20	40	70	2.5	1.9	1.4

* Computed from the average of the five relevant accounts receivable balances: opening January 1, March 31, June 30, September 30, and ending December 31.

other customers, the father defended his loose control with the statement that these customers had kept him alive during the Depression and he would not offend them or get tough with them now.

Only after one of the old customers went bankrupt did the father realize that a nostalgic relationship was less important than rational business policies.

This example brings out two important points: (1) The past (as evidenced by the relationship between the father and certain customers) can impose a constraint on sound decision making. (2) Simple analytical tools, such as the trend of accounts receivable aging and the return on receivable investments, can be quickly and inexpensively used to help make better decisions.

Analysis of changes in customers and products can go far toward creating understanding of and responsiveness to product and service life cycles. Though it is a truism applicable to most firms that 20 to 50 percent of present sales are based on items that did not exist five or ten years ago, a high percentage of small companies still do not work at anticipating the consequences of aging in their products. Small firms are prone to stick to the products and services they have provided in the past. Larger firms have much less product loyalty, and if there were no other factors to be considered, that one alone would put them considerably ahead.

Here are three practical suggestions for small firms:

1. Analyze the trend of each major product or service for at least

three to five years in terms of sales dollars to total sales and, if possible, determine the gross profit or variable income (sales less all variable costs) produced. Emerging trends should be explored and, when the potential looks good, exploited.

EXAMPLE:

A CPA firm in the Midwest was called in to help a small hospital install a recordkeeping system originally designed for a giant urban hospital. After successfully completing the engagement, the firm looked around and found that other small hospitals usually had no one to turn to for systems help. Within ten years, as a result of specializing in the field and being recommended to other hospitals by satisfied clients, the firm was deriving half its income from systems and audit work related to hospitals.

2. Call on an outsider or two who can challenge the proportion of efforts you are devoting to present products or services and customers and can ask whether you are missing the boat in untapped or inadequately serviced areas.

EXAMPLE:

An industrial supply firm originally sold its products entirely in bulk to industry and retailers. It moved successfully into the packaging of items for the household, do-it-yourself market served by chain, department, and discount stores after a partner in its accounting firm noted a decline in the size of the average sale to regular retail customers. The accountant's investigation showed that the retailers were losing out to the other distribution channels and he recommended a shift. The company's management quickly invested in the packaging equipment necessary to service the new markets.

In a parallel situation, alert textile rental companies, traditionally concerned with flat goods, found profitable expansion opportunities in wearing-apparel rental. The diversification made them less vulnerable to the competition of on-the-premises laundries (hospitals, schools, hotels) that primarily handled flat goods.

3. Ask customers what they want, what they will need, how you can offer them new or better products and services. Remember, for most small firms innovation takes the form of refinement, modification, and specialization more than invention, expansion, and generalization —all of which involve greater risks. Radical innovation can be engaged in by small firms without undue risk mainly by pooling resources in their trade associations for major technological research. For example, the development of a concrete block that can sustain heavy load-bearing stresses was supported by the National Concrete Masonry Association.

The design, engineering, testing, approval, and promotion of the product were beyond the capacity of any single firm.

Measures of performance are doubly valuable when their application requires the establishment of a data base for the future. Analyses of sales, inventories, customer buying patterns, salesmen activities, and so on are important in themselves. But when made regularly, they become trend lines that can often tell a great deal about the future. Small firms miss great opportunities by failing to estimate what they will want to know five years in the future and then tailoring data collection for that purpose.

The point is sufficiently important to merit repetition: It is rare for a firm to *anticipate* its knowledge needs. Much of what it needs consists of trend information, and such information cannot be developed unless data have been accumulated in advance.

The benefits of having trend information are illustrated by the case of a small grocery chain. It collected data on changes in sales mix, location of customers (from charge accounts, delivery records, and quarterly giveaways), size of order, and traffic and population patterns in its trading area. Then it used this information not only to analyze present performance but also to determine the direction in which it should move in the future: opening and closing of stores, merchandising policies, services to offer.

Service organizations are not likely to know why they lose customers unless they have regular and relevant information on all customer complaints and dissatisfactions.

EXAMPLE:

By checking into all claims against his shipping company, the vice-president of sales learned where operations had fallen down seriously —in some cases, to the point that customers felt strongly enough to sue. He then followed up by investigating and upgrading the operations which the claims revealed were not functioning properly.

Most small professional organizations find that the ratio of billable time (in hours or standard billing rates) to total time worked provides the single best measure of efficiency: how people's efforts are being managed, what income can be expected, whether breakeven volume has been reached.

Another example of an operational measure is that of a wholesale distributor (approximately $4 million volume) who controlled the efficiency of the warehouse, a major cost center whose operations critically affected customer service, by monitoring the number of invoice lines picked daily by each man.

Figure 1 shows a card given to customers of an installment jewelry chain. One of the top managers follows up on the problems mentioned.

Figure 1

Please Fill Out & Mail - NO POSTAGE REQUIRED

Are you satisfied with your purchase? _____

Did you receive courteous treatment from salespeople? _____

Is your name spelled correctly on envelope? _____

Have you any suggestions for improving our service? _____

REMARKS: _____

PLEASE PRINT

NAME..

ADDRESS..ZIP CODE..........

CITY...APT..............

ACCOUNT NO.......................................

CASH SALES SLIP NO...............................

RETURN ON INVESTMENT AS A PERFORMANCE STANDARD

The complacency that is so common among managers of small firms is sometimes based on a sense of insularity or on the assumption that the firm is too small to be considered a competitive target. Owner-managers, however, are more often complacent because they have an adequate personal income and they are not enthusiastic about taking on the burden of comparing the results of the firm's operations with those of other investment opportunities. In such cases, a comparison can be made simply. The following case shows the application of a comparison using return on investment.

A real estate investment and management firm was managed by a 50-year-old, third-generation owner. Because his company had held much of the property for more than half a century, its depreciated cost was small. The owner drew a modest salary, and the low return (5 percent) on the low book value was enough to satisfy him.

His accounting firm sought to convince him that he should reappraise his situation. From tax bills (based on recent assessments), insurance company appraisals, and estimates of the knowledgeable owner, the accountants determined a more realistic and current value of the company's assets. Using that figure they recomputed the return on investment and found it close to 2 percent. Further investigation showed that increasing the rate through increased income would be an arduous, long-range task because of existing lease terms and local real estate conditions.

Reducing the investment base seemed the most practical idea. The accountants showed the owner that selling all his property and investing the after-tax proceeds in insured savings accounts would actually increase his income. Although he could not dispose of all the property, the owner did sell several parcels. It galled him to think he could earn more by not working than by working. So, instead of investing the money in interest-bearing accounts (which had been used as a minimum standard), he invested the proceeds in income-producing real estate which had to meet a new goal: a return on investment of at least 10 percent. In short order the financial performance of his firm was sharply improved.

The example shows that small firms can get a lot of mileage out of common performance standards such as ROI. The failure to benefit from such standards usually comes from not using them.

INDUSTRY SOURCES OF INFORMATION

Parochialism is one of the possible consequences of small size. An almost total concern for the present, a need to operate tightly, and a tradition of holding information close to the chest prevent many small business managers from making realistic comparisons. Fortunately, there are successful techniques for expanding the measures of reasonableness with small risk, cost, or embarrassment.

The first is to use the full resources of the trade or professional association in the firm's industry. Most associations have tabulated financial and operating data which can be used as a measure of performance. Categorized by size, specialization, area, or quartile of profitability, this information offers a lead to investigation of possible problems. For example, if the average direct labor percentage to sales is 25 and yours is 32, the difference is material enough to warrant investigation.

Requiring higher involvement but offering a richer reward is the informal association of noncompeting firms in the same industry. The degree of involvement and data sharing varies, but in almost all cases the association has these characteristics:

- Members are asked to join because their geographical dispersion limits their competitive threat.
- Detailed financial information is shared, sometimes in a code which hides the identity of each company from any reader except the members.
- Operating ideas are exchanged on selling, production, personnel, inventories, and so on. Meetings can take place on the company premises of the members and are used to investigate in detail all the operations of the host company.

In one case a number of noncompeting regional retail jewelry chains were brought together by a management consultant. He acted as administrator; planned the semiannual meetings; issued monthly financial reports; wrote a monthly newsletter which carried stories of successful advertising, merchandising, personnel, or credit-granting techniques; and kept the enthusiasm from waning. The comparative data were especially valuable: The reports included detailed information on percentage of sales and profits produced by each type of merchandise (such as large diamond rings, wedding bands, name-brand watches, house-brand watches, portable TV sets) and fixed and variable expenses, which were a source of ideas for cost reduction (in everything except the salaries of the president-owners, which were in the top quartile). When the group met at the home office of a member, his stores were the beneficiary of a detailed, professional examination he could never have obtained in any other way.

In another case the managing partners of seven independent public accounting firms from seven large cities, whose practices did not overlap significantly, spent two days and nights talking about tough problems which could not be easily discussed with anyone except peers. Their agenda included partner admission, earnings, distribution, retirement; firm decision making; staff hiring, training, evaluation, scheduling, fringe benefits; handling the partner or staff man who has stopped growing professionally; methods of expanding the practice; the advantages and disadvantages of merging with smaller firms or with a larger firm; the place of the computer; the use of paraprofessionals. Not only did each of the firms benefit from the many new ideas its managing partner brought home, but the frankness of the discussions and the willingness of all the men to tackle the individual problems of the others created a camaraderie that continued over the years. Most of the partners who attended felt free to call others for suggestions in handling specific questions as they arose.

The advantages of sharing information and problems apply to noncompeting firms in any industry or profession. It takes initiative and some care in choosing firms of approximately equal size. (In the retail jewelry store case, branch operations were a major operating problem. A single store, however large, did not face the problem and was therefore inappropriate for the group.) Above all, it takes a willingness to exchange confidential information. The benefits are well worth the effort and the disclosure.

CHANGING ATTITUDES TOWARD WORK

If a firm's survival depends upon its filling needs in the marketplace, then survival is contingent on keeping up with the changes taking place in its markets.

But not all the important changes in a firm's larger environment impinge directly or solely on customer needs. There are dimensions to the external environment other than the firm's customers and markets or the demographic and economic aspects. There are those aspects of the environment summed up by the phrases "cultural patterns" and "social behavior." Of the many social behavior variables that have influence upon a firm's fortunes, nothing may be more influential than attitudes toward work. This is a variable small firms should pay particular attention to.

At this point in the Industrial Revolution, which is in its third century and still going on, attitudes toward work at all levels are changing faster than ever before. Studies have demonstrated convincingly that an increasing number of people find their work unsatisfying or dissatisfying. The finding is not particularly revealing; most workers have probably not been satisfied by their work since the Industrial Revolution began. What is noteworthy is that the attainments achievable through work, so highly prized to date, are changing. The ethic of climbing the company ladder, work as a virtue in itself, and achieving social acceptance through work are being challenged widely and apparently successfully. Many people are beginning to see alternatives to achieving success through corporate membership. Psychologically, they can afford other ways of living, with the result that their goals and priorities are changing. The company game is moving out of first place.

The discontent formerly restricted primarily to lower-level personnel has reached the managerial level. A recent survey report * revealed that for many businessmen and executives there are goals more important than money and status. For example, almost half of the 2,800 executives and businessmen questioned said that meaningful success in business can be measured not by the rewards earned but only by the worth of the work done. One-third of the respondents felt that success meant the realization of goals lying quite outside their business careers. Over a third questioned whether the organization for which they worked could satisfy their personal goals. The survey results also suggest that about two-thirds of lower and middle managers do not think of their work as supportive of their life goals or their employers as being concerned with these goals.

The significance of these changing feelings about success in the business world and the gap between the realities of life in urban America in the sixties and seventies and the Puritan work ethic is not yet decipherable. We do know, of course, that any organization in which all decisions are made for economic reasons only, without consideration for the personal aspirations of its staff at all levels, is going to have trouble in utilizing and keeping people. But it seems likely that small companies can more easily capitalize on such characteristics as their informal and more individualized job structure to create a workable fit between the needs of the individual and the needs of the enterprise.

This is not to suggest that widespread concern for the personal aspirations of people working in an organization should take precedence over the survival needs of the firm. In meeting the needs that are the reason for its existence a firm will on occasion have to put individual needs second. Despite that necessity, the evidence shows that the more individuals' goals are considered, the greater will be the contribution from employees.

The signs of change in work attitudes are obvious to all but the obsessive elitist. To make anything productive of them will require perception, skill, and work. Making use of them, however, is likely to produce a substantial competitive advantage.

A later section explains how management by objectives helps to bring together personal goals and corporate objectives. For those man-

* Dale Tarnowieski, *The Changing Success Ethic,* AMACOM, 1973.

agers who find MBO difficult to implement, other tools can be used to allay the insecurity and overcome the sense of isolation from executive decision making that disturb many employees. The financial strength of a large company provides an umbrella of security. In the absence of a strong economic base, small companies may need to open the organization in such a way as to insure wide participation in goal setting and at the same time reduce rumors. Managers will find it helpful to issue news bulletins, carry on regular conversations (not lectures) with work groups, and make a conscious attempt to show employees in every way that the company has a purpose, is being managed with an eye for the future, and is trying to stay alert to changes in the world.

KEEPING UP WITH CHANGES IN SOCIETY

In externalizing, a firm not only must establish pipelines to the outside so as to learn what the present state of affairs is but also must keep abreast of the changes taking place. No aspect of the small firm's total environment is changing faster than the social.

Full discussion of the changes occurring in society, including changes in the speed of change and the problems that individuals and organizations have in adapting to change, is of course impossible here. But it is of value to show that small firms need not be without help in keeping abreast.

Take legislative changes. Even though the course of legislation can occasionally be affected by trade organizations or other interest groups, a small firm whose business is closely tied to legislative acts is not totally at the mercy of legislation. For instance, a factor bearing importantly on the sales volume of construction equipment distributors is the timing of the release of highway funds. These funds are released to serve local or national political purposes, and the timing and amount are substantially beyond the influence of the individual dealer-distributor. When the money flows into local highway construction, contractors buy or rent machinery, and equipment dealers do well. Conversely, their fortunes ebb when the faucet is turned low or shut off.

Although the equipment dealer's survival and growth are tied to factors over which he has little influence, he must be aware of changes in these factors as far in advance as possible so as to arrange for inventory, personnel, and financing that will allow him to make the most of the changes or at least survive them. Successful dealers pick the brains of those who keep abreast of the disposition of highway trust funds (for example, legislators and trade association experts) and the likely effect on local conditions.

EXAMPLE 1:

A concrete block manufacturer believed that the two most significant factors affecting his business were local building codes and new architectural designs. As new products came into the market and new building commissioners replaced the old, the competitive position of concrete block changed. Architects called for new shapes, sizes, textures, colors. The daily struggle to keep up with internal operating problems made the manager realize that he would never get out from under until he stopped merely reacting to building code and architectural changes and began to anticipate them. Altering his focus and adjusting his priorities reduced the manager's problems in keeping up to date, and he began to benefit from being in a position to exploit the changes as they came.

EXAMPLE 2:

The program at a convention of hotel and motel managers included the traditional subjects of cost control, security, housekeeping, insurance, and keeping guests happy. Significant additions to the agenda, however, were the Occupational Safety and Health Act; how to deal with the consumerism and ecology movements; and the possible effects on the industry of new air fares, federal programs to increase foreign travel to the United States, and the changing patterns of vacations and long weekends. Many of the managers admitted that they were at ease with the traditional subjects but were not yet comfortable with the subjects that arise outside the industry and are only partially subject to its influence. Yet it was the outside factors that had affected the preceding year's performance the most and promised to be the most significant in the years ahead.

Let us turn to some of the techniques that can help us keep in touch with environmental and social changes. The three following seem most likely to give the small firm a window on the outside world.

The first is an adaptation of a planning technique used by large organizations. It consists of asking and answering a series of future-oriented questions that are essentially elaborations on the general question, What will our world be like five and ten years from now? In asking the question, small firm managers must be sure that the world they envision includes not only customers, suppliers, competitors, and employees but neighbors and governments as well; not only resources and technology but also social and demographic aspects that may affect them. The specific questions are similar to these:

1. Are we likely to have less competition? The same amount? More? Will we be faced with foreign competition?
2. Who are our customers likely to be, and in what ways will they be different from today's customers?
3. Will the services or products that we are now offering be more important than they are now? Less important?
4. What changes are likely to occur in the organization of our customers' firms? Our distribution system? Our industry?
5. If we were to change our product, service, distribution, price, and so on, would we expand our markets in areas where we are not now doing business? How?

EXAMPLE:

A chemical manufacturer was strong on research which made its specialty products acceptable to large, sophisticated textile firms, and it had always been able to sell on terms of 1 percent up to 10 days, net 30 days. Average receivables were about 15 days' sales to these large customers. To expand sales to smaller, less strongly financed customers, the company merely changed its standard of receivables collection to 45 days for these firms.

More questions need to be asked and answered. What share of the market do we want next year? In five years? These questions require a starting point: What is our present share of the market? They also require a definition of the markets now serviced and, even more important, those that are not serviced but might be.

Another technique is the analysis of returns, allowances, lost customers, and suits against the company to determine how present products or services are *not* satisfying customers. Often the subject of jokes, customer complaints are too serious, too sensitive an indicator of marketing effectiveness, too rich a source of ideas to be left to anyone but an executive at a top policy-making level.

In the example of the shipping company whose vice-president of sales investigated every lawsuit against the company, the vice-president believed that each lawsuit spotlighted some aspect of service which had disintegrated to the point that the customer felt he had no other recourse. But the vice-president also was astute enough to recognize that each suit offered an opportunity to find out precisely what was wrong with the service his company was offering. Because of his investigations, many customers were saved.

EXAMPLE:

The president of a company that made outerwear textiles sold his fabrics to retail organizations that contracted for the manufacture of garments from the material. The president wanted a direct, unfiltered reaction to his products from the end users—the people who wore the clothes made with his fabrics. He gave finished jackets, slacks, and other items made from his textiles to cab drivers who drove him around in the cities he visited on his selling trips. In return, he asked only that they wear the garments every day and send him a postcard monthly, telling him their good and bad impressions of the fabrics. He even kept track of the drivers and on repeat visits would call them when he had time. The cost of the hundreds of garments he gave away each year was insignificant in relation to his company's sales volume and to the value of the information he collected.

Even small companies can use a consumer panel, a group of customers whose opinions are solicited, listened to, and used to improve the product or service. Some firms make participation in a consumer panel attractive by providing a meal, a small fee, discounts, or movie and theater tickets. In turn, the panel provides feedback on company products in areas that sales volume alone cannot reveal.

EXAMPLE:

The executive partner of a professional service company who has little personal client contact calls each client who leaves the firm to find out what caused the change. Whether the reasons lie inside the firm (late reports, unprofessional conduct by the staff, fee differences) or outside (required services not provided by the firm, other firms offer broader or more personal service), the executive partner has learned to listen to former clients and be alert to any evidence of a pattern which requires a change in the firm's policies or strategy.

Keeping a finger on the pulse of customers' changing needs is a vital concern of all management. In small firms, managers sometimes continue to perform the pulse-taking ritual as a way of honoring their sales-oriented past. Because they dealt with customers in the early days, and because activities that are directed to the customer are rarely criticized, managers personally call on long-standing customers under the guise of keeping in touch with the market. What is wrong with this approach is that these client contacts are often an excuse to avoid tough management problems; calling on old friends rarely generates disagreeable information or represents a fair sample of all customers.

EXAMPLE:

The president of a manufacturing company, a man in his seventies, made quarterly calls on old cronies who were owner-managers of about a dozen of the thousand or so active customers his company serviced. These visits were preceded by fanfare and followed by detailed accounts of the homage, friendliness, and personal concern the customers had displayed. New ideas for the line were attributed to these visits.

Probably closer to the truth was the reaction of a young executive who said: "The old man loves to tell stories with his cronies, get their adulation, and have them confirm what he has already decided to do. Meanwhile, we have a long list of unresolved problems that he should be working on. But the problems are thorny and don't give him the kick the visits do. Some of us doubt the value of sampling a dozen customers out of a thousand. But until he permits a real debriefing of our sales force, we have only this trickle of questionable data on our customers' reactions to our products."

In the short run, taxes, unions, laws, credit availability, and attitudes toward success and work are outside the power of an individual or a small firm to influence. But major changes in society strongly influence the firm. For example, the son of many a small company owner is unwilling to join his father in the family business. The overextended tenure of the father may be one reason for the son to stay away.

But a more powerful reason may be that the challenges and opportunities offered by the family business suffer in comparison with work in social, cultural, educational, or scientific fields. Why sell shoes, bolts, factory supplies, cars, tractors, or houses when you can help people more directly? Some sons and daughters choose not to engage in business because social responsibility or esthetic excitement attracts them elsewhere.

A large retailer took advantage of this environmental factor and bought some 10 or 12 stores, thus capitalizing on an observation by its president: The sons of the founder-owners of downtown stores were not interested in joining the family business because of the long hours, poor environment, lack of work satisfaction, or low status. The result was that as the owners reached 50 or 60, they did not know where to turn to dispose of their businesses. The larger company offered to buy the smaller companies, proposing a variety of individually tailored deals that gave the owners an acceptable way out. Through long-term payouts and a substantial 15-year loan from an insurance company, the acquiring company was able to digest the acquisition financially. And it met its own management needs by training new managers who recognized growth opportunities.

In another case, a small group of investors formed a company to buy out the owners of small- to medium-size businesses with the distinguishing characteristics of dullness and slow growth, attributes unlikely to attract the sons of owners or large conglomerates. The new company identified prospects with the help of a computerized credit information service that searched its files for companies whose size, location, and industry met the specifications. Then the owners were approached with a deal similar to the one that was offered by the large retailer.

These two cases touch on a few of the reasons why owners of small businesses do not succeed in convincing their children that they should join the family business. Other reasons are to be found in the differing concepts of economic security and independence. These do not mean the same things to the 25-year-old and the 50-year-old. To the older person, symbols of security are often material things, such as shares of stock, real estate, cars, money in the bank, little or no debt, perhaps furs or jewels, and a vested interest in a profit-sharing or pension plan. The typical 25-year-old, on the other hand, is more likely to equate security with competence. As the possessor of specialized knowledge, the younger person wants to choose how he will work, where he will work, and for whom. Having grown up in a period of high economic activity sustained by massive governmental support programs, he has never known economic depression and, therefore, the need to be very cautious in making career decisions.

Recognition of these new attitudes by the manager of a small firm will affect the way he hires, trains, and delegates work to young professionals. If he does not expect lifetime loyalty from a new employee, he can fashion a program to provide the younger person with the professional challenge and growth he wants while corporate goals are at the same time moved ahead. The company will not suffer if, during a less-than-lifetime stay, a young manager contributes ideas, energy, and technical expertise in exchange for the hands-on experience he wants.

MEETING SOCIAL RESPONSIBILITIES

With consumerism, sensitivity to ecological problems, the articulation of long-suppressed demands by minorities, and the ascension of managers who are aware of social problems, social accounting and responsibilities to society have become of increasing interest and concern. Much of the publicity on corporate social programs, both the successes and the failures, has focused on giant companies. Although the small company is less frequently the subject of attack for failure to live up to some as yet undefined standard of corporate responsibility, the manager cannot escape being involved. His time, his resources, his opportunity to make a significant change in society are all limited. Assuming he wants to do something, what should he do?

Aside from whatever financial support he gives to organizations in which he is interested, the manager of the small firm should concentrate his acts of social responsibility in only a few areas. For example, he might focus on local issues such as pollution control in his own business, training and employment of the underprivileged and the handicapped, or positive action to improve consumer education or consumer safety as it affects his products. Such measures can have a direct and immediate result in socially sensitive areas that will be productive and satisfying. It goes without saying that all these activities should go beyond those required by law.

In sum, if you want to succeed, concentrate your efforts in the area of social action as in all other significant areas.

BUILDING BRIDGES TO THE FUTURE

Efforts to gain understanding of trends and events in the firm's larger environment have their final and best expression in the projections and objectives the firm sets for itself. Firms that make sincere efforts to discern the needs and opportunities in the marketplace are likely to have more realistic and rewarding goals and forecasts than firms that do not.

Setting objectives and forecasting are two parts of the planning process that should be dealt with from the outside in. Each must have a practical external orientation if the effort invested in detailed planning is to yield the best payback. That is why the setting of objectives and forecasting are included in this book in a different chapter from the other parts of the planning process.

Planning is not homogeneous but is a common name applied to different activities performed for the same reason; namely, to improve a firm's prospects. The establishment of goals and objectives differs greatly from all other aspects of planning just as the process of establishing a hypothesis differs from the process of drawing implications from it. Goals and objectives derive their strength as much from judgment as from analysis, and realistic forecasts are as much the expression of creative thinking as they are of arithmetic. Corporate objectives and forecasts are products of the marriage of the subjective and the objective.

This does not accord with common thinking. Most managers cause or allow objectives and forecasts to be built on the basis of arithmetic and consensus, and apply their imagination most creatively to the selection of strategies for accomplishing them. This is backwards. There is more room for creative thinking and initiative in setting goals and projecting sales than in building plans for implementation. Therefore, it behooves every firm to found its intentions and expectancies on sound knowledge of the realities of the outside world rather than on such things as polls taken within. The path to bankruptcy requires little vision to traverse; for those whose eyes are turned within, it is the route most often chosen.

In most small businesses, goals are of the gut variety. They are felt rather than cognitively arrived at, talked about rather than written and communicated. But worthy goals are not so derived; they are based on an analysis of what the company does well and a continuing reading of its market. The goals are then shaped by having all company executives discuss, challenge, test, modify, and agree to them. Such goals unify direction, strengthen policy decisions, and make meaningful the team concept of management.

Such goals are also rare in small firms. Firstly, as can be judged from the foregoing description, arriving at them is a complex process. Secondly, most small firms are not sophisticated enough to see merit in dealing with uncertainties. And lastly, most firms are unwilling to spend the money that destiny planning undeniably requires.

Nevertheless, the value of establishing explicit and well-founded goals and objectives cannot be challenged, even in the smallest of firms as defined in these pages. And the task of setting them does not have to break the firm's back.

Following are several goals that one small service firm set for itself:

> Although there is now, and probably will continue to be, a trend toward increasing size of organizations, we are confident that the medium-size business will remain. The needs of these firms will continue to be unique, and an organization that can serve these needs will have an economic reason to exist.

> We think that people will want more satisfying and challenging work. An organization that wants to attract and keep the good people it

needs if it is to prosper has to create such work deliberately and consciously.

The relatively informal atmosphere that most members of our firm enjoy is as much a function of our size as of anything else. Studies of groups have confirmed that it is possible to maintain this atmosphere as long as the total number of people does not top 500. The size of an organization can therefore be taken to be a primary factor in the satisfaction of employees. We intend to increase the size of the firm through normal growth and acquisitions until we have reached approximately 500 people. To retain an ideal size we will seek to acquire new and more desirable customers and drop those who are both unprofitable and troublesome. It may also be sensible to decentralize our line operations into several offices to permit each individual to feel that he is a part of the organization.

The areas served by our customers have expanded geographically. Because we respect family life, we intend to restrict our offices primarily to metropolitan areas; expand within the next five years through the acquisition of other firms; and, when proper, establish a decentralized base. We will then have local offices with staff members who are deeply involved in their communities and whose travel obligations and customers' needs are so balanced that their personal lives and comforts are not jeopardized.

To exist in the economic world requires the provision of service at least equal to that of other organizations; to grow requires the ability to offer superior service. A number of firms in our area offer products and services on a par with ours. Why then should a customer stay with us, and why should a prospective customer come with us, unless we can offer something special? The answer lies in having a staff that is superior in motivation and knowledge. Each staff member, then, must have an equal opportunity to do challenging and diversified work while providing exceptional service to customers.

When we look back over the past ten years and realize how dramatic have been the changes in society and in our field, we must assume that change is normal and accelerating. To equip ourselves with the new knowledge that high-quality service will demand, we must make a commitment to lifelong education. The firm will seek to provide for our employees as much of the knowledge and the opportunities to absorb it as possible.

Starting with these assumptions, we propose the following company goals:

We intend to conduct our operations so that the highest business ethics will be the minimum performance standards that we will try to achieve. It is important that each person consider his work rewarding. We accept the fact that the self-image of most of us is substantially based on our feelings about our work and the respect we get from the people for whom and with whom we work.

We will go on trying to provide personal security, opportunity for growth, respect, and fair compensation for each individual's unique contribution to the success of the organization.

The ideal is to merge the goals of customer service, organizational growth, and personal aspirations so that they are consistent and each gains strength from the other.

This firm's goals included specific points on the service it would offer in an effort to create a unique marketing advantage; the services and customers it would *not* take on because of incompatibility or lack of profitability; the training and educational support it would provide and expect from its staff; and the specific steps it would take to attract and compensate the outstanding individuals it needed in order to provide superior service.

Once specific corporate objectives have been set, each department should take the lead in setting its own objectives. This includes departments that have no direct contact with the buying public, such as purchasing, manufacturing, and accounting, as well as marketing, sales, credit, service, and public relations. When internal contributions have been made, and possible side effects have been considered, the final plan should be pinned down in writing.

That is no simple task; in many cases you will be talking about intangibles. But even objectives relating to intangibles—such as attitudes, images, or individual development—are worthy of being planned for and written down for all to see.

FORECASTING

Forecasting is one of the most poorly performed parts of the planning process. Contrary to their avowed role to help companies maximize utilization of their resources in reaching for the largest share of their markets, forecasts more often constrain utilization and market position. That is because most forecasts are generated wholly out of internal views of what the world of tomorrow will be like rather than out of a balanced analysis of information from all relevant sources.

A good starting point for a small business manager determined to put a solid foundation under the planning process is to make forecasts of the major cost elements of his business. He should first carefully analyze their historical trends and then add predictive information for the next two or three years. (Few small businesses can predict beyond this period with any accuracy.) The forecasts should then be broken down by principal categories of expense for budget formation, investment decisions, and pricing as well as the usual projections.

When forecasting is an extension of trends, modified by economic indicators and changes in the firm's asset position, it has limited value. It helps in the development of a pro forma budget, which in turn satisfies some managers' craving for appearance. But it does nothing to force attention to a firm's opportunities. Projecting sales and challenging expenses on the basis of painstaking fact-finding and the analysis of alternatives (the essence of planning) produce immensely useful results. Unfortunately, many small firm managers are uneasy about putting on paper what they think their business will be like three years ahead. To reduce the uneasiness, the manager can use a what-if tool in the form of computer time-sharing programs that analyze a range of possible factors and their consequences.

Better decisions can be made if reasonable alternatives are considered. Assume that a company's sales have been rising at an average rate of 10 percent a year and the anticipated growth rate for the next few years is between 5 and 15 percent. A manager can use programs available through several computer time-sharing facilities to get a sensitivity analysis of each material factor in the projected financial statements at several levels of sales.

Thus the manager can see what the effect on profits, cash, inventories, and receivables would be if sales were to grow or shrink at 5, 7, 9, 11, 13, or 15 percent a year; if receivables are outstanding for an average of 35, 40, 45, 50, 55, or 60 days; if inventories are required to be available 40, 50, 60, 70, or 80 days prior to projected sales. All these alternatives can be presented easily, inexpensively (about $100 for the total package), and quickly. Many banks, data processing service bureaus, and accounting firms make such programs available.

The results of the what-if or sensitivity analysis can provide a range of possible choices that put the stamp of reasonableness on forecasts, a powerful tool for planning.

The process of spelling out the wanted results—that is, translating the felt destiny of the firm into statements that can be understood, tested, and agreed to—is the beginning of introducing order into the affairs of a firm. It is, in short, the beginning of rationalization. From it, courses of action can be set out that maximize resources, one of the prerequisites of superior corporate performance.

In sum, if we assume that servicing customer needs economically is one of the bases for business survival, an indispensable and unique function of management is to determine what the company's resources are and then to reduce the risks of randomness in the environment by picking the services, customers, and procedures to exploit those resources with economy. Planning puts the inside world of the company and the outside world of the environment, including customers, together rationally. Its results are seen when managers do something they could not have done if they had not planned.

We have emphasized that the route to decisions on a firm's conceptual mission, its purposes, and the planning process that results in establishing its service–product–customer strategy starts in the outside world. From there it leads to analysis of the strengths, weaknesses, resources, style, and limitations of the individual firm: the choice of goals which will satisfy expected customer needs; the plans to reach those goals; and the measurements and feedback that show how operations compare with the plans.

4

RATIONALIZATION

IN THIS ERA of the computer, it was probably inevitable that systems thinking should come to color all our thinking about business. We now often hear it said that a well-run business forms a system, a collection of coordinated parts, each essential to the operation of the system as a whole.

Few views offer such rich rewards for probing and understanding the nature of a business enterprise. In addition to its value as a tool of understanding, the systems view has practical value. When vigorously employed in problem-finding, it can lead to discoveries that can significantly raise the quality of decisions. Among other things, the systems view forces one to deal with the firm conceptually, a perspective that produces decisions necessarily different from (and potentially more valuable than) those resulting from dealing with particular problems or situations by themselves. The systems view obligates one to deal with a business as a whole when engaging in decision making, a relationship that is enormously productive in trouble-shooting and setting the course for the future.

Two activities are vital to business survival and prosperity. Each is highly conceptual. One concerns the selection of a firm's destiny— the purposes for which it will exist. That has been covered in the chapter on externalization. The other concerns adaptation of the system to the goals or purposes envisioned. The process of adaptation we call rationalization.

As has been noted, small firms generally do not deal with the conceptual aspects of their businesses as effectively as large ones do. The small firm manager rarely stops to think about his firm's mission, even less often postulates it, and can be challenged to consider it only with greatest difficulty. A rejoinder that typifies the attitude of the manager is, "Who do you think we are, General Motors?"

Though each firm forms a system, that does not mean it has a chosen destiny that confers particular benefits. Though a firm does not choose its destiny it has a destiny nonetheless. By default, it will have a homeostatic one—the destiny of a system doing no more than maintaining itself.

Systems in which maintenance is the leading function are passive and vulnerable. Though durable enough in fairly stable environments, they cannot last through crisis. Without a sense of direction, they lack the competence to mobilize quickly and redirect their resources. Without much contact with the outer world, they have little immunity to economic ills.

The firm that constitutes a rational system can be readily recognized. It has clear, relevant, and reinforcing goals which have been disseminated, a goal-supporting planning activity, clear assignment of job responsibilities and performance standards, and a control and feedback system that keeps operations on line with targets and provides input from the outside to modify the plans.

PLANNING FOR ACTION

Planning for action, or fulfillment planning, entails making rational selections of strategies from realistic options; correctly proportioning and assigning the physical, human, and economic resources required to make the journey; and establishing control over the process of implementation. It is a detailed, complicated job that involves hard choices. In that sense it is an intellectually demanding pursuit. Most firms do it poorly, and many small firms do it not at all.

In a company of any size, planning is critical to keeping resources from being overtaxed by commitments. Because they respect that concept and know the benefits of planning, large companies give planning much attention. However, the majority of small businesses do no planning worthy of the name, even though their resources are scarcer and therefore more precious than in large businesses. Many small businessmen feel their firm's flexibility and closeness to their customers make planning superfluous. Those who feel less secure or want to appear progressive are content with sales forecasting and budgeting. Both are useful planning *tools*, but neither is true planning.

The need for planning, its advantages, and its problems are too well known to repeat. But the enormous outpouring of material on the subject must be largely sterile because few businesses plan as well as they are capable of doing. Most managers do not seem to care for or are afraid of planning, as evidenced by the little effort they make to understand the planning process and their preference for action rather than reflection.

Perhaps looking at the work managers do will yield an answer to the paradox. In *The Nature of Managerial Work* * Henry Mintzberg shows how the manager's diverse, reactive, multirole activities poorly prepare him for planning functions. Planning starts with reflection and conceptualization, neither of which can be done in fits and starts. Yet the demands upon managers tend to be urgent and unremitting. The unbroken time spans for seeking out, identifying, and laying the plans for exploiting the firm's opportunities are seldom available to managers. Executives in small firms are in the worst position of all. They engage in more numerous brief and fragmented activities than executives in large firms. They are also more directly involved in the primary operations of their firms and have to be ready to step in as a substitute operator, primarily because of the small number of people employed. The picture is one that readily explains why true planning is not generally found in small firms.

In planning, however, companies probably have their greatest opportunity to achieve superior performance. No matter what measure is chosen—sales, earnings per share, stock prices, earnings on common equity, earnings on total capital—studies have shown that economic performance and formal planning are strongly and positively related.

Although the relationship between planning and thinking as an element in business is direct, it is rare to find action based on acceptance of the view that "the ultimate essence of management effectiveness lies in rational thought processes . . . ," that "it is the quality of thinking behind the actions that determines the quality of management." † The ability of a firm to add some economic or social value to the world is almost entirely rational. Unfortunately, the attitudes and practices that prevail in planning suggest that most small firms have a long way to go before their corporate heads bump against the ceiling of their capacities.

* New York: Harper & Row, Publishers, 1973.
† Merritt L. Kastens, "Cogito, Ergo Sum," *Interfaces*, May 1972.

The shortcomings in small companies with respect to planning stem largely from three deficiencies:

1. Small companies tend to be exploiters rather than creators of opportunities.
2. Small companies usually commit themselves to action without the benefit of a program for achievement.
3. Small companies react to rather than anticipate situations.

Small companies tend to wait for opportunities to become apparent rather than expend effort to find, identify, and set about exploiting appropriate opportunities. Small business managers tend to focus on operating problems and handle their day-to-day chores with greater skill and pleasure than activities with deferred feedback, such as planning.

Consider the sense of importance derived from the pile of letters, memos, and phone messages facing the executive when he returns from vacation. They reinforce his sense of place in the firm's history, his central position in daily operations, and his reluctance to take time off for an activity as remote to him as planning. As a result, small business managers do not build much experience in planning and find the planning process strange and difficult. This is unfortunate since without competent planning small companies cannot help but let opportunities slip by. Those who are planners know best what the opportunities are, which to go after, and how to exploit them.

As to the second deficiency, managers of small businesses tend to commit their firms without the support of detailed programs that specify resources, authorities, deadlines, controls, and so forth. Oddly, the very ability that enables small firms to survive in the first place—cutting corners, watching pennies, avoiding unnecessary risks, being on top of daily operations—may be what prevents them from developing a planning process capable of insuring their survival. Knowing so well what is going on day by day may lead the small business manager to feel he is equal to whatever the future may bring. That arrogance is often the first sign of aging in an otherwise young enterprise.

The difficulty in switching from a reactive to a planning basis is small compared to the difficulties of implementation. Managers in small firms tend to defend fiercely the much vaunted small firm's flexibility and thus find it difficult to be steadfast in the implementation of plans. One small business manager, who had struggled through the planning process to the first frustrating stages of the changes brought on by the plans, said: "Ideas are easy; putting them to work is hard."

Judging from the general quality of plans, few managers have the patience to engage in the complex and sophisticated work they entail. Reliance on the here-and-now skills demonstrates managerial competence but leaves a firm's future virtually unprotected.

Finally, the manager's preference for reacting to rather than anticipating events is only partially size-related. The pressures under which all managers work force them to be more concerned with stimulus–reaction than with planning and other conceptual, reflective activities. With a thin staff (usually the case in small firms), the function of looking ahead takes a low priority in the long list of undone tasks.

Planning is not less needed or easier in a small company than a large. The small firm also has to be in control of its progress into the future if it is to prosper. But the planning problems of each are different. For example, a study we conducted for the American Management Associations in 1969 showed that executives generally see planning as being harder to do in small companies and keeping things on course harder in large companies. Whether valid or not, these views undoubtedly lend a good deal of support to the reluctance of managers in small firms to plan and the common excuse that large companies can do it more easily. But planning is not necessarily easier in large firms, as their better resources are often offset by conflicts of interest and views between unit and headquarters personnel far exceeding those between the key people in small firms. On the other hand, planning is not easier in small companies, because they are more subject to rapid market and production cycle changes than large firms and, overall, have fewer alternatives to choose from. The large company needs to focus on carefully scheduling the large investments required by long production runs and personnel acquisitions; the small company needs to be kept free of harm and to be helped, when possible, to benefit from the frequent changes forced on it by the market or the economy.

The fact that current problems keep the small business manager's hands full probably constitutes the strongest planning constraint. Planning requires taking executive time from today's problems and operations, which have immediate payout, and applying it to the reaching for future benefits, which are always less assured. The shortage of executive time to do the planning, combined with the relative lack of planning experience, makes planning in the small company especially difficult.

Because planning is difficult, is only occasionally used effectively in small business, and has a disproportionate return for properly applied effort, we will outline in some detail the steps to be taken by a small firm to implement a practical plan. Most of the steps require answers to tough questions. The first questions are strategic:

- *Internal.* What do we do best? What do we have to do that requires improvement? What are our resources in terms of products, people, finance?
- *Market.* What do our customers want? Why do they do business with us? How do we compare with competitors?
- *Environment.* What is happening in the outside world that is likely to affect us, our markets, and our customers in terms of government action or political, cultural, and social trends?

These questions are only a beginning. Though factual answers to at least these questions are fundamental, planning requires far more detail in areas of special interest, strength, or opportunity.

The mechanics of planning are best developed by posing the key questions to a group of top managers (and perhaps outsiders) a few weeks in advance of a scheduled one- or two-day meeting. It is helpful to assign the fact gathering to individuals and to schedule the planning meeting away from the office. This not only lends deserved dignity and importance to the process, but allows open-ended, uninterrupted discussion and the development of team spirit.

One or two outsiders can bring with them the necessary objectivity and balance and can fill knowledge gaps. If the company lacks expertise in personnel selection, finance, exporting, organizational analysis and development, or any other significant area, an outsider can provide not only the facts and experience but a friendly skepticism on overall plans.

Following general agreement on the conclusions drawn from the internal, market, and environment situational analyses, a three-year plan should be drawn in broad outline. It should be laid out in three-month segments and should describe the balanced objectives of the company in terms of products or services, profits, markets, sales, people, space, and finance. A detailed one-year plan should be prepared in monthly segments. The three-year plan should be updated quarterly; the annual plan, monthly. This means that at all times the company will have a broad three-year plan and a detailed one-year plan. Perhaps the most important result of this regular updating is to make planning a process rather than an isolated, occasional act.

Plans require controls and feedback so that the people responsible for them know how they are doing; therefore, measuring and monitoring points must be set up to provide data individually tailored to the needs of managers in different jobs and with different levels of under-standing of the planning process. As much as possible the feedback information should be quantitative and verifiable so that it will be accepted and used to stimulate action rather than be challenged and serve as a digression. Individual goals should be tied to corporate goals so that there is common understanding of the overall purpose. The best reinforcement of corporate goals is a compensation and promotion program that rewards results and behavior that are in tune with the goals.

For two reasons this discussion has provided only the barest outline of the planning process. First, there are many good texts and articles on planning; it is the essence of management. Second, we are concerned with planning for the small company. The long-range planning departments, and other procedures and paraphernalia of planning in large firms, are not only impractical but intimidating for the small firm.

For successful small firm planning we emphasize these elements: (1) Investigate the factual bases of the company, its customers, and its environment. (2) Develop alternative opportunities based on the resources of the company and the anticipated needs of the customers. (3) Plan no more than three years ahead, unless there is a proven need to do so. (4) Make planning a group participative process. (5) Keep it alive through updating and feedback. (6) Reward people (at least in part) on their ability to plan. (7) Assign responsibility for getting the job done to one person, preferably the chief executive. His backing is always necessary; his direct involvement makes success more likely.

The recommendation that small business managers exploit planning as a competitive advantage is not an exhortation that they follow the example of large businesses; for, in fact, the need for planning is in considerable degree influenced by the character of organization structure, managerial style, and executive capabilities as well as the technologies and markets involved. The amount and scope of planning needed, for example, are directly related to the distance between supervisors and subordinates, the span of control, the degree to which authority is distributed, the variety of products or services provided, and other factors that vary more or less directly with business size.

The importance of fitting size and character together is indicated in a letter sent by the president of a chemical firm, now a division of

a conglomerate, to the authors after their initial venture into writing
about small business.* He wrote:

> A division such as mine, while a small company as measured by your
> definition, behaves, nevertheless, much like a large corporation be-
> cause of our being owned by a conglomerate. The net result is that
> the division, though small, suffers from some of the disadvantages of
> a large corporation. Specifically, we do not have the flexibility that
> small companies have. When we were independent, if an opportu-
> nity arose for us to purchase the machinery of a used plant, we did
> it on the spot. Now, if we haven't included the item in our capital
> appropriation requests, prepared in the prior year when we had no
> idea the opportunity existed, we lose the chance. If we go through
> the motions of getting approval of the administrative committee, it is
> usually too late because a fast actor has seized the opportunity.
>
> The same thing applies to our salary program. The parent company
> has set up ranges of salaries among its many divisions for presidents,
> marketing managers, research directors, and so forth. While there is
> flexibility within each range, I am dissatisfied with the limitations
> imposed on us. Not only are we limited in what we can pay key
> people, but they have set up a program of salary grades.
>
> To get the same pay, our controller must be in the same grade as a
> controller for what they consider an "equivalent" division. I question
> their definition of equivalency. Nevertheless, here is another example
> of a small company (now a division) being restricted by the same
> kind of thinking as exists in a large corporation.
>
> Among the programs a small business can use is a profit-sharing plan
> to attract an entrepreneurial person. Large companies find it hard to
> have profit sharing. If they grew by acquisition, they could not have
> such a plan in one division and not in the others. If not, they are well
> past thinking of the motivation profit sharing offers. Instead, because
> of uniformity, they have pension plans. Actually, the small firm's
> profit-sharing plan was usually in lieu of a pension plan and payments
> from it could be paid only on retirement, death, or other circumstances
> as deemed appropriate. Actuarially, the employee may be better off
> with a pension plan because of the stability of payments being made
> to it. Nevertheless, the kind of motivation offered by profit sharing in
> its sensitivity to profits holds great value in a small company.

Large firms have several planning advantages that are not available to small companies. The first advantage lies in the greater manpower resources of large companies, which reduces the consequences

* How Management Is Different in Small Companies, AMA, New York, 1972.

of faulty decision making. Plans are subject to a much greater variety of views and competences in a large firm. This virtuosity, though it usually slows down the planning pace and limits dramatically novel ideas, offers some protection against potentially disastrous planning decisions. Planning in small companies, on the other hand, is subject to the scrutiny of fewer (and, often, similarly inclined) minds. The danger that a bad plan will slip through is consequently greater.

The second advantage in a large firm is that it is better able to support the costs of planning—not just the costs to which plans commit the company but the direct costs of the planning activities themselves. Though it is not often expressed, the cost of moving a company safely into the future can be one of its greatest single expenses. Small companies, accustomed as they are to watching dollars, find it difficult to allocate funds to the development of sound plans, which may involve purchasing outside research, spending a weekend away from the plant once a year for an overall review of performance and a goal-setting session, and establishing feedback procedures to keep track of the implementation of plans.

The third advantage is more voluminous and varied information. Consider two strategies, both apparently based on information about changing population patterns. In the face of a declining birthrate and attendant smaller baby market, Gerber Products Company, primarily a baby-food producer, expanded into baby clothing and insurance for the newborn. In this way it is holding onto its customer acceptance and increasing sales by selling more to the same market. Johnson & Johnson has directed its ads for baby powder to men (to smooth their rough skins) and its baby shampoo to babies' big sisters and mothers, a strategy aimed at reaching new customers by stretching the appeal of accepted products.

All generalizations about planning must be brought down to the level of each small company's individual situation. Therefore, the starting point for planning is a definition of present status: what the company does well and poorly, what its strengths and weaknesses are in people, products, finance, markets, and so on. From this analysis, planning can move to the establishment of corporate objectives that take into account not only the results of the analysis but economic trends and changing environmental conditions. Clearly, the individual character of the facts involved and the objectives chosen (from which plans develop) means that planning has to be carefully tailored to each company, not mass-produced.

Following are some of the questions that can be used to start the analysis of where the small firm is. Each question should be answered in the light of the firm's strengths and weaknesses: the strengths to be identified, then protected and exploited; the weaknesses to be overcome.

Products-Services (P-S)
What are the P-S for which customers come to us?
What are the most distinctive P-S we offer?
What are the new P-S? The fading P-S?
What are our plans for developing new P-S?
How do we compare with competitors?
What economic (value added) factor do we provide?
What are the most profitable P-S we offer? The least profitable?

Customers
What business do we do with what customers at what profitability and investment?
What markets do we now serve?
What new markets should we serve?
How do our customers see us?
What do they think we do well or poorly?

Prices
How are our prices set?
When were they last reviewed?
How do they compare competitively?

Profitability
How do we compare with the industry? With our own best period?

Facilities (Plant and Equipment)
Do we have the facilities we need?
Do we know what is available in the industry?
Do we have controls over productivity? Over obsolescence?

Finance
What is our flexibility for growth? For recession?
What sources of funds do we use? What sources should we use?
What risks are we exposed to?
What controls do we have over cash, receivables, inventories, debt?
What controls should we have?

Information
What are our sources of information as to what's going on in the outside world?

What action do we take with the information we have?
What action would we take with additional information?
Do we know its cost-effectiveness ratio?
Where do we stand in relation to computerization?
Do we have adequate input from external sources?

Decision Making

What decisions are critical to our business?
Who makes what decisions on what bases? (a key question)
Are our decisions based on adequate information?
How can our decision making be improved?

People

What do we know about our present management and technical
staff in terms of age, skills, potential, turnover, and retirement?
How does our fringe benefit program compare with that of other
firms? With the expectations of our staff?
How do our people feel about the company? About its prospects?
About their own future?

Dangers

What would we do if substantial changes took place in our products-
services; customers; competitors; key staff; location-environment;
sources of supply?

Effective planning in the small company reflects the recognition
that orthodox planning, with its point-to-point coverage, rigid objectives, and fixed expectations about outcomes, is insufficient. What the
small firm needs is more comprehensive and integrated planning and
forecasting. Planning in progressive companies is being broadened to
include identification and continual monitoring of progress toward
major corporate and unit objectives, formulation of policies needed to
attain desired and desirable futures, allocation of resources, and development of productive internal and external relationships. This is
a new kind of planning directed at securing changes in whole systems,
enabling the enterprise to adapt effectively in complex environments.
It differs from merely manipulating such variables as capital investment, production, and staffing within existing subsystems.

The new planning is goal-oriented, ongoing, and sophisticated, involving a substantial broadening of the criteria used in the approach
to complex problems. It emphasizes integration of planning in two
axes. The vertical axis encompasses policy as well as strategic and tac-
tical elements; and the horizontal axis encompasses the full range of

business functions and organizational elements. The new planning also requires extensive feedback and less than the usual emphasis on top-down planning. It promotes contribution from every level and involves substantial individual participation.

Introducing such planning into organizations committed to obsolete organizational forms or incremental decision processes poses serious problems. Small companies that are wedded to such organizations and processes must work hard to change these forms and processes before they can do effective planning.

Planning in small companies should focus on the short range rather than the long range and on maintaining the ability to detect and respond to or bring about change rather than on maintaining stability in operations. Changing circumstances affect small companies more than large. Accordingly, a major concern in setting up planning procedures in a small company must be to provide a means for modifying plans to meet such changes. This almost certainly means that the plans of small companies need not extend as far into the future as the plans of large companies do since the changes affecting small companies come more frequently and are less predictable. This point receives support from views such as the following:

> Many small companies have been frustrated in their attempts to plan ahead because they have tried to follow the familiar advice offered from the safety of the seminar or lecture platform: "Decide what business or businesses you want your firm to be in ten years from now. Determine through market research the potential volume of these businesses. Then decide what share of the market you want for your company."

> These procedures may be sound in the corporate giants but are wasteful in small concerns. Planning in the small company must be realistically scaled to the limitations of time, energy and data available.*

Since the data relating to the future are more limited and less accurate in small companies than in large ones, planning in small companies should be directed more to finding and exploiting opportunities than to creating them.

The necessity for focusing on the short range is readily demonstrable. Take the example of the small plane, the Piper Cub. It is vital that the pilot of such a plane do a thorough job of exploring the visual

* The Research Institute of America, Inc., *Research Institute Recommendations*, Sec. 2, September 1969.

envelope, the world he can see, rather than to explore conditions beyond the range of his sight. In contrast, the pilot of a large jet needs to be much more interested in what weather he faces several hundred miles ahead than in what the sky looks like in the immediate vicinity. Because of the rate of speed of the jet, the pilot's visual contact has far less meaning. Since he cannot handle his cockpit responsibilities and also keep his eyes on his immediate environment, it is much more important for him to look into the future.

Similarly, small companies should devote far more effort to shaping the near future than the distant future. For the small business, it is a waste of effort and an exercise in daydreaming to have definitive plans (as opposed to broad goals or objectives) for a long period.

Small firms should focus on strategy more than on operations because their operational affairs are well controlled and "operating" is their greatest skill. The small business generally uses its money more intelligently than its other resources and should seek to improve its use of nonfinancial resources. Many a small company is guilty of poor planning; many another has no plans at all. What they do have instead are controls of all kinds. Yet it should be the other way around. Large companies ought to focus on the establishment of viable controls because they plan rather well, but their planning oftentimes does not work because they have much more to control and their controls are weak or inappropriate.

The informality of the smaller company is the source of some control problems. Smaller companies need fewer and simpler controls because they have fewer organizational levels, managers are closer to operations, and operations are often simpler. But they do need the feedback that even the simplest controls provide. Small companies, which traditionally have relied on personal management for control, should pay particular attention to the control requirements of plans; that is, to the establishment of control standards, information generation and transmission, performance appraisal, and so forth.

In small companies the chief executive is often the planner. This can impose limitations as well as offer benefits. While planning in such cases can be efficiently done, it is likely to suffer from one-sidedness. When a small company president plans, he often finds that his plans are resisted by members of the organization because they are his alone. The planning he does is usually in the light of his personal financial interests. His assumptions and the results sought are difficult to communicate, and it is equally difficult to gain understanding and support. Effective planning requires talk with others, inside and outside the firm, and clear, unambiguous statements of objectives. To the small firm, help from the outside is especially valuable for its objectivity and practicality.

In both the planning process and the content of the plans, managers should keep in mind that the organization chart is an inadequate, limited picture of the firm. It excludes individuals and groups who are part of the organization although outside it: customers, vendors, unions, banks, governmental agencies, local community groups, and professional advisers (accountant, attorney, insurance agent). Full systems planning includes using the knowledge of people from this list and considering the effect of specific plans on them. A decision to import an item previously manufactured locally should consider input from or at least reflect sensitivity to the reactions of customers (feeling about foreign goods), vendors (delivery time, alternative sources), banker (willingness to provide credit, help in paperwork), unions (impact of imports on local labor force), and CPA, attorney, and insurance agent (new accounting, tax, legal, and risk problems).

The benefits of planning are not limited to its direct consequences, such as improved use of resources and reduced waste. Planning also produces a whole range of secondary benefits. When properly executed, for example, the activity entails periodic evaluations of the company as a whole as well as of its major functions. In that way planning can show up areas where improvement is needed or where opportunities lie. Bringing assets to bear on problems is greatly facilitated in a company that does sound planning. Another secondary benefit is that setting objectives has profound implications for many aspects of the business, including organization structure. Planning also has motivational value because it requires the participation of those who are going to implement the plans.

The small business manager should recognize that his on-the-job experience does little to prepare him for planning. The work of planning is a specialty, different from selling and different from designing or producing a product—as different as tennis is from golf. Contrary to common opinion, it is not intrinsically a part of these and other fundamental activities. An offshoot of this is the myth that because small company managers "wear many hats" they are natural planners. Planning differs from other functions not only in the form of activities involved but also in the faculties involved. It takes reflective thinking, self-analysis, and ways of looking at the company and its people which at times will be uncomfortable.

Small business managers must recognize that plans will die if it is assumed they have a life force of their own. Establishing a plan is only the first step in attaining an objective. Once committed to a plan, a company must keep it alive by keeping it in the forefront of everyone's consciousness. This involves more than establishing reporting procedures and controls. It involves human attention—which is not easily engaged and still less easily commanded. Planning must be integrated into the company's value system. Only then can planning benefits be realized. Planning can influence a company's future only when it is congruent with the most basic motives and interests of the firm, whether these are obvious or buried beneath the surface.

One objection against planning is based on an assumed relationship between growth and plans. Planning does not imply or require growth. If a small company manager decides to maintain the size of his organization, work fewer hours, and provide for the firm's continuity without increased sales or personnel, he will have to plan to reach these goals; they will not happen by chance.

A manager who is at the starting point of planning is in a position to ask Peter Drucker's famous questions: "If you weren't in it, would you go into it? If that fellow didn't work for you, would you hire him?" A few examples will prove the power of the questions.

EXAMPLE 1:

A retailer had problems with one of his stores 100 miles from his home office. Despite 15 years of trying all his tricks, the store remained marginal. Asked the question, "If you didn't have a store in this town, would you open one?" he replied, "Of course not." The next question was, "Why not close the store?" After struggling with the problems of a lease, separation pay for employees, and his own emotions about giving up, the retailer closed the store and eliminated the headache.

EXAMPLE 2:

A service organization had built its early reputation by expert work in one area of specialization. Although the importance of this specialty had declined, as had the firm's unique expertise, oldtimers attacked any suggestions that the service be curtailed or modified as though virtue itself was at stake. The result was a stalemate that ended only when a group of younger managers asked the question, "Without criticizing the past, but considering our present alternatives, would we go into this specialization today with the same investment of time, money, and people as we now have?" The answer had to be no, and the shackles were at last cut loose. New services were brought in and the old specialty became proportionately less significant.

EXAMPLE 3:

For years the head of a manufacturing company complained to his attorney about the inadequacy of his factory superintendent and the difficulty in dealing with the man, who was a holdover from his father's time. Loyalty to his father and unwillingness to face the short-term practical consequences of letting the superintendent go were finally overcome when he was asked, "If Charlie were not working for you, would you hire him?" Obviously not, so he let Charlie go quickly, gave him a generous severance check, and replaced him with a more competent and personally acceptable manager.

INFORMATION AND COMMUNICATION

For any company to survive and grow its managers must make timely, balanced judgments and effectively control the company's activities. Both judgments and control are information-based. It follows, therefore, that survival and growth are information-dependent.

Businessmen are paying increasing attention to information. But information still is not managed as a resource in the way that money and inventories are. Information is commonly viewed as a necessary evil of doing business, and the bulk of management effort directed to it aims at minimizing its cost and the time it absorbs. Few managers look upon information as a resource, something potentially worthy of being put on the asset side of the balance sheet. This chapter considers how information can be a greater asset in small firms.

One of the limitations in being small is that the opportunities for significantly improving performance are fewer than in a large firm. Most of the means by which small businesses can establish themselves, survive, or improve earnings either are subject to size-related constraints—such as capital and knowledge shortages—or are equally available to firms of any size. Consequently, the small business manager has to be unusually creative to come up with a profit-improving production, marketing, or administrative procedure, method, or technique offering special advantages to his firm.

Because of the rarity of profit improvement opportunities, managers in small business tend to ignore them and cling to familiar, tried-and-true methods. Most of these managers learned early in their careers to become dollar-watchers but never learned that decisions with the most direct and obvious payout do not necessarily serve their firm's long-range interests.

But the very scarcity of improvement opportunities in small firms makes it important that they be searched for diligently. Competition from large firms, for example, is no longer so bound to long production runs as it was, and the vaunted flexibility of small firms is rapidly declining in the presence of an increasing capacity of big business to meet small needs in the marketplace. Consider how individualized a Chevrolet or Ford can be made (the computer is changing the character of business in more ways than one). Even between small firms, competitiveness is increasing as managerial competence rises. Therefore, a significant and uncommon direction in which small firms can profitably look for improvement opportunities is the fuller and better use of information.

Small firms tend to have a profound information skew. The total amount of information, formal and informal, used in decision making is tilted in the direction of the personal, the subjective. Much of the knowledge that managers use they pick up from personal contacts and observation, and much of it is oriented to their own needs rather than the firm's needs.

It is true that the typical manager in small business sees directly a good deal more of the activities under and related to his command than the typical manager in large companies. But this cannot be taken to justify an excessive dependence upon personal observation and experience. Managers in small firms also need what they too seldom have: objective information about costs, profits, sales, and whatever else is germane and economically procurable.

The key terms are "germane" and "economically procurable." Because of the scale of operations and number of uncertainties affecting large companies, a vast amount of information floats around in them, much of which is excessive to their needs at any given moment. No small company can afford to be in such a position. On the other hand, the notion that small business managers should have as much accurate information at their command as possible is equally erroneous. Information is all too "possible"; even breathing in its direction tends to stir it up!

Information is expensive to generate, process, and use. Excessive information clogs the channels of communication. Information is not excessive merely because one person or unit of organization declares it to be. What wastes one man's time is greatly needed by another. Therefore, in our information-joined society, the power to know and let others know should be shared. In a study conducted by *Industry Week* magazine, only 2 percent of the 1,000 managers surveyed felt they received more information than they needed; nearly 40 percent felt they were receiving too little information.* Because of the secrecy

* April 23, 1973, p. 33.

with which many small companies are managed, we think it likely that an even larger percentage of small firm managers want more information.

Closely related to the information problem is the problem of communication, thought to be the bigger problem by large company managers. The small company has advantages here, since greater organizational size increases a man's distance from the people who influence his activities. Opportunities for an overview of the whole operation become scarcer as size increases. A modern foreman, for example, can easily live out his life in a large company and never meet a man who sells the product he makes. When men involved in related activities are out of direct contact with each other, their perceptions may become dangerously distorted. Because free and open communication becomes more complicated with growth, a man at any level becomes more isolated from others at the same level. Direct communication with distant decision makers is almost impossible, with the consequence that in large companies subordinates focus a considerable share of their energies on finding out and verifying potential decisions for consistency.

The small company does not have this problem in the same degree. Yet benefits from improving the quality and use of its information bank cannot be realized without also improving communication. The most critical factor in keeping all the lines plugged in properly in any company is communication. This requires that some portion of the communication system be formally designed and procedurally maintained. Without such formality there is slim assurance of free passage of directives and results to and from all areas.

One significant advantage gained by the small firm in formalizing the design, documentation, and maintenance of its information and communication system is protection against managerial subjectivity. Where the same person generates and uses information, as is the case in many small companies, objectivity may be severely curtailed or altogether destroyed. In large companies the user of information seldom generates it and therefore cannot materially influence its shape. In a small company, however, there are ample opportunities for the decision maker to be secretive about the information used in making decisions. Formalization diminishes this so-called information privacy.

As explosions will, the information explosion is making its mark. Probably no sector of society has been more profoundly affected by it or has responded more definitively to it than industry.

Most large companies have set up some kind of organizational unit for monitoring the flood of external information. Even when small company managers are aware of the profit potentials in being well informed, they don't quite know how to become so. Caught between the need to know about the powerful, subtle, possibly dangerous forces in the environment and the need to cope with daily operating problems, small business managers have few guides to help them allocate their time. Being in the smallest segments of markets, they cannot easily see which, among the alternatives facing them, has first call on their time.

A few guides: No small company can afford to marshal all the facts needed to determine the consequences of all feasible courses of action. The information it gathers, processes, and uses must be limited to be cost-effective.

Another guide springs from the first. If information must be limited, it must be tailored to the ongoing needs of the company if it is to be effective.

What are these needs? For one thing, to survive, which entails being able to identify market opportunities, perceive threats, and control costs. To compete successfully entails limiting the small firm's activity to the field in which it is capable of generating profits. That, particularly, requires having the right information.

It is a peculiarity of small businesses that they are so much at the mercy of consumer preference changes. Therefore, another measure of the rightness of information is how well it alerts managers to such changes. Good information is customer-oriented.

SURMOUNTING THE INFORMATION BARRIER

If we define rationalization as the bending of resources to the intentions and opportunities of a firm, then planned sharing of information becomes a feature of rationalization.

Transmission of knowledge should be the concern of small firms more than the retention of it. Small firms tend to be secretive; they do a poor job of seeing that employees get the knowledge they need to do superior work.

No one can really decide for others what information they need. Therefore, people should have a say as to the kind of information made available to them. Managers in small businesses, particularly when they are owners as well, tend to create barriers to the free passage of information within their firms. The barriers are not obvious because of the ways that dominated firms operate, but they are there nonetheless. If any attention is to be given to communication in small firms, it should be on improving the flow of information and knowledge to people.

Admittedly, the information barrier is a hard one to break. Sales, profits, and owner salaries and expenses are treated as top-secret material. Faced with the question as to what they would do if the company went public and SEC disclosure requirements had to be satisfied, thoughtful managers realize that the disadvantages of secrecy are greater than the advantages. True, some company heads regret going public because they feel as though they are living in a fish bowl. But chief executives of that stripe usually do not appreciate management so much as privilege. No firm's profitability has ever been limited by freeing information from elitist service!

To improve the quality of information in a small company requires a clear view of how information on current operations is being collected and used. The past has its uses; it offers a basis for looking into the future and testing the reasonableness of change. No company can afford to neglect these uses of recorded information, the history of performance which is relatively easy and economical to obtain.

Managers must know at least the data relevant to the areas they control. In one metal fabricating company, the effect of distributing the monthly financial statements to its eight top executives was to improve the sense of company profitability without reducing the concern for departmental activities. The end of parochialism marked the beginning of a dramatic improvement in economic results.

One manager put it this way. "I spent 22 years breaking down knowledge barriers, and that was not too difficult. But I couldn't put the knowledge to work until the owner died. Knowledge without the freedom to use it is of little use."

Since effective communication is a two-way exchange, the most productive results come from situations in which a manager and his employees can respond to each others' ideas and feelings. In one case, the administrative manager of a service organization every few weeks arranged informal luncheons with a half dozen different members of his firm. He always asked two questions: What type of firm do you think we should be in five years? How can we improve our operations now? He used the luncheons not only to listen to suggestions and complaints but to express some of his own ideas about the future and hear reactions to them. In the long run, the staff's challenging questions sharpened the goals presented by the manager. Furthermore, the staff's understanding of the goals was far greater than it would have been had they been the target of a preconceived and frozen program.

DATA PROCESSING IN THE SMALL FIRM

Another aspect in improving the quality of information provision and usage has to do with the way data are processed. Traditionally, small business has had to depend almost exclusively on manually produced historical information, having neither the markets nor the resources to support the gathering and processing of data on current activities for the guidance of future business activity. That's where the computer comes in. In an astonishingly short time EDP has been made versatile and inexpensive enough to handle most of the needs of small businesses.

The benefits of high-volume, high-speed, low-cost data processing are no longer limited to large companies. The earliest computer systems were so expensive that small companies could not afford them. But this is no longer the case. The rapidly diminishing costs of memory and computation power and the rising costs of human effort are making computers an economic necessity for many small companies. The small company that does not consider computers as a tool for obtaining accurate, up-to-the-minute information that can help management give the business positive central direction may well be missing the boat. This is why small companies should seek to use data processing as soon as possible, but with caution as to cost.

Small companies should not rush into computerization, much less acquire in-house facilities. The company without direct computer experience probably should not begin with an in-house installation because the big item may not be the cost of buying or renting the hardware but the cost of the people needed to utilize the computer's power. Computer people are not easily kept moving in the right direction and productively occupied.

Service bureau computers are available on an hourly basis to process almost anything the typical small firm requires. The development of shared time (using terminals in an office connected by telephone to large computer facilities) is moving rapidly ahead and may be expected to meet increasingly sophisticated needs at declining costs.

Productive use of the computer requires that managers decide what information they need in managing and what information they need in improving the business. The two are not the same. But now the computer can provide managers with information power never before possible. For example, a computer can economically produce regular sales analyses broken down into almost any required format, as well as many other kinds of statements that could not be prepared manually. It can also be used for production or financial modeling and simulation, yielding alternatives for manufacturing, marketing or investment decision making. The computer allows a small company to improve its present performance and at the same time lay the groundwork for a more profitable future.

Small, general-purpose computers promise to greatly improve the manageability and competitive strength of small firms. For the first time the minicomputer, as it is familiarly called, raises the possibility of bringing information under management control.

There are many reasons why computers have not come within the reach of small companies earlier. From every viewpoint the early machines were costly. First, they were expensive to build and, in view of their short life, expensive to own. Second, they required a costly environment, with controlled temperature and humidity, raised floors, sound-deadened walls and ceilings, and "clean" electrical power. Third, they were expensive to operate. They could be communicated with only in complicated languages, which required human and mechanical translators to convert the information to be processed into holes on cards or magnetized bits on tapes. Fourth, they could handle only one task at a time, forcing the accumulation of like items into batches to be processed together. Last, they could not be communicated with directly at the convenience of executives; they were not designed to respond to the varied and often unpredictable needs of decision makers.

Small firms could not afford to put up with these shortcomings and experiment in learning to use the computer profitably. A small-scale computer with capabilities comparable to larger machines required several breakthroughs in design and manufacturing. With those breakthroughs the minicomputer was made possible.

Although information requirements vary somewhat with company size, small companies need proportionately as much and as varied information as large firms. Until now they have had to do with far less. With the coming of the minicomputer the balance can be restored.

Mines of information lie untapped within most firms. The information may not be concentrated in one place; it may not be in useful form; the manpower or process to transform or access it may not be available; or managers may be too busy to look at it. In addition to these obstacles, small firms generally could not afford to put the information into usable form.

EXAMPLE:

A firm with gross annual sales of $7 million was in a transaction-intensive business, where small dollar amounts generate many information transformations. This created a staggering amount of data which the firm could not afford to process for more than the minimum information needed to keep alive. Its minicomputer will now bring within economical reach answers to the following questions: (1) What is the profit contribution of each product, class of products, salesmen, and sales territories? (2) What are the marginal costs of sales by class of customer size? (3) Can we meet a customer's immediate need for volume merchandise? (4) What is the best level of inventory for each raw material or subassembly? (5) Where or to what customers in our sales territory are we not selling our products? (6) What items are selling above or below our expectations?

The lack of answers to questions such as these has constituted a handicap in being small. Possessing the answers may well determine a small firm's future in the marketplace, and most small firms can now afford to use computers to get them.

There are as many definitions of minicomputers as there are people who want to sell them. The machines generally fall into three categories.

1. *Electronic accounting machines* (EAM). These machines usually have direct keyboard entry and slow printers (10 to 30 characters a second). They range in price from $5,000 to about $50,000. While these machines meet the government's definition of a computer (which means only that they have internally stored program instructions), they are not flexible and have such limitations in speed, capacity, and compatibility that they are not usually well suited to a firm's general information and reporting needs.

2. *File-processing machines.* These have faster input and printing speeds (100 to 300 lines a minute). They are more expensive, ranging from about $25,000 to more than $100,000. These machines are true computers and can be used in the management of information.

3. *Process machines.* These originally were designed for fixed purposes such as industrial control, message switching, and communication. Purchase prices range from $3,000 to about $80,000.

The business minicomputer is generally recognized as having evolved from the category of process machines. The list of new vendors of business minicomputers is long and still growing.

We choose to call any general-purpose computer a minicomputer if it can be rented for $2,500 a month or less or can be purchased for $80,000 or less. Under the impact of technical advances and competition, prices will undoubtedly come down. We anticipate that smaller firms will have computer systems for as little as $1,000 a month.

Minicomputers have a number of cost-related features that especially suit them to the needs of small firms, operating costs being the most important. The costs of buying or leasing a computer are significant, but the monthly operating costs of full-scale data processing installations at last count were about two and a half times hardware costs. Minicomputers bring that ratio nearer one to one.

Minis can do this because they do not require highly trained in-house specialists. Most minis use a simple computer language (RPG, BASIC, or some variant). Employees can learn to design programs for their own work by taking a vendor's one-week basic programming course or by reading a manual and trying it.

Further, minicomputers do not have to be operated by specialists. Minis are interactive; that is, they can be "spoken to" directly without having to go through an interpreter such as a keypunch operator. The interactive mode not only makes it more difficult to introduce errors but greatly reduces operator training. It is common for a newly installed system to be staffed with people on the payroll.

Computers that can catch most errors before they enter the system—and minis are among them—offer great benefits. Because most large computer systems lack this ability, they have to verify operator-entered data by having a second operator rekey the same information or require the information to be rekeyed and reentered when it proves incorrect.

Direct input offers a benefit in that the limitations of punched cards (still the most common means of input) are avoided. Punched card systems are limited to 96 columns of data per card. A record that exceeds this limit requires multiple cards that must be punched with duplicate data to link them together. Video terminal input lifts such limitations.

The benefits of interaction do not end there. Executives can raise their effectiveness by calling, through the interactive mode, for information which is in the system and available for the asking. Printouts at different levels of detail can be requested. If printed copy is not needed, available information can be obtained on demand through a cathode ray tube, which looks like a small television screen. By 1980 there will be video terminals on the desks of most key executives.

Another positive feature of minicomputers is their ability to handle more than one task at a time. A manager can inquire about a particular account balance, inventory level, or other situation at the same time that accounts payable are being processed. The interruption will not be apparent because the inquiry/response occurs at electronic speed. A practical result of this capability is that it is no longer necessary to accumulate efficient batches of like items for processing together.

A small company that can use a general purpose computer should be prepared to spend between 1 and 2 percent of annual sales up to $10 million for data processing (on a declining scale as sales volume rises). Large companies are spending between 1.5 and 2 percent for their data processing. Their higher costs stem mainly from the higher ratio of operating costs mentioned earlier.

Since business computers were introduced, integrated systems—systems that make multiple use of the same input—have been an ideal. Minis may bring us closer to that goal. Information entered only once can now be programmed so that it affects all related records and files.

Entry of a customer order ideally can do all or most of the following:

Validate credit and credit limits.
Retrieve name, address, and other fixed information.
Check inventory levels.
Create shipping documents.
Store backorder information.
Issue purchase or production orders.
Update inventory.
Look up prices.
Extend line items.
Apply appropriate discounts.
Print an invoice.
Update accounts receivable.
Compute profitability by customer and product lines.
Generate sales and other statistics.
Calculate commissions.
Post the general ledger.

Although a mini can handle all these functions, it is rare in practice to find such integration. The reason is that it takes so much time to freeze the specifications and program the system, and it is so expensive, that most small companies properly accept separate pieces which solve immediate problems.

Data bases can now be created for small firms by placing in minicomputers the information produced in daily operations to perform such calculations as:

Cash flow analysis.
Financial planning.
Cost projections.
Inventory turnover.
Forecasting and budgeting.
Marginal income analysis.
Breakeven analysis.

An example of the usefulness of such calculations lies in capital expenditure decisions. Significant decisions should be influenced by managed information in the form of analyses of asset payback, discounted cash flow, make-or-buy, and lease-or-buy, all within the capability of minis. Minis can be put to many other uses. The main constraints are imagination and energy.

In defining information, many managers of small firms restrict their thinking to traditional accounting and financial terms. The computer offers an opportunity to expand the information horizon to other profitable areas that were previously too costly or time-consuming.

EXAMPLE:

A contractor developed a minicomputer program that estimated his firm's capacity to apply labor factors in hours and dollars to each construction operation that involved labor and material. Labor rates and different overhead and profit factors were easily changed as costs went up, bidding strategy changed, or alternate plans were considered. He was also able to accumulate data on the quantities of material specified throughout a total contract. With this information, which could not have been collected economically in any other way, he was able to negotiate purchasing savings that annually were worth several times the cost of operating the minicomputer.

TURNKEY CONTRACTS

One of the fears small businessmen have had to overcome in putting their toes in the EDP water has been that the costs would far exceed initial estimates, a fear certainly justified by experience with computers to date. For that reason, with the development of minicomputers has come the turnkey contract.

What makes the turnkey contract attractive is that it lets the businessman know in advance what he is getting and how much it will cost. At a minimum, such a contract should cover four general requirements.

1. *System design.* Someone who knows what is needed tells the vendor's systems analyst the firm's requirements, which the analyst then translates into programming specifications and costs.

2. *System sign-off.* The businessman approves proposed input and output as acceptable to his needs. This is perhaps the one act most critical to success of the live operation. It requires a willingness to spell out the needs so that program writing, a precise art bound by system specifications, can begin.

3. *Sample run.* After the vendor has written the program, the businessman runs some sample data through the system and verifies the results.

4. *Installation.* Once the system as demonstrated has been accepted, it is installed on premises. This, too, has sometimes been an agonizing experience because of communication failures or second thoughts. Most vendors are reasonable about making modifications up to 10 percent of the original program cost quotation; beyond that, expect to pay for the extras.

In sum, profits can result from the management of information. The small businessman now has available to him, at a price he can afford, a key that may unlock these profits: the minicomputer. There is no one right answer for everyone, and installing a minicomputer will guarantee nothing. But, as with all items in his bag of tricks, the businessman must be sensitive to the full potential of this new tool and must be prepared to exploit it.

In the early 1960s computer investment represented 4 percent of total plant and equipment investment; by 1975 it is expected to exceed 15 percent. The trend is unmistakable. The fundamental problem of managing information in the small business can be resolved by the minicomputer if it is used to make money, not save money.

THE MANAGEMENT INFORMATION SYSTEM MYTH

It's a large step from the dream of a total real-time management information system, or MIS, which would tell every manager whatever he wanted to know immediately, to the patchwork systems that are to be found even in the largest companies.

To the small business manager, a system that simultaneously records a sale, creates the receivable, reduces the inventory, initiates the replacement order, computes the commission, and analyzes the sale by type of product, customer, and area—as a start—sounds like the answer to a prayer. With his imagination stimulated by the predictions of computer manufacturers or aggressive consultants, he may feel that an MIS of this complexity would solve many of his planning and control problems, especially as the business grows and his direct control weakens.

The problem, simply, is that systems of such complexity are rarely economically feasible. They take extraordinarily long to develop, thus creating their own obsolescence in the specification of output stage. They require skills in systems analysis, programming, and operations that are rare and therefore costly. The incremental benefit of the information, when developed, suffers in comparison with the cost of development.

An application of MIS more useful to the smaller firm is the modular one: Pick an area in which savings or profit opportunities can be found, or which is causing problems, and develop a system that fits the needs of the company now and for the next three years in that area. When the people using the system feel comfortable with it and the ratio of value derived to cost incurred is positive (more dollars out than put in), it is time to move to the next operation. Common areas include the order entry, sales, receivables, cash receipts system and the purchases, payables, disbursements, inventory system.

It is *not* necessary that the system be real-time (transactions recorded as they occur and available on demand) or integrated. Changes in desired information take place at an increasing rate as managers and systems people learn to communicate with one another. But the changes are not in all areas simultaneously. While the sales manager requests more detailed data on sales by customer, no one else in the company may care. The modular system permits change with the least disruption.

Computerization is also best applied to internal rather than external information. The latter tends to be more conceptual and less subject to mathematical limits. How do you record the effect of OSHA, the local pollution laws, the changing styles of the young and the elderly, or the effect of import and export policies?

The important pieces of information that each company must have deserve top management attention. Fortunately, there aren't many of these. Internally, they generally deal with value-added factors, asset turnover, liquidity (cash), and the human organization. Externally, the factors may be harder to define, unless specific legislation or appropriations are involved. Because they are less precise, they take more effort and imagination to identify—and have a bigger payoff when found and digested.

THE ENTREPRENEUR

We cannot leave the subject of a firm's efforts to meet the opportunities and threats arising in the outside world without commenting on one of the principal barriers to rational behavior in the small firm— the entrepreneur.

Many things can come between the needs of a firm's markets and the recognition of these needs and selection of appropriate ways to fill them. Few can match the entrepreneur's power to perceive the needs— or his interference in filling them. The capacity of a self-motivated, gifted person to smother initiative and competence around him can be awesome.

The small firm, it is said, is the perfect place for the entrepreneur. To understand that commonly voiced principle, it is necessary to understand what an entrepreneur is.

The ordinary definition of an entrepreneur is a risk taker, a man distinguished from others by his extraordinary capacity to lay his resources on the line in seeking to win higher stakes. Although not a false definition, it is far from adequate. Perhaps what is missing is this: The entrepreneur is a person with a keen perception of what he wants accomplished who brooks no interference in attaining his goals.

Most entrepreneurs have difficulty in working for others. Their single-minded view of the results they want is generally incompatible with team behavior and with the processes required to make large enterprises work. That is why they never stay for long at the head of large companies and ordinarily come to roost at the head of small firms. And that fact is the workshop in which is fashioned one of the crosses that small companies particularly have to bear.

In many ways the problem of the entrepreneur places the problem of a business's small size in perspective. The entrepreneur provides the driving force needed to give a firm the power to surmount barriers and attain its goals, but provides little opportunity for the realization of the desires or capabilities of others. Forthright dealing with the problem is rare, and the failure to do so has driven some companies to the wall.

The view that a business can't have too many entrepreneurs and should sprinkle them throughout the organization fails to consider that entrepreneurs live by a territorial imperative, and any approach that has them working together within the same environment is unrealistic.

Still, while the creative business mentality cannot anywhere be accommodated easily, small firms are in the best position to benefit from its employment. This was pointed out by John L. Burns, who has been vice-chairman of Booz, Allen & Hamilton, president and director of RCA, and chairman and chief executive officer of Cities Service Company: ". . . big businesses have a distressing tendency to smother the entrepreneurial spirit. . . . That's why some smart young competitor running his own show can often run the big company right off the track in the small segments of its business." *

Entrepreneurs do have vision and the courage to try new ideas (or the inability to resist them), but they are seldom good managers. Many of them feel that every minute spent in managing is a minute taken away from the things they do well. The truly successful entrepreneurs, meaning those who have kept their companies alive while being entrepreneurial, know their limitations and the necessity of supplementing their talents with those of others. "The most important thing in business," said Nelson Harris, a prominent business builder, "is having people work with you, not for you." William Lear said, "The greatest mistake I ever made was hiring the second-best man for the job. You pay a terrible penalty for that." Sherman Fairchild agrees: "One thing I try to do is regard my executives as partners. My father used to say to me, 'Son, don't worry about how much money you'll be going to make. Get the right guy and make *him* make a lot of money and that's all you'll need.' I've always followed that advice." Presumably, these men were not just talking about the advisability of hiring order-takers.

Perhaps the last word on entrepreneurs was voiced by Fairchild when he said, "What I want is to surround myself with entrepreneurs. A foreman in a shop can be an entrepreneur. If he takes existing things and puts them together in a new way, he usually ends up being head of the company." In so saying he probably put his finger on the most important point about entrepreneurship: that all men have their own individual contribution to make and should be encouraged to make it.

* *Forbes,* July 15, 1970, p. 57.

This mixture of entrepreneurial views suggests several things. Small businesses are the best vehicles for entrepreneurs, but they must organize as much to contain the risks of having them as to exploit the advantages. Entrepreneurs are more concerned with self-expression than with organization building. To them, an enterprise is little more than a means to the end. To the effective manager it is far more than that. He recognizes the firm as an entity deserving of continuance long after any specific goods and services have been discontinued.

Many people feel that management of small business can be highly individualized but management of large business cannot. As one executive put it, "The small business is generally an extension of one man; others are his arms but his is the only brain. This may permit a capable organization, say, up to $50 million a year. Above this amount, generally speaking, it is fatal." He may be right, but that does not necessarily also mean that the closer personal relations in the small company permit it to be casual about providing the channelizing effects of administration devices. The executive cited above must agree, because he also said, "One of the major problems that small businesses face is in organizing the work of others."

To successfully operate a small business, giving maximum sway to individual differences, demands that not too many people be involved and those involved be mature persons with broad vision. Many small companies have the small number of people required, but few have enough people who meet the second criterion. Fully developed and relatively selfless people are rare; hence, almost every company must carefully attend to the work of providing guides for and hedges against individual performance.

A point in opposition was made by a group vice-president of a major chemicals company:

> I believe that the president or chief executive officer must be the leader of his company and must be the driving force behind the company's plan. The company should reflect the personality of the chief executive officer, and the final long-range plan will be his to live with. He is the one who must decide what business the company is in; and, of course, he must bear the responsibility for the success or failure of the company.

Though we respect these views and recognize that most executives share them, we differ strongly. We know of no reason why a company should reflect the personality of its chief executive; the facts, indirect though they may be, argue quite the opposite view. Businesses behave as systems, and a system responsive to one person or personality has doubtful abilities to relate to the real world. A business responsive to disciplined collective thinking does better.

Organizing for the entrepreneurial spirit is an individual problem. One small company president put the matter well:

> The number of effective people available is extremely limited. A small company president will tailor the jobs of the company to such effective people. Where the employee is an entrepreneur, the president should leave him alone but limit the expenditures that the entrepreneur is allowed to make. Where the employee is not an entrepreneur but a doer, then the small company president should lay out the program for the individual. Generally speaking, the latter program is the most successful because the self-starter entrepreneur is not usually available as an employee to the small company.

5

INSTITUTIONALIZATION

WHEN TWO MEN get together for some purpose external to both, they need written agreements if they are to work jointly for long. The formality of drawing up agreements has never been viewed with affection, but it has earned grudging respect from those who recognize that some bureaucracy is better than bloodshed.

Though rarely accepted by entrepreneurs or economic buccaneers, institutionalization is a worthy human accomplishment. We define it as the formalization of procedures and differentiations that foster the application of resources in keeping with management's knowledge of present and future events in the outside world. Without it the modern world could not have come into being. Without perfecting it, the modern world will probably not mature.

As they grow, small firms cannot escape being institutionalized, however much the view prevails that they are counterinstitutional in character. They, too, must take pains to institutionalize those elements that become wayward when not documented and controlled.

This chapter deals with three features of business life that small firms should take special pains to formalize; that is, set up organizationally and procedurally to be identifiable and viable. The features are administration, innovation, and organization. They have been chosen because their effectiveness suffers from negative assumptions concerning a small firm's need of them.

At least one of these items, innovation, is usually dealt with in books on management under headings that connote imagination, creativeness, and inventiveness. Here it is coupled with institutionalization. This will seem odd to anyone who regards institutionalization as the enemy of change. It is included in this chapter nonetheless, because the need to make innovation structured and ongoing is most important in small firms. Justification for the unusual classification is based on the view that progressive, timely, economic change takes place less through accident than through discipline and control.

A word of explanation about the order of the three items may be helpful. Administration comes first because, as related to the maintenance of corporate health day by day, it is critical in providing the matrix of action—the connective tissue that holds different things in place. Innovation comes next because under sound administrative control it most affects corporate survival through time. Organization comes last because it influences corporate performance only *after* all other factors affecting performance have been taken care of.

ADMINISTRATION

Each business has a source of decisions that determine the actions taken and the responses made to change. In many small companies where that source is one person the concentration of power does not necessarily damage operations or prospects.

Up to a certain size, which varies with the product or service, one man *can* manage an organization effectively. But the accomplishment often has a price: One-man management tends to remain long after the firm has outgrown one man's capacity to manage.

One reason is the sweet taste of power. Business and political history are replete with examples of men who failed to change the nature of command as the environment changed as well as with examples of old men who lost every skill except that of retaining power. Unfortunately, even when the one-man manager is competent he is often insensitive or hostile to the idea that his firm look to its administration if it is to survive and grow.

This is unfortunate because the failure to spread decision making through the organization has two deadly effects. One is the imposition of monocular vision; decisions are based on only one view of the business. The second is the widening of the decision gap; the firm's capacity to respond and to innovate is severely limited by having one man make every important decision. Either effect severely damages the firm. Taken together, they will eventually kill a growing company or force it back to a size that can be managed by one man. Late decisions, failure to use relevant facts, and prejudices founded on obsolete experiences are some of the signs that one man has the final say on everything.

EXAMPLE:

In a professional organization one of the older principals was indignant when a group of supervisors proposed a reduction in the hours worked during the peak season. The supervisors were sensitive to the reluctance of younger staff to work 60 hours a week. But the principal's reaction was, "When I entered this field, we worked 80 hours a week, every week, for three months. Anyone who won't face up to the workload is not a professional and should be fired." Fortunately, he did not have the final say; the issue was settled by a new overtime policy. The point of the story: The principal's standard of conduct was based on his own experience of 25 years ago, not on current attitudes and needs.

The tendency to think of administration as a problem that grows with size impedes recognition that many small companies could significantly improve their performance by raising their administration levels. If the variety and complexity of decisions needed by a small firm are more limited than those of a large one, the requirements of versatility, adaptability, and discrimination are oftentimes greater because most small businesses survive in an environment dominated by large businesses. The requirements can best be provided through systematic administration, whatever the size of the company.

A number of prejudices constrain the use of rational processes in the small firm. One of the strongest is the view that the best basis of stewardship is ownership; in other words, if somebody owns something he will behave responsibly toward it and take care of it. That view is groundless, as shown by the irresponsible behavior of many owner-managers toward their enterprises. Made of the same stuff is the view that small businesses are by nature flexible. No evidence points to such a relationship. Some of the least flexible of businesses are small, and their rigidity would quickly bring a large company to the brink of disaster. It is as much in the nature of a small business as of a large to be inflexible, a point to be noted when thinking about the need for administration in small firms.

The most powerful of the mind-sets is elitism of a kind not often met in large firms; it finds expression in the phrase, "I am the business" or "I built the business." Any person who says that is really saying, "I am the only one to decide." This mentality is all too common in small business. Obsession with the privileges and rights of ownership is incompatible with productive administration.

Another restraint is an obsession with being small. These are its sounds: "We're only a small firm, what can we do?" or "We're too small, we can't afford it," or "We don't need that; it's for big companies." Small size is the biggest excuse for not having a desperately needed management tool such as planning or, even worse, not being rational in decision making. The small company that puts size before other factors cannot grow, probably cannot survive. Among other things, the obsession precludes development of a measured administrative function, the lack of which has an early rather than late effect.

A company can no longer do without an administrative process, regardless of the quality of its leader, when three kinds of work first make their appearance together: when (1) primary work, such as making and selling, and (2) supportive work, such as financing and inventory management, are joined by (3) connecting-link work, such as is performed by foremen and other supervisors. Given these three different thrusts, a small firm can no longer put off establishing a formal administrative process if it wishes to keep its gains or continue to grow.

Because management tends to be more informal, less integrated, and less visible in small companies than in large ones, managers in firms of all sizes regard administration as mainly a problem of big companies. That was shown in a survey conducted by the authors in which two-thirds of the respondents said that management is more difficult in large companies.* That most executives in large companies should feel this way is understandable. But, surprisingly, 55 percent of the small company managers who responded to the study's questionnaire agreed. Only a little more than 40 percent took the opposite view, that managing in small companies is more difficult.

Other constraints restrict the building of a small firm's administrative function. A powerful one rests in this. Because many managers in small firms do not have a clear understanding of the nature and methods of administration, they are prone to make two kinds of errors: First, they underestimate the complexity of the job of running a company, and second, they slavishly follow big business practices and methods.

Concerning the first, management is not simple. Those who think it is recognize that running a small business is hard work but overlook the complexity of the job. Small businessmen face a variety of prob-

* *How Management Is Different in Small Companies*, AMA, 1972.

lems that require disciplined thinking and analytical ability. Yet managers in small businesses often feel their size permits and even favors seat-of-the-pants, ad hoc management. The facts do not support this view. Small size permits informal management, characterized by few details and few documents. But it does not justify being less systematic than in large companies.

Concerning the second error, managers in small firms adopt methods and practices used in larger firms rather than develop techniques and applications tailored to their specific needs. This form of imitation not only brings about equipment and procedural inefficiency but severely handicaps development of an administrative system suited to each small firm's needs. Techniques adapted without change from large firms fit about as well as a size 44 suit draped over a five-foot boy.

Trying to fit big company techniques to small companies is part of the universal management practice fallacy that what works for one company will work for another. The following anecdote shows the consequences of such a practice.

EXAMPLE:

When an old, well-established retail house came into the hands of the second generation it seemed lackluster and flaccid to its new operators. They decided to streamline the business and brought in a new president who had been vice-president in a much larger New York City firm. One of the first things the new president did was to order a management information system. After the system was processing the data received from stores, buyers spent many evenings poring through massive computer printouts to see what was selling, what was coming up, what was fading. Not long afterward an automated, complicated open-to-buy system was installed and the firm fell apart.

After firing the president the owners scrapped the system and sent the buyers out to the stores to find out what was selling and why. The president, who had said that he didn't need to know about the commodity being sold because he was a professional manager to whom one product was like another, went back to a large company. A management information system makes sense for companies of all sizes, but like a garment it must be tailored to fit.

Those who view management as a discipline with one body of principles applicable to every kind and size of company make a big mistake. Coping with the irrationalities of our economy and fitting them to the goals of a company are more important than applying managerial generalizations. Yet the experience underlying the principles of management is for the most part that of large companies, and administration is largely a description of the methods that have worked in large enterprises. It has popularly been assumed that the ways in which the big producers solve their problems are the best ways for *all* business. That is not usually the case. Commonly accepted management knowledge does not sufficiently recognize the unique management requirements of the small firm.

A practical, best-cost administrative function in a small firm starts with the recognition that administration is an abstraction that does not exist in the real world. It is a term for a collection of activities that take many forms, depending upon the behavioral and procedural patterns entering into them. The term does denote activities common to all firms, but the system it refers to varies greatly between companies. Therefore, "administration" takes on specific meaning only when it .refers to the mechanism tying together the elements and subsystems at work in a particular company or organizational unit.

The basis for administrative design lies in (1) the general characteristics of small business and (2) the specific characteristics of one particular small business. To recognize the characteristics and needs of small businesses is the first step in the creation of an administrative process that clearly meets its needs. The second step is to perceive the characteristics and needs of one business in particular.

Granted that many management methods have fairly common application, not all are useful in all companies. Therefore, you must select a method suited to the needs of your firm if you are to have effective administration. One business is not the same as another across the street, even if the business across the street is identical in terms of externals, sales volume, and profitability. The human organization and the style and patterns of work are different, and the administrative processes will also have to be different. An enterprise's administrative organization cannot be built out of homilies and generalizations.

What kind of administration would make sense? We are not in a mathematically precise area where statistical evidence can be offered in proof of the differences. A model is needed. To make clear the distinctions between the administrative requirements of a small and a large business, consider our aircraft analogy again. The small Piper Cub with its fore-and-aft seating arrangement for two people is one of the simplest of all aircraft and a far cry from the Boeing 747. The basic processes in flying the two planes are the same, but the configurations are vastly different. The economy and the effort expended to do what has to be done are completely different in each case.

A Piper Cub has a stick, rudder pedals, three or four instruments for altitude, attitude, and direction, and perhaps a simple radio. It is a wholly manual system. On the other hand, the 747 requires an apparatus to amplify manual motions that takes more horsepower than the total output of the Cub's engine. Its pumps, amplifiers, cables, and conduits are probably eight or ten times the total weight of the little Piper Cub, including the glue that holds it together. Further, as we pointed out earlier, the Piper Cub pilot, flying at 90 miles an hour when there is a good tail wind, must be in visual contact with the outside world to a far greater degree than the men in the 747, who scarcely bother to look out the window. The Piper pilot's safety depends upon his knowing what is happening in his immediate environment. Happenings beyond his horizon are of no immediate concern, because it will be some time before he gets there.

The 747 crew members, on the other hand, have little interest in the world they can see because in a minute or two they will be out of it. Their interest is in what is happening several hundred miles away because they will be there soon. The energies involved in flying differ vastly between the Cub and the 747, even though the basic procedures are the same. To apply 747 equipment and specialization to the Cub not only would prevent it from getting off the ground, but would crush it flat. Similarly, applying the sophisticated planning, control, resource allocation, and compensation methods of a large company to a small one would result in disaster.

The relevance of the aircraft example to the administrative procedures of small and large firms should be clear: not only are small firm administrative processes more direct, simpler, faster reacting, of shorter duration, and closer to the environment but they are also fit and proper for the small firm.

Because small business management is personalized rather than institutionalized it is unlikely that more mileage can be squeezed out of personal qualities; small businessmen have always used them to the hilt. While it is true that the qualities must be preserved intact where they are serviceable, the small firm can sharpen the advantages of personal knowledge and skills by introducing practices that lend consistency and pervasiveness to certain aspects of the company administration.

Take job descriptions as an example: Few small companies bother with documentary statements of key jobs. Yet the absence of job descriptions is as likely to cause problems in the small company as in the large one. Aside from gaps in functions that are left unrecognized and untended, confusion arises over what is expected of personnel in terms of responsibility and level of performance (a good performance appraisal is almost impossible without accurate, previously agreed-upon job descriptions). Agreement on job objectives and performance standards is hard to arrive at in the small company because of the informality that exists between the few executives. But it is precisely this informality that causes the need for written job descriptions; without them, assumptions and understandings are likely to conflict.

Further evidence of the need for moving small business management toward formality is to be found in the area of repetitive procedures. When more than one person regularly performs a task (how a sales return or allowance should be handled) or is affected by a personnel code (when vacations are earned; who is assigned a company car), the company requires a formalized procedure. Without it, unnecessary and possibly contradictory decisions will be made. With a written policy, explained to all concerned, management and staff can stop fretting about these details and devote their time to their primary tasks.

Another consideration in designing the administrative function: Small companies are usually weak in activities concerned with renewal and survival, such as providing for key management, setting up a routine for finding and training new personnel, establishing policies covering recurring situations and conducive to the widest understanding, and developing new products, processes, and markets. Because smaller companies are better at doing today's work than at planning for tomorrow, investment in administrative procedures (using current assets for possible future benefit) is not given high priority. The typical small company should give particular attention to these activities.

The designer of the administrative function must keep in mind that there is a difference between informality and absence of administration, between formality and management. The existence of informality is not evidence that administration, the proper direction and control of the business, is lacking, nor does the presence of formality prove that sound administration exists. At any point in the effort to control an operation there is danger in becoming too formal, whether the company is large and diversified or small and unified. Everywhere, managerial rigidity is on the way out, and nothing that is not absolutely necessary should be allowed to impair an enterprise's flexibility.

Against this view must be balanced that of the benefits of administrative formality in providing protection in risk taking. The highest rewards almost always stem from taking high risks, but the highest risks are also most often fatal. Formality of procedures, structure, and control can protect the small company from slipping into unwarranted risks or dealing carelessly with assumed risks. Budgeting, return on investment, performance standards, ratio analysis, management by objectives, and integrated planning are examples of formal procedures with generally high productive yields in small businesses.

At some point size alone requires that informality begin to be replaced by policies and procedures that can be communicated. That generally is around the $5 million sales mark. Up to that point, staff members can usually communicate adequately and keep things in view. Beyond it, however, informal methods begin to fall short of administrative requirements and a company needs procedures.

The number of people and the proximity in which they work, rather than sales dollars, can be measures in deciding when administrative procedures should be installed. Coordination of 20 manufacturers' representatives scattered throughout the country probably requires carefully worked out written procedures, whereas 100 people working in a single factory or office might need fewer written policies.

Because of the size of the smaller firm's base, its growth usually results in changes that are proportionately more dramatic than those in larger firms and requires frequent and radical administrative moves on the part of management. The step phases are closer together. The doubling of sales from $5 million to $10 million is much harder to digest than is a $5 million increase in a $100 million company. The administrative machinery of the growing small firm must be prepared not only for the constant change that all organizations live with but for change that will challenge its basic structure and organization again and again. Any simplistic view of management will not permit or support this kind of change.

The recent upsurge in the professionalism of management probably has opened at least as many doors as it has closed to small business. Though there are size levels (which differ with the product lines) below which businesses cannot make effective use of certain advanced techniques, professional management is the main reason that companies survive and perform well irrespective of size.

The small businessman who earnestly works to understand and then apply proven and relevant management concepts can bring to his firm the benefits inherent in his company's size. Without such effort, size-related benefits cannot be realized, only size-related handicaps.

INNOVATION

The company that specializes in turning out indifferent products or services at indifferent prices does not live long.

Small companies should take special interest in innovation and seek to innovate especially well because their markets are so vulnerable. Small businesses become established and profit from filling the interstices of markets but have no special protection from the competition of large firms. Any shift in technology, taste, distribution, or imports can seriously erode or wipe out a small company's market. Further, as the economy grows, the demand for a product or service that was too small to attract large companies may become big enough to introduce economies of scale in production and distribution.

Against these or similar eventualities, the small company earns a measure of security by exercising tight financial control. But that alone is insufficient to keep the firm going. A sounder if less common strategy is to innovate according to plan. Whatever their size, firms that innovate on a planned basis do better than those that leave innovation to chance.

Innovation in a small company can be effective only if it fulfills that most critical requisite, the freeing of executives from mundane tasks so that they can give enough time, attention, and support to the work of steadily and safely moving the company into the future. That is a formidable accomplishment because it usually involves changes in procedures, policies, systems, organizational relationships, and management philosophy. Specific techniques that have worked include setting aside a few uninterrupted hours a week for discussions, brainstorming, forward thinking; and getting away from the office for a day, perhaps with an outsider who will ask the tough questions or bring the wild-eyed ideas within the bounds of reality.

Innovation is like strong medicine; the dosage must be carefully calculated. Managers in small businesses who are determined to achieve improved results through innovation must ask themselves, How much is enough? Small firms can die as quickly from too much or misguided creative work as from none. As one consultant put it, more small firms go broke from overambition than from inertia. Successful innovation begins with a search for guidelines that are realistic and fit the style and limits of the individual company's personnel, finances, and facilities. The following list contains a mixture of propositions generally true for organizations of all kinds and sizes.

1. Every commercial enterprise, whatever its size, exists for the purpose of spending money to create value in excess of the money spent.

2. A small company makes its living by producing products or services in response to variables inimical to large-scale production, such as short delivery time or custom featuring.

3. The small company does best in a stable market that is stable for its products (a small business that must continually fight product obsolescence has picked the wrong products).

4. The small company is favored by products that have short production runs; the longer its production runs, the more vulnerable a small company is to competition from larger companies.

5. Great variability of demand, seasonally or volumetrically, favors small company operations.

6. Small companies should look for products that are required in high quality; high-volume methods (which favor large companies) often leave something to be desired in the quality of the article or service produced (exception: high-volume, uniform-quality items, such as steel plate).

7. Increasing product variation and complexity create new opportunities favoring exploitation by small companies.

8. Companies serving markets highly sensitive to product features must take pains to avoid getting trapped into product stasis. (Market *stability* at times results from design *mobility*.)

9. Small companies should strive to maintain recognizable degrees of exclusivity for their products or services; because the investment capacity of small companies does not permit them to invest heavily in equipment, they benefit less from freezing product designs than large companies.

10. Small firms are sheltered when their products or services cannot easily be combined with other products or services, either in production or sales.

11. Small companies should resist having a full product line if it diminishes having a distinctive line. The small company competes most effectively when its items are appealing because they are distinctive rather than because of gradations among them.

12. Small companies that risk large portions of their resources

in projects which do not offer the possibility of learning early whether the innovation will be successful engage in unjustifiable and, possibly, deadly risks. (Seven out of eight hours of technical time devoted to product development in this country are spent on projects that do not achieve commercial success. This is another argument for small companies to combine their resources in trade associations for technological research.)

13. Small companies should avoid products that require heavy investments of time; risks rise in direct proportion to the stretching of time between the first investment and the earliest possibility of payoff.

14. Opportunities for small business relate to the state of maturity of the industry or product involved. Small businesses tend to be important producers or suppliers of components of products in early stages of development, while large firms tend to dominate the markets for older, established products.

The risks of innovation require the small business manager to apply objective analyses to even the most exciting idea. It does not take many dead issues or unfavorable financial or personnel changes to overwhelm the thin resources of the typical small company. Mistakes are of greater consequence in small companies and are more likely to prove fatal.

Ideas for change should be measured against a variety of standards: technical feasibility, compatibility with the company's market and marketing resources, the likelihood of bringing in an adequate and early return on funds invested in development, the availability and cost of the talents required to make the change, and so on. However, application of a financial measure, such as return on investment, is the simplest and surest method of quickly analyzing the worth of specific investments. Whatever the small company's situation is with respect to other resources, it must be able to operate until the funds invested are recovered from the net cash earned by producing and marketing the new product.

There are three principal constraints in bringing about change on a systematic basis in small companies:

1. Managers are conditioned to make do with less. Having less than the total market, less than enough staff, less than the best financing terms, managers in small firms tend to do without some of the options lying within their grasp, such as adequate planning. With everything being used to the full and no reserve staff, procedures, or equipment, the running of the enterprise takes all the company's available energy and leaves practically nothing for self-improvement.

2. Managers in small companies reject the thought of spending money for things that can't be seen, measured, or resold and regard themselves as primarily managers of money and material assets rather than of people.

3. Small firms that do innovate (as exemplified by "brain companies" headed by inventors or scientists) often confine themselves to exploiting the competences of their founders or a small group of extraordinary individuals. Once this has been done, the same competences often become barriers to the introduction of new ideas. Innovation is acceptable only if it stems from top management.

Each of these blocks to innovation must be removed if the small company is to become or remain prosperous.

Because it must take a distinctive approach to innovation, the small company must look to imitation as a major survival and growth strategy. Imitation is not only more common than invention; it is also a much safer road to profits and growth.

The opportunities for incremental innovation are more plentiful than the opportunities for wholly creative innovation. Existing products, processes, and services far outnumber those for which a new market is waiting or has to be created. Exploitation of what exists holds more potential and less risk for the small company than trying to bring into existence something new. Small companies can usually produce product variations at less cost than large ones, provided they are concerned with the right kind of products in the first place. Small companies can discern the possibilities or need for changes in existing products, test the changes, and make go, no-go marketing decisions earlier and faster than larger, slower-moving competitors.

New product development is best handled by firms with diversified and large-scale resources because it is almost always exceedingly costly, time-consuming, and troublesome. Most small businesses cannot afford the aggravations and high costs of finding and building acceptance of new products. The small business manager will, therefore, do well to focus on refining or expanding existing products, processes, or services rather than developing and introducing wholly new ones.

And yet, while it is true that new products generally emanate from big business, this should not be taken to mean that small companies are frozen out; it often falls to a small firm to get the way-out invention going. The safety razor, xerography, disposable cigarette lighters, and rechargeable flashlights were brought to the marketable state by small companies. There are two main reasons for this: (1) The initial markets for some new products are only large enough to be attractive to the small company, and (2) large companies often have large investments in going products that they do not want to jeopardize by launching competing products. Even if the product pioneered by a small company turns out to be useful in a much larger way than anticipated and attracts competition from larger companies, the small firm will not be badly hurt if it has not overextended itself.

Still, small companies should adopt a conservative posture with respect to product development. In all but the most unusual circumstances they should avoid products or services that by their nature require heavy development or marketing expenditures, no matter how attractive the profit opportunities appear. Unless a company is large enough to support a development effort of, say, $100,000 a year, it is unlikely to get much out of the effort. Further, unless it can afford to assign at least two men to work without interruption on each long-range project, no project is likely to have the variety of competences required to produce the results sought. Even the task of improving a product that is completely familiar is inherently difficult. The comment of one manager, "We had three shots at improving our lines in ten years, and we got nowhere every time," is indicative of how difficult the task is.

Innovation in the small company should not focus exclusively on existing products or services. The real reason for innovation is to do something better. This can mean doing something cheaper than competitors, or of higher quality than competitors, or earlier than competitors. And this implies that innovation in the small company also should be extended to manufacturing, marketing, inventory management, recordkeeping, data processing, the service organization, and many other aspects of the business. But the aspects to be worked on should be chosen with care since small size is of special disadvantage in a number of operating areas, such as the handling of inventories. A small company's innovative efforts should therefore be directed to projects likely to yield above-average payouts.

EXAMPLE:

Anticipating the need for large-capacity cranes to handle containers in an eastern port, an equipment company invested heavily in the best machinery available to do the job—and jumped the gun on its competitors in the process. By virtue of its presence, knowledge of the special problems of the emerging container industry, and personalized service to shippers and freight forwarders, this firm practically dominated the market for many years.

The manager who intends to make his small company truly innovative needs to know that innovative companies are characterized by the free flow of information. Companies that are not innovative, on the other hand, are highly stratified; there are sharp breaks in the information flow between the executive, middle-management, and lowest supervisory levels. The firm that is organized and run along traditional lines is least likely to be innovative.

The small company manager interested in innovation also needs to know that creative firms have their members interact with the outside world through community participation, consulting, teaching, board memberships, and other activities that bring men and ideas together. The key people in innovative small firms are generally open and inclined toward participative decision making. In any but that rarest of companies headed by a creative genius with a keen administrative and marketing sense, team effort is vital to successful innovation.

The participation and close coordination needed to provide a sound and economic innovative activity do not arise naturally or accidentally. The survival of large companies requires their managers to take formal steps to coordinate their work across a wide range of functions. In small companies, on the other hand, work usually takes place within a framework of understanding so complete as to minimize the need for formal action to achieve coordination. This feature of small company managerial life is not all positive; the very fact that it reduces the need to "work to make things work" diminishes awareness of the commitment and renewal functions, such as planning and innovating, which have high information and control requirements. For this reason, small companies that want to maximize their chances of surviving and prospering should formalize their innovative efforts.

Formality is reputed to be the enemy of newness, and small companies are counted fortunate for not having to contend with as much of it as large companies. A bit of reflection will show that change deliberately undertaken, to be accomplished within a defined span of time, and at a precalculated cost (a good enough definition of innovation) can be effected only under tight control.

If control means anything, it means formality. In the company that does not deliberately allocate its creative energies within a structure of effective planning, close control, and organizationally recognized responsibilities, the resources of money and especially executive time are used in daily activities and problems and not in building a better future.

If innovation is viewed in the broadest terms, its legitimate preoccupations range from the most basic kind of work simplification to the rarest kind of operations modeling. Because innovation is a vocabulary-oriented and logic-oriented discipline, the language and thought processes employed strongly influence the discovery processes. We see things differently and operate on them differently as we define them differently. Take working capital. As a rule it is viewed as the assets tied up in cash, receivables, and inventory, reduced by current liabilities. However, if it is viewed in terms of *time*, as a cycle that begins with producing something and ends with receiving payment for it, we will deal with working capital differently.

Small companies wishing to innovate should move with conviction tempered with reasonable care. A number of safeguards can be applied in determining and controlling the extent of changes: budgeting, market research, proper record maintenance, operations auditing. Though improvements in product features or the way things are done should be considered for introduction as soon as feasibility has been established, the manager has to know whether or not he can afford the changes. Constructing a budget tells him that; it provides a planned standard and a yardstick against which to measure the affordability of a change. It specifies amounts of money, time, and space set aside for the development of specific innovative ideas as well as for innovation generally: keeping in touch with industry, the market, and personnel and organizational changes of which the company must be aware.

A singular advantage in budgeting for innovation is that it permits comparison between the outlays of similar organizations. Progressive companies assign a percentage of sales to innovation, and such percentages are often reported to credit organizations and industry associations for comparison.

As to market research, few small companies use it—perhaps because it is reputed to be costly. The reputation is not always deserved, however. For example, surveys to help spot and define a potential market do not always have to be large in scale or expensive. Because small firms have little margin for error, they cannot afford *not* to test new ideas with market research facts. Many sources can assist a small company in its efforts to find and assess new possibilities at a minimal cost. These include employees, customers, government agencies, trade or industry associations, banks, and academic institutions. Note the occasional crossing of the conventional lines between big and small business in relation to invention and market exploitation of new products or processes. Large companies are increasingly the source of projects for small companies to work on. Major automobile manufacturers, for example, have made awards to small firms for pollution control and propulsion systems.

In dealing with the problem of improvement, formalizing the information gathering can be helpful. Innovation makes greater knowledge demands than almost any other business function. It is therefore advisable for the small company to put the collection of new ideas on a continuing basis so that it can identify emerging trends and capabilities. A file can be of great assistance in collecting facts and ideas under such headings as products, production methods, packaging, sales methods, advertising and sales promotion, and financing.

Though financing may not seem subject to change among small companies, one survey of the 200 largest companies in the country showed that two out of three already had or were about to set up a venture capital department to finance research and product development projects in small companies. This is not generally known to small companies and is deserving of a file heading under which relevant information can be collected.

The last item in our list, operations auditing, is suggested as a safeguard for small companies because the operating responsibilities of their executives usually take precedence over future-oriented responsibilities. Large companies always assign some portion of their staff to full-time appraisal and modification of significant aspects of the enterprise. Since smaller firms cannot afford such specialists, their analyses usually occur only when troubles explode into crises.

The small firm should therefore look for alternative means of obtaining objective appraisals of its operating modes and overall performance, so as to avoid gambling with its future. Consultants and CPA firms are prime sources of such assistance to small companies.*

At this point it is probably fitting to repeat the cliché that change for the sake of change is purposeless. The objective of innovation is not to make change but to make corporate life secure, exciting, and rewarding.

Make no mistake about it. The number one reason for innovation is that deliberate change is the central requirement of business survival. A manager who will not be content with mere survival must do more than change when possible; he must *make* change.

ORGANIZATION STRUCTURE

It is axiomatic that there is a direct relationship between corporate size and complexity. In other words, the bigger the company the

* Roy A. Lindberg and Theodore Cohn, *Operations Auditing*, AMA, 1972.

greater the variety of talents, functions, and interfaces required to run it successfully. On the other hand, it is by no means as clear that a similar relationship exists between corporate size and structural differentiation.

According to our research many small business managers believe their firms can benefit from being as formally structured as large companies.* That belief runs counter to the widely held view that informal relationships (and the attendant lack of structure) are among the strengths of small companies.

The objective behind a given organizational design should be the creation of conditions most favorable to the attainment of desired results. Such results come out of jobs designed to attain them. Since the results that are attainable depend in considerable degree on the size of the company, so must the jobs. Hence, organization structure also should relate to corporate size.

Despite the conviction that organizational differentiation is as important to small firms as to large ones, most small business managers either ignore organization or design their companies after the models of large firms. It is the rare manager who acts in accordance with the views that structure makes a difference in performance and that small companies require organizational arrangements unique to their size as well as their character.

Large companies require a high degree of differentiation and formalization to achieve the integration of effort needed to reach their goals. Small companies, which operate in the most volatile part of the economy, do not need and are often impeded by extensive organizational differentiation and formality. But their choice is not between the intensive organization of large companies or none at all. A small firm needs only the minimum of structure, but it should not be designed less carefully because of that.

That organization structures of big and small companies must differ in major ways cannot be doubted. Graicunas showed years ago that relations between 5 people involve 10 channels of communication; between 10 people, 45 channels; between 100 people, 495 channels; and so on. One lesson to be drawn from this is that an organization suited to a company when it was one size is inapplicable when it is another size. For example, a communications network suitable to a 100-man firm made up of four subgroups will probably not work in a firm of 1,000 men distributed among seven subgroups.

The fact that structural differentiation and the scale of goals have

* *How Management Is Different in Small Companies,* op. cit.

a patterned relationship carries with it other lessons, one of which has to do with the ability to change. Because organization on a large scale can offset even the best innovative and initiative efforts, the organization of a large company should be designed to increase the ability to respond to *introduced* change and facilitate the implementation of plans. In a small company, on the other hand, the organization should be designed to constrain *gratuitous* change.

In other words, organization in large companies should be designed to offset the gravitational pull of bigness on the change functions. The organization of small companies, on the other hand, should be designed to keep the firm from flying into space because of overreactions to environmental fluctuations and impetuous decision making. The differences in these two objectives make it clear that large and small companies should organize differently.

Although small companies need organization to keep on course, they must guard against gaining that benefit at the expense of their ability to innovate. The warning is necessary; the benefits of structuring are far more noticeable than the constraints it imposes upon subtle and complex managerial processes that make for progress.

In small organizations managers often carry responsibilities that would be divided among several individuals in large concerns, and the wearing of many hats makes for economies in communicating, decision making, and so forth. An executive in a small company may handle several unlike functions such as finance, purchasing, and personnel relations; foremen in small shops commonly shoulder responsibilities which are separate staff services (such as personnel) in large companies. The benefits are that fewer segregated services are necessary, the communication burden is minimized, and relations between supervisory and nonsupervisory employees have little or no formality. Hence, the conditions of control and coordination are simplified.

The problem is that they are often simplified to the point where small firm managers stop being concerned about them. The reduction of interfaces, redundancies, and interactions between disciplines has its value, but if it goes too far it also increases the likelihood of error. The second-guessing, the countervailing opinions, the wait for another's approval do make decision making slow, but in appropriate measure they also increase its quality. A swift decision can be fatal, just as a slow one can, and it can be fatal sooner.

Suitable organization can reduce the error index in small companies. When one man can no longer keep all activities in view, he has to use other means of retaining the productivity level that existed when he could see and coordinate all the work under way. Unless structure is introduced as the boss loses sight of things, chaos and decay will become the order of the day. Organization is the correlative of the self; when men begin to achieve things through the efforts of others, organization is needed to impel and channel the efforts into a stream with power and concentration.

Structure assumes economic importance when a firm becomes larger than one man can run. Unfortunately, no bells ring to alert the top man to the need for increased differentiation and formality. More often he responds to the growing needs of the firm by taking on greater responsibility himself and by adding personnel to do his bidding. The first is impossible to accomplish; he probably can't do much more than he is already doing. And trying to stretch himself merely lowers the quality of his authority. Adding personnel is also a mistake because it adds complications without offsetting benefits. Executives or assistants who cannot exercise independent judgment bring about actions that create more work than they eliminate. What is more, the owner may be reluctant to accept a competent, strong person whose professionalism could show up the flaws in his own style of management.

Even after a top executive decides to share his work he finds it hard to do so effectively. In many ways, some subtle and some obvious, some conscious and some unconscious, he is likely to go on doing things as he did before. Unless authority is divided when the company outgrows one-man management, the overall quality of administration declines. The company then falters and usually falls back. That is one of the reasons why growing companies are sometimes moving toward bankruptcy or weaknesses that can be overcome only through acquisition by a larger firm.

There is a direct relationship between the size of a business and the number of variables affecting or operating in it. As size increases, so does complexity. The relationship cannot be quantified but it is fairly constant. Organizational formality, unlike size, does not progress linearly; it grows by a step process. Up to $250,000 a year in sales there is virtually no specialization in organization, just a broad, featureless landscape. But at $500,000—give or take a little for the nature of the business—the first organization barrier must be scaled.

EXAMPLE:

One service company (whose barrier was apparently at the $250,000 level) was run by two men who built their business to annual billings of $300,000 but could go no further. In frustration they alternately blamed each other for a lack of understanding, then accused the employees of irresponsibility. The solution was to reorganize by separating the functions previously shared by the men or not handled at all. One man was designated administrative head of the firm; the other assumed responsibility for technical matters. Regular meetings with an outside adviser helped clarify firm goals and priorities, define responsibilities, and reduce redundancy of effort. Within a year the firm was handling $400,000 in billings and was geared to move easily to $1 million.

Beyond the $500,000 stage, organizational barriers are encountered at approximately $5 million, $25 million, and then $500 million in annual sales. Three factors may affect the timing: (1) the life cycles of the firm's products or services; (2) the ranges of diversity of the products or services; and (3) the levels of special skill or knowledge entailed in the firm's activities.

The point at which organization becomes critical in a growing company depends upon the nature of the work performed, the capacities of the top man, and the managerial attitudes in force. In one company, one-man management may become inadequate when it has 25 people; in another, not before it has 200. Separate work groups seldom form in companies with annual sales below $500,000. Companies with sales of $1 million to $3 million a year often have two or three formal departments; those with sales of $3 million to $6 million, three to five departments; and those with sales of $6 million to $20 million, five to eight departments.

Small businesses have begun to differentiate organizationally much earlier and with greater virtuosity than they used to. Production and sales are still the functions most likely to be separated first. The next units are likely to be research, personnel, data processing, and product research.

Although a small business should be concerned with structure it should organize conservatively, lest it organize itself to death. Small firms should differentiate further only when the benefits on some tested basis appreciably exceed the penalties. They should always keep in mind that solving one problem does not mean eliminating all problems. Successful reorganization at best means substituting smaller problems for the ones replaced.

Despite what their managers *say*, in practice small businesses cling to the traditional view that they don't need organization because they are small. It is true that one of the strengths of small firms is their ability to do a great deal without structural sophistication and that excessively formal organization would be deadly to a small business. But in assuming that small businesses are naturally open and flexible systems and do not need formal organization, we lose sight of the fact that some formal organization is mandatory in small business.

Earlier we said that the differences between small and large business are not absolute but are significant nonetheless. Organizationally, the differences are such that managers in small firms should work at opening the organization more than building it, or increasing communication flow and individual involvement without equally increasing organizational differentiation.

The small business manager should focus not so much on assigning authority as on detecting authorities that are missing or not being used. In big business, because organizational changes take time, and because distance from the home office filters bad news, one must be very careful where and how power is placed and with what limitations. Not so in small business. Here the need is to detect what is missing in the way of power to make the machine work properly (planning, controls, innovation, succession) rather than to decide where to put it. In other words, the big danger in large firms is the assumption of unauthorized power; in small firms the big danger is failure to exercise power because the need to assign it has not been recognized.

In opening the organization, the small businessman should work toward employee involvement and extracting the most from manpower rather than trying to get people to conform or be acquiescent. It is a myth that small businesses are great places to work because they put fewer constraints on individual initiative. The fact is that small businesses are more conducive to the repression of initiative than large firms, where one can often get around the system. The elitist who is convinced that he knows what is best for his business is far more common in small firms. And the typical small business employee may give less than he is capable of because of the limits imposed by one-man rule and a closed authority system.

The sum of this is that the small business has to exert itself to be open and provide an effective environment for people. There are certain necessities in being large that force large companies to create adequate communication flows and opportunities for personal growth. This is not meant to suggest that large companies provide more natural environments for the skilled, the ambitious, the responsible. It does mean that improvement in the condition of the small company is worthy of attention.

Closed systems, systems that are sealed off from the world and dominated by small power groups, are probably most common among small companies. Lunch with the Elks or the Chamber of Commerce may provide an aura of openness, but in many cases an idea originating outside the business has not been in evidence for years.

The complexity and ramifications of growth in a small business organization are demonstrated by the following examples:

EXAMPLE:

A service organization with $1.2 million in annual sales operated in most areas of one state. The president proposed to install an incentive compensation program for three managers, each of whom had some responsibility for a specific geographic area. Two of these men had special skills which were needed in all areas, and all three were paid equally. The president wanted a plan based on a percentage of the excess over a base figure of gross fees less controllable expenses. On the surface the plan seemed sound; the standards and accountability seemed reasonable, and each man appeared to have the same opportunity to produce income.

On probing, however, it became apparent that an incentive compensation plan would not work without organizational restructuring. Since the geographic division had to be tested or an alternative—perhaps a functional centralized organization—had to be set up, the compensation plan was deferred until the structure and assignment of responsibilities in the company could be reviewed. Though the president had responded rationally to a personnel problem, he had not taken heed of the changing nature of the company. On becoming aware of the impact of a compensation plan on organizational structure, he quickly changed priorities and attacked the structure and responsibility questions first.

As noted elsewhere, organization should be planned to achieve long-term objectives, not simply to solve current problems. In planning or redesigning the organization structure, the small company manager should be aware that the character of the changes will be shaped in considerable measure by the corporate objectives chosen. Organization therefore follows corporate objectives. Only in this way can the new organization be prepared to deal with the problems it will face.

EXAMPLE:

A fuel oil dealer in a suburban northeast area decided to balance his seasonal operating cycle by taking on the distribution of swimming pools. He reasoned that his service and repair crew could be trained to handle the maintenance if not the original installation of pools, and his existing customer list of thousands of homeowners was a solid base from which to start selling. Fortunately, he also considered the organizational implications of the new move and brought in an installation engineer through whom all estimates passed, subcontracts were let, and service calls were directed. He also found that a two-tier selling effort was more effective than a single salesman and designated one of the fuel oil supervisors as sales manager to improve the ratio of sale closings.

Controlling redundancy in decision making is a vital principle of organization as well as of cost control. To economize on effort and time, authority should generally be exercised by the one person responsible for accomplishing the task. When responsibilities are unclear (a common condition in unorganized companies) a great deal of time is wasted in unnecessary consultation and cross-checking before action is taken.

Such waste can be reduced by providing clearer guides to action in the form of statements of the firm's objectives and policies as well as statements of each manager's responsibility and authority. This recommendation does not run counter in fact or spirit to the sound advice that a small business stay loose. When standards of performance and corporate results are explicit, self-appraisal is possible in higher degree than in all but the most unusual or undifferentiated firms.

The organization structure that works best at a given point in the life of a small company will be novel to it and strange to all other companies. Organization is the most pragmatic of the major business functions. Its concerns are objectives and results. No principle distilled from other corporate experience, whatever its scale, can take precedence over that.

Whatever form an organization takes it must maximize the use of human resources. Many a small businessman treats his business as an extension of himself—"the lengthened shadow of a man"—which is both unfair and unwise. Each business has a life and character of its own, and each must be kept separate from every other. Putting it another way, no individual's wishes can be put before the corporate life. Countless small firms have perished because personal interests were placed before corporate needs.

Yet to say that the interests of individuals can safely be ignored is like saying that because structural integrity does not make an airplane fly, it can safely be ignored. Employee needs, aspirations, and participation must be included in firm goals. Managerial efforts should be addressed to special projects or task forces that can be deliberately used by small business managers to increase participation, cut across departmental lines, create a sense of movement, and, incidentally, test young managers.

EXAMPLE:

In one firm a number of task forces were formed to research the feasibility of a computer, review the personnel evaluation and compensation system, plan training for new staff, create new services based on a market survey of competing services and possible future needs, and investigate acquisitions. Different employees were assigned to the groups, and each group existed only long enough to complete its mission. Other special task forces have been used for determining plant location, office layout, factory expansion, lease-or-buy and make-or-buy decisions, and staff reduction.

Although most organizations have individuals or departments under whose nominal responsibility each of the above tasks might be assigned, the advantage of temporary groups is that they open participation in the firm to personnel who might otherwise not have the opportunity to use their interests, skills, and knowledge so soon.

A summary of many of the preceding ideas is in the following adaptation of a letter written to the head of a company doing $10 million a year in sales volume. We include it because the relationships between organization and results are generally applicable.

> If we agree that the term "organization" refers to or is synonymous with work differentiation, many small companies do not need to be reorganized so much as they need to be managed differently. The distribution of authority is far more limiting in its depth than in its pattern, requiring not so much a basic change in the existing divisions of executive work as giving more authority and setting up the means to make sure it is used well. The chief executive officer is far too prominent in the operating affairs of the company, and his people do not act sufficiently on their own but feel obliged to have his approval before they act.

> The firm pays a high price for this concentration of authority: Both the CEO and his staff operate below their peak levels of competence. Worse, many relatively unimportant things take up the great bulk of the available managerial time while critical things are starved for attention.

> Since the best risks are those that offer the best chance for survival and profit, and since most small companies make money primarily out of taking high risks, the best efforts of a firm should be directed toward improving the quality of the risks selected and limiting the

threats stemming from these risks. To accomplish this requires that (1) the number of risks of equivalent value that are looked at be greatly increased and (2) the screening of risks that are potentially assumable be much more intensive and thorough. The two can be accomplished only by increasing the responsibilities of the executives reporting to the CEO for operating decisions and keeping the bulk of his time free for discovering, contemplating, and selecting the firm's major investment opportunities.

A test of how the firm's present needs are being met can be made by measuring the proportion of the time spent on cutting-edge or risk-taking activities. The CEO should be spending at least half his time on such matters. The administrative side of the business should take no more than one or two hours each day.

To accomplish this task, the CEO should take action to (1) increase the authority of each key member of his staff, (2) set up the means to keep informed of progress and measure performance (through exception reporting, monthly profit and loss statements, and so on), and (3) restrict his accessibility and the demands on his time to matters deserving of his attention; this will require the establishment of clear policies for the guidance of others.

Most firms can well afford to take the foregoing actions. A firm can easily afford—and it is very costly to avoid—some waste in activities at the lower levels of the scale of importance. What a firm cannot afford is waste in activities or a lack of activities at the higher levels. Because most firms are not doing enough of the things that are most important for their own safety or profitability, the CEO spends too much time in his office.

The following observations and opinions are generally relevant to small companies.

1. Key people are work-oriented and selfless; in other words, they are what we usually speak of as loyal and faithful.

2. Executives have a positive relationship to the CEO, respect him, and identify their work with his personal interests.

3. The staff puts in too many hours, which shifts the emphasis from quality to quantity, increases the incidence of errors of judgment, multiplies the problems of coordination, and increases the tolerance for significant waste.

4. The company focuses excessively on corporate leanness, with the result that learning is limited to direct experience—a slow and costly way to learn.

5. Key people are for the most part amateurs in their fields, and as

vacancies occur they should be replaced by professionals; this is because the lowest cost decisions are made by persons well versed in
their fields.

In trying to balance organizational formality against organizational flexibility, small companies should pay special attention to clarity of job content. Our experience in hiring executives for many positions indicates the need for a written definition of three key areas of
an executive's job. Unnecessary problems can be eliminated if a manager and his superior agree upon the following items in writing from
the start.

1. What are the priorities of tasks and results for which the manager is to be held responsible?
EXAMPLE 1:
A controller was told during his hiring interview that his experiences in the preparation of prompt, accurate monthly financial statements was one of the reasons he was being given the job. With this
as a clue he spent too much time getting out the first month's statements and left untouched such routine chores as checking to see that
cash discounts were taken. The controller's misinterpretation of this
clue almost cost him his job. The solution was to write down, in order
of importance to his superior, the things he was to do and on which
he was to be judged.
EXAMPLE 2:
A plant manager ran into trouble when he devoted his ten-hour
days to trying to increase production and reduce a backlog which was
causing service problems with customers. The president of the company complained to the executive search firm that had found the manager that he was not training foremen, attending to personnel procedures, and purchasing supplies, all part of his job. Again, a meeting to
clarify the priorities saved the situation.

2. What amounts and types of expenditures can the manager
spend without approval?
EXAMPLE:
A factory manager who had been told he was to run the factory as
he saw fit got into trouble when he ordered a new $5,000 piece of
equipment he believed would pay for itself in six months. In the mind
of his superior, the manufacturing vice-president, "to run the factory"

did not include spending $5,000 without approval. The solution was to define the value of individual items ($5,000 in this case) and the total annual budget ($50,000) over which the manager had discretion.

3. What are the manager's responsibilities for people, and what are his relationships with others on the job? Who can the manager hire and fire? To whom can he give raises and rate changes? Can he approve vacations or hours and days off which do not conform to personnel policy? Also, an introduction to the mysteries of the firm's informal organization can be reassuring to a new manager and may prevent embarrassing or unpleasant episodes.

EXAMPLE:

A new treasurer was told he was to be part of a three-man management team. But when he hung his coat in a closet used only by the firm's two principals, he violated an unwritten rule and started down the road to failure.

A small company must focus less on the development of methods than on their control. Methods in a small company become ingrained, fixed, restrictive, chiseled in granite. How many small firms have something as simple as a periodic review of methods? A thorough annual or semiannual review of methods in force will usually result in a substantial payoff through the elimination of obsolete procedures. To make the review most productive, it is not enough to challenge paperwork procedures. We now make four copies of this form; should we increase the number to five? reduce it to three? eliminate the form entirely? Organizational relationships and the location of decision making must also be challenged. Should each executive have his own secretary, or should we use a secretarial pool? Should we ship from our warehouse or use public warehouses? How many salesmen should a sales manager supervise? How many people should be involved in hiring, firing, and promoting key people?

Small firms run by entrepreneurial managers suffer an organizational disadvantage. Entrepreneurial management does not structure the organization to accomplish objectives but to extend itself throughout the firm. Other members of the firm are dealt with not as autonomous decision makers but as representatives of management. It is their size that permits most small enterprises to be organizationally dominated by the entrepreneur, by the chief executive or some other individual, or by a small group. With all their informality, small firms are usually not as open or procedurally democratic as large firms that can institutionalize and monitor participative management or open communication. In the small firm, one person can decide to do things in his own way, often without opposition. If he has any plans deserving of the name, he can keep them to himself, disclose no operating information, and set up procedures that suit his whims and disregard company needs. For example, in one small manufacturing company the site of the new plant was a location equidistant between the winter and summer homes of the owner. In companies where outsiders have a voice, decisions on plant location would not be made on such a basis.

No small company can afford the staff of full-time specialists that helps big firms. Yet a small firm has to do substantially the same things as a large business. Like pilots of the Piper Cub and the 747, who do the same things, go through the same processes, but allocate their time and efforts differently, big and small companies do many of the same things and go through many of the same processes, but their scale of responses varies considerably.

To handle the range of variables organizationally, the small company should amplify or increase the knowledge, the experience, and the special competences at its command. Special competence will probably come from the outside because of deficiencies in the variety of views, perspectives, experience, knowledge, and sensitivities inside. There are a number of formal ways of doing this, among them such techniques as advisory committees or management committees and employee or consumer panels.

One successful way to break out of the bind of limited knowledge and perspective is for the small company to set up an advisory or management committee consisting of two or three outsiders and the key internal managers. A well-constituted committee can act as a catalyst in setting goals, help establish standards for executive and corporate performance, be a resource for information on new and strategic trends, and make up for staff deficiencies in dealing with problems not large enough or long-term enough to justify full-time staffing.

Because activities in the small company may stay within a narrow range, managers often miss the experiences that make broad-gauged decision makers. A properly constituted advisory committee can compensate for that lack and act as a sympathetic audience when the chief executive needs to discuss his problems. In such a discussion, he will often find his own answers and in the process expand his experience.

Advisory committees serve some of the functions of a board of directors with a few significant differences: They have no legal status and advise rather than decide; they help but do not make the final decision in choosing management; their existence and the choice of individual members are entirely subject to the wishes of the chief executive and not the stockholders.

Members should be chosen from business-oriented outsiders who have been successful (we are not interested in learning how to go broke) in larger companies (because growth problems are usually significant to small companies) and who agree to serve for a reasonable fee and the intellectual satisfaction of helping a company solve its problems and grow. People from different industries bring a fresh and critical eye. For example, the advisory committee of an equipment distributor included contractors from two different markets it served, a sales consulant with a manufacturing background, a bank trust officer, and a management consultant. Other committees have called on executives from many industries, loan officers from insurance companies, and investment bankers.

After choosing the members, the chief executive sends them background data on the company along with an agenda for the first meeting. The package identifies serious problems and long-range opportunities and also separates from committee consideration those nagging difficulties which require a tough management decision but not extensive analysis. The first meeting usually lasts three to five hours, includes an introduction to the company, deals directly with several problems, and serves to break the social ice. Common subjects covered include these questions:

- What are the company's strengths and weaknesses?
- What are its goals? If there are none, how can they be formed?
- What plans are there for new products, services, or markets? for management succession?
- What is the status of information and control? Should we computerize?
- What are our people resources? How do employees feel about the company?
- How can we handle new competitive, legal, and social factors?

Specific problems are also proper concerns for the advisory committee, especially when they involve unresolved conflicts of interest.

EXAMPLE:

One small businessman whose company created an advisory committee of executives and outsiders said that the committee had made clear for the first time who was responsible for what. Recent growth had stretched job responsibilities, created interpersonal tensions, and threatened nonfamily employees. Systematic management in this case required simple delineation of job duties and limits, a procedure which executives of large companies learn early in their careers. Once established, the committee undertook as its first order of business the determination of responsibilities of each key staff member. Later it functioned as an appellate body, hearing and resolving jurisdictional disputes.

Normal meeting techniques should be observed; someone should prepare and distribute minutes, and individuals should be assigned specific duties with fixed completion dates. Project groups should be formed for delving into areas that require additional background, and a date should be set for the next meeting.

Outside advisory committee members are paid a fee of $150 to $500 plus expenses for each session, usually based on the length of the meetings. It is diplomatic to pay the same fee to all members, except for a premium to an outside person who initiates and leads the meeting. The original invitation should make explicit internal management's right to end the committee or drop any member after the first meeting. Paying a fee puts the relationship of the company and committee members on a professional basis and makes a little easier the occasionally difficult act of not inviting someone back.

Since all corporations already have a board of directors which legally must meet, why do we recommend the advisory committee? A functioning, effective board of directors is a rarity in a small company. The weaknesses:

• The board represents the personal interests of the important stockholders, not those of the company. There may be a difference.

• Its members are often incompetent or subservient to the wishes of the dominant stockholder(s), or they may be relatives who serve merely to comply with the law but play no part in running the firm.

• If there is a difference of opinion between the stockholders and the officers, the board represents the stockholders and does not provide the support the officers need.

• If the outside board members are in the majority, the stockholder-managers can expose themselves to temporary loss of their jobs.

The result is that outside members are rarely a majority and therefore, effectively, have only a consultative position.

• Competent, independent, sophisticated people are reluctant to accept membership on the board of directors of a small company because of the legal liability that is attached. Members can be held personally responsible for acts of management over which they have no control. Faced with a thin management team, infrequent meetings, and less than total participation in decisions, the outside board member is somewhat at the mercy of the inside managers.

These limitations on the board of directors in the small company are not what should be, or what need be, but what is generally true. Because of the difficulty in changing or working around the basic power structure that causes these board problems in an owner-managed company, we have found the advisory committee practical in answering the needs of the small firm for information, testing of decisions, and setting goals and performance standards.

An advisory committee permits first-rate people to serve the needs of management without liability and as long as their counsel is respected and acted on. Busy, competent members of an advisory committee will not suffer the frustration of helping to define problems and come up with answers which management fails to act upon. One committee lasted two meetings. Two weeks after the second meeting, when nothing had been done, the members called one another and decided that they would resign unless management acted on the recommendations of the committee. Management was informed; committee members checked two weeks later, met with more procrastination, and resigned in a body.

Sometimes the tough basic questions asked by an advisory committee are too uncomfortable for management to handle if the long-held self-image of a successful, masterful manager seems to be under attack. Committees die quickly when they meet that attitude. The consequence is that committees work best with successful managers who have the strength to admit that they do *not* have all the answers and want help.

Advisory committees do not always succeed in bringing about change. One of the most successful businesses we know depends on a man whose customer relationships amount almost to a love affair. Combined with his great sense of quality and style, this relationship has carried the company. As long as he is there, he will probably continue to produce his mix of successes to sustain it. But heaven help it when he is gone! He has an advisory committee which meets irregularly, but it has influenced him only in introducing some minor institutionalization of personalized customer service and some design and quality control.

Because membership on an advisory committee seems enormously attractive to busy businessmen, you should aim high in asking people to serve on a committee. The attraction is based on both flattery and challenge: flattery because the invitation to join implies that the person is qualified to help; challenge because the work of an advisory committee in helping a business grow is enjoyable and satisfying. Once involved, committee members give time, attention, and the benefit of their experience and judgment.

Among the people who have served happily on the advisory committees of companies in the $1 million to $25 million annual sales range (most of them below $10 million) are the executive vice-president of an airline, the president of a $40 million retail chain, the financial vice-president of a $100 million service company, the retired merchandising vice-president of a $500 million retail discount chain, the group vice-president of a $50 million chemical company, the manager of a $125 million cooperative, the vice-president of a Wall Street investment banking house, an account executive from a large advertising agency, and a variety of successful managers of small firms who had benefited from an advisory committee in their own businesses and wanted to spread the gospel.

Let us review the economics of an advisory committee. Assume that three outside members each receive $300 for every two and a half or three hour meeting they attend and that four meetings are held per year. The total after-tax cost at a 50 percent tax rate is $1,800 for a year, or perhaps $2,000 if some travel expenses have to be paid. It would be hard to find any other investment of comparable size that is likely to have as beneficial an effect on the firm's survival and growth. One other cost should be mentioned, that of internal managers' time to prepare for and attend the meetings. Although the number of hours can be significant, they are well spent because they force planning, choosing, and thinking to become part of the regular pattern of management's activities.

Another approach to increasing organizational effectiveness was used by a company which formed a group of employees to make recommendations to top management on any aspect of the business that struck them as needing improvement. Not only did these employees develop into knowledgeable bird dogs who were close to incipient problems, but top management proved by its willingness to act quickly to solve the problems that it believed in participative management.

This approach works for smaller companies because it gives heed to the need to increase involvement through formal and informal organization structures and because it reduces the dominance of one or two top managers.

EFFECTING CHANGE

Small firms are probably not much different from large in the gaps that exist between ideas and their implementation, particularly in basic management policies. Probably not more than one good idea in ten requiring changes in management becomes a reality. But there are other reasons for managerial rigidity. For large companies, their size makes changing direction a tremendous undertaking that usually takes several years. Managers in small companies, particularly owner-managers, are often hesitant or recalcitrant about taking steps toward rational management procedures which may affect their status or require a change in their style.

Small size can be a useful lever in making change when properly handled. Dependence on a major vendor or customer can be used to compel a small business manager to take steps in the direction of change. The pressure of such a supplier or customer is almost irresistible.

EXAMPLE 1:

A successful equipment distributing company with annual sales of $6 million to $7 million was owned and run by two men. One of them, a man in his late 50s, was a fine salesman, close to suppliers, and personally involved in most of the buying and selling decisions. The other, a man in his early 40s, was trained in engineering and eager to bring planning, budgeting, decentralized decision making, and other management tools to the business. The older man did not want to risk his image as the company's leading personality and accepted few of the many recommended changes which directly affected him.

Frustrated with the slow progress of his plans, and the older man's argument that the firm was among the most profitable in the industry and could not do much better, the younger manager accepted a suggestion to use the clout of a major supplier whose manufactured line accounted for more than 40 percent of total sales. The distributor was known primarily as a dealer in the equipment of the major supplier and could not afford to weaken the relationship or have the manufacturer question the firm's stability.

The manufacturer's vice-president of sales casually asked what plans the two owners had for the continuity of the business if they died or became disabled. (He'd like to meet the next level of managers.) How did they intend to react to the area's changing population and transportation trends? What had they budgeted for purchases for the next three to five years? How did they plan to finance, house, and service the larger inventory? The older owner now saw the younger manager's plans in a different light. Suggestions from the younger manager or outside consultants were annoyances that could be deferred. But continued good relations with the prime source of supply made change imperative. The result was a change in the buy-sell contract, freezing the value of the older man's interest, paying him a lifetime consulting fee and retirement salary, guaranteeing the redemption of his stock at his death through the use of insurance proceeds, and opening up the acquisition of stock to other employees.

EXAMPLE 2:

In a comparable situation with similar results, the sole owner-manager of a specialty electronics manufacturer finally moved toward formalizing previously vague plans when his major customer put pressure on him to bring in new people, establish budgets, and routinely provide for inputs of new technology. Without these changes the customer felt insecure about continuing his annual purchase contracts. Call it pressure, persuasion, or anything else. It works.

IS CHANGE EASIER IN A SMALL ORGANIZATION?

Following is an excerpt from *Behavioral Sciences Newsletter* * which relates size to organizational change and spotlights the roadblocks caused by personal, one-man management:

> A lot of literature produced and read by organization development specialists and other change agents assumes [that change is easier in a small organization]. But some problems we have heard about in small organizations convince us the *generalization doesn't always hold*.

> Let's start with the influence of the chief executive officer on change —a much debated topic even aside from size considerations. *A small*

* September 24, 1972.

organization—either a company or a fairly autonomous unit within a bigger structure—*is far more likely to reflect both the virtues and the defects of the CEO.* If he is committed to change and adept at fostering it, then his small organization might well be able to move faster than its bigger counterparts, simply because there's less inertia to overcome in getting things moving.

But what if he's not committed, or adept? In that case *it may be harder to initiate change in the small organization.* First, the resources of time, money, and specialization may be in short supply. Second, in a smaller organization, the consequences of significant change are likely to be greater, the stakes high, the cost of failure more drastic—and resistance tougher.

A crucial fact is that *it may be harder to assemble the "critical mass" needed for change.* The number of inputs suggesting change will be smaller. And if the man at the top has been close to the hiring process, as is usually the case in small organizations, he may tend to build a group of lieutenants picked in his own image.

Conflicts about the desirability of change and ways to accomplish it are more likely to become more explosive when enclosed in a small space. Proposals for change will be typically argued face to face; *if there is any underlying clash of personalities, it is likely to be buffered by the communication channels* that usually intervene in larger organizations. There will be fewer opportunities for the disgruntled to find other opportunities or slots without leaving the organization.

Finally, because there is more face-to-face contact and (probably) less codification of decision criteria, *personality factors, as opposed to objective criteria, are likely to play a bigger role in the evaluation of change proposals.*

All this is not to insist that change is harder in a small organization. But the claim that it is necessarily easier should be viewed very critically.

We close this section with some thoughts on things managers should keep their eyes on.

Good managers always seem to know how their firms are doing. This relates to their knowing the critical factors in their industry and business, and to their insistence that the information they receive be the kind that will alert them to coming problems.

Take early warnings first; every manager should see that the information he receives is not all backward-looking. Every manager must have his quick-and-dirty thumbnail measures for on-the-spot, up-to-the-minute size-ups of the state of the business. Examples are the prison guard who is alerted by total silence in his block and the general manager who measures production levels by looking at the scrap barrels.

Whatever the measures, whether substantial or thumbnail, they are concerned with three elements: *wanted products, lean costs, and satisfaction in work.* This says it all. You can't have all three without making a profit in the long run. Anything that takes away from one of these, however good it may be in itself, will seriously injure your firm because these three elements are essentially interlocked.

6

PROVIDING
WANTED PRODUCTS

BUSINESS SURVIVABILITY depends on the provision of wanted products and services which fulfill needs. A loaf of bread, a bottle of beer, an antibiotic, a tennis court, music, a hula hoop, a Rolls Royce—all are felt needs. Not only the survival but the profitability of a business depends upon the fulfillment of those needs.

No business creates needs. The notion that it does misses the point. The most that one can claim is that he identified an existing or potential need and satisfied it. Henry Ford did not create the need for low-first-cost, cheap-to-operate, individualized transportation. But he was the first to anticipate the need and meet it.

The concept of profit is also a source of confusion. Profit cannot be the immediate goal of a business. The immediate goal is to satisfy needs over time through a multitude of transactions, the majority of which are economically favorable; the result of meeting that goal is profit. In other words, survival must be the overriding concern and profit the subordinate concern. However, through time, profit must be the top aim. If in the long run nothing is left over after all the work is done, a firm will starve to death. The starting place in the process is the provision of wanted products.

A small business cannot be insensitive to the concept of market needs without seriously endangering its future. If the top executive is not the sales manager, which he often is, he must be in touch with major customers and changes in product design or scope of service. In view of the slim marketing resources (especially in research

112

and planning) and the high workloading of sales personnel in the typical small firm, it can easily become insensitive to impending changes in its markets. Our point is one of emphasis, the conscious allocation of resources to maximize the survival and growth attributes in the provision of wanted products and services. To define and segment the markets, keep the product unique and up to date, provide the proper staff, delivery, service, and backup, detect the effect of competitive moves, dig deep into end uses—all for the purpose of fulfilling constantly changing customer needs—these steps require basic planning. The planning must commit top skills, time, and money in large enough pieces to monitor the customers and external world.

This is not big business magic brought down to small size; it is a process that each company must provide in its own fashion. For example, the service organization must go beyond analysis of accounts receivable arguments and find out what its customers really think. The reason for losing customers must be analyzed and generalizations developed; every new customer should be considered a source of information as to what the company does well. Perhaps all it does well is selling, since a new customer, by definition, has had no chance to taste the service. If the company bids on jobs, all lost engagements should be checked to see what could have been done differently and what the winning bidder offered. Loss of jobs because of high pricing is also worthy of investigation.

MARKET SEGMENTATION

The small company can benefit from the concept of market segmentation because smaller segment size and individual tastes favor it. It is not easy to define a market segment. Only a few companies took the lead and won the initial advantage in appealing to the youth market, the trend toward informality, the changing symbols of success, the interest in health and organic foods, the desire to get back to nature in the form of camping, backpacking, and boating. Each of these markets was capable of being serviced by small companies; many were.

A useful analysis that helps define a market or segment is the time frame in which the customer or prospect sees the buying decision. When a company chooses an insurance agent, CPA, or attorney it usually commits itself to a long-term relationship. These services may also require the prospective user to judge professional competence in areas he is rarely qualified to assess. For these reasons choosing a new insurance agent, CPA, or attorney takes time. Further, breaking the existing relationship is unpleasant and procrastination comes easily.

Consider, on the other hand, the decision to find a new electrical repair service or a scavenger to remove waste and garbage. Both decisions would be made much more quickly and without personal problems. The purchase of stationery supplies does not involve the same time frame as the purchase of a $100,000 machine. The small company that tailors its marketing policy to the customer's individual needs and the time frame in which he chooses his product and service may find a unique advantage in the way it fulfills needs.

UNIQUE SERVICE

Another tool that is rarely exploited by small firms in providing a unique service is to tailor the product to the end user and not to the immediate customer. In some cases this will require a marketing emphasis on services offered rather than a basic change in product design. One component manufacturer, for example, developed almost untouchable relations with his prime customers by sending his engineers into the field with the customers' salesmen to check on and improve the ways in which his product was incorporated and utilized by its end users.

In another case, a builder developed a successful word-of-mouth promotional program by following through in solving the inevitable problems associated with a new building. He specialized in pre-engineered offices for professional men. In a typical case he promised delivery of the completed structure on a specific date and kept his promise—in itself unusual. When the keys to the office were handed to the new owners, he told them that although he had done everything possible to make the building perfect, it was inevitable that the owners would find things wrong. In the event of an emergency they should feel free to call at any hour of the day or night. For more routine problems—tile loose, window stuck, paint sloppy—a repairman would be around every 30 days for the next six months to solve them. And the builder delivered on this promise.

The costs associated with this follow-up program rarely exceeded half of one percent of the total construction costs, and in all cases the result was a substantial number of referrals for new business. The builder did not initiate other promotion or advertising and needed none, since his strategy of anticipating complaints not only softened their impact, but differentiated him from builders who may be hard to find once the formal contract is completed.

In forming a strategy aimed at providing a unique product or service to fill a need, the small business manager needs to know three things: the competitive situation, his own costs, and his customers. Knowledge of the competitive situation requires an investment in learning about comparative techniques of selling and distribution as well as products. Knowledge of his own costs is basic; it requires a good cost accounting system, focused on the marginal or incremental costs associated with products, lines, customer class, salesmen, and areas. Knowledge of his customers probably offers the greatest payoff in terms of the uniqueness of the information produced and the action available. Evidence of the value of comparing selling techniques is to be found in the following case.

EXAMPLES:

A medium-size service organization had enjoyed reasonable growth through traditional methods of promotion: a heavy emphasis on exploiting existing personal and professional contacts, exposure to potential clients through writing articles and giving speeches, and provision of good service that kept present clients happy. Determined to increase the practice, one of the principals looked into the sales development methods used by the large firms in the field. Since they did not have to establish their legitimacy in the public's mind, as the smaller firm did, the large firms concentrated on establishing their expertise in fields where they felt a potential for new business lay and, more significantly, zeroed in on specific potential customers. They did this by finding clients or other contacts who were willing to introduce their representatives to prospects across the luncheon table. A direct sales pitch would then be made. Within a month, the smaller firm had put this technique to work with positive results.

Since we deal with usable cost data elsewhere in these pages, let us turn to the third of the approaches to finding and fulfilling needs: knowledge of the customer. Most marketing texts are based on experiences with large firms and deal in market rather than customer information. For most small firms, the market is too big a universe; further, it does not offer the same opportunity to concentrate and individualize service, thus maximizing the small firm's skill in personal relationships and speed of reaction to changing needs.*

EXAMPLE:

A wholesaler of industrial supplies worked out individual shipping schedules and maintenance of inventory levels for its major customers. Its salesmen kept in weekly contact with the purchasing agents or buyers of the customers to give the special service needed. Although this firm's prices were higher than those of larger competitors that concentrated on bulk shipments and long credit terms, it had analyzed customer buying and inventory patterns and had found an unfulfilled need in the immediacy of service.

A similar approach is reported to be used by a giant retail chain which wanted to capitalize on the entrepreneurial interest of local managers and the regional differences in merchandise taste. Central headquarters could not detect these local differences. By setting overall financial controls and performance standards, management was able to take advantage of a small firm quality. Decentralization of this type thus offers a major competitive threat to the small firm, since it backs individual motivation and local sensitivity with economic power in buying.

One of the large national chains that supply fabric and sewing needs used model garments to promote the sale of fabrics and patterns. These model dresses, which were displayed on mannequins, had to be sewn in such a way that the home sewer could examine a dress inside out, see how it was put together, and ascertain how difficult the task of duplicating it would be. A small garment manufacturer offered its services because it was located in a labor area with access to many full-time and part-time home sewers. After closing a test order, the firm flew a group of seamstresses and supervisors to the main office of the customer to learn the business in its training schools. The result was a close relationship with the customer and a long-term contract to make model garments.

Large firms are organized to sell the typical customer in a large market. And where the result is recognizably lower prices, the exercise of individual taste is often forgone. Since not all customers are typical, a small firm in an industry dominated by large companies can profit by catering to individual tastes.

The selection of the small company's place in a given market

---

* See Mack Hanan, James Cribbin, and Herman Heiser, *Consultative Selling*, AMACOM, 1973.

must be made with great care, as shown by the large number of auto-mobile companies that died seeking to cater to individual tastes, only to find a shortage of customers willing to be individualistic or to put taste before price.

Many small companies are in trouble now because they under-took to serve markets that could be profitable only in prosperous times. The small firms that are healthy now probably looked at market opportunities with jaundiced eyes, subjecting them to merciless profit-ability analysis, and restricted their new ventures to the portion of the market they could serve with some advantage and therefore some likelihood of retention.

Big companies have begun large-scale programs for studying to-day's changing social conditions and estimating the probable effects on their markets. Small companies, on the other hand, have not made a start on finding out the effects on their markets. Among the trends that should concern them and that require interpretation are:

1. Increasing technical competence on the part of customers.
2. Rising demand for product quality and reliability.
3. Growing emphasis on individualism, leisure, and socially use-ful occupations.
4. More spendable income as more women join the work force and families become smaller.

TILTING WITH THE COMPUTER

The following case illustrates the weakness of trying to preserve old ways of satisfying needs by providing service without considering the effects of change, in this case change brought on by the computer.

EXAMPLE:

Members of a state society of CPAs urged the society's executive committee to press for legislation prohibiting banks from offering bookkeeping services (not auditing) to their customers. Several banks had excess computer capacity and saw financial statement preparation as a competitive selling tool to attract small business depositors. These banks had been offering to do bookkeeping tasks leading to simple financial statements. The CPAs saw this bank service as a direct threat because they were dependent on write-up work for steady income and for keeping in touch with their clients. Many of them had made little effort to upgrade their professional skills, aside from tax work, the major service which brought clients to them.

To many of these small accountants, the computer was an unfair, incomprehensible monster. Their response to the competitive threat of bank financial statement preparation was to seek restrictive legislation rather than improve their own offerings. The executive committee turned down the request.

What is the lesson in the example? To know your markets and your competitive strengths and weaknesses. The threat to the CPAs was not from banks but from computers. The computer is beyond the control of any practitioner or even any profession. It was the machine's ability to do at a fraction of the cost and in a fraction of the time what accountants had previously done manually that was the source of the threat. Rather than tilt like Don Quixote at changes in the environment, the CPAs should have taken the approach of other small, progressive practitioners, which was to learn about computers and adapt them to their uses. By installing small computers in their offices or becoming expert in service bureau applications, these progressive accountants exploited the opportunities that computers presented, increased their practices, and used the hours freed by the computer to provide higher-level and more remunerative services such as the installation of budget and cost systems and estate tax planning.

Fighting changes in the outside world is all but impossible for even the biggest firms, to say nothing about small firms. Therefore, being attuned to impending or actual changes, analyzing them to see how you can cope, and either turning them to advantage or turning away from them is the only course open to small firms. (The research and marketing resources of a large company can create new markets of a size and with a speed that are impossible for the small firm to match; witness nylon, Pampers, Trac II, McDonald's. But the small firm may be in a position to capitalize on the existence of the new markets.)

MOVING WITH THE MAIL

The computer is so pervasive an influence on business and society that it is probably in a class by itself as a factor in strategic decision making. Nevertheless, it serves well to illustrate the changes taking place in the environment that no firm can afford to ignore. Though most changes are not as apparent, as well publicized, or as dramatic as the computer, they must be watched for. Consider the effect of something as mundane as changes in airmail patterns in serving customer needs.

EXAMPLE:

An East Coast manufacturer of small items (average package size $2'' \times 2'' \times 1''$) opened a branch facility in California in 1946 to provide its West Coast customers with better service. Although work coming from areas west of the Rockies was directed to California, about 25 percent of the service generated in the West had to be handled in the East because certain sophisticated manufacturing could only be done there.

For years there had been a disagreement over establishing other local offices and over the need to continue the one in California. The argument in favor of expansion was based on the assumption that fast service by branch offices was needed in order to compete with local companies. A study revealed that the substantially larger East Coast plant could absorb the western production with little or no increase in variable costs and at a considerable out-of-pocket saving. As for shipping, except for customers who hand-delivered their goods and picked them up (less than 1 percent), there was no meaningful difference in cost for the round-trip mailing of an item 50 or 3,000 miles. Airmail speed had reduced distance as a factor, and overnight delivery was generally dependable enough not only to justify closing the California office but to make impractical the opening of any other regional offices.

Although the company had used airmail for years, it had failed to analyze its growth and relate it to proper strategic concern for fast customer service.

SALES STRATEGY

Because the background of small company chief executives, particularly the founders or participants in the founding, so often includes a good deal of sales experience, salesmen in small companies are usually given their heads and not held down by the many constraints that are imposed on the sales personnel in large companies. Most small company sales efforts are made without the benefits of an overall marketing strategy, a preplanned sales presentation, or a policy framework. Price, delivery, quality, warranty, return, and credit policies are open to negotiation or are subject to evasion because they are not policed. Without consistent strategies, presentation controls, and policies a

firm cannot hope to create an effective sales operation. It must endure
chaos or put up with an uneconomical number of repetitive management decisions. These are among the reasons for establishing policies
and also for testing them at least annually against customer acceptance, competitive policies, and internal efficiency.

In becoming concerned with the establishment of strategies and
consistencies which seek to maximize individual selling effectiveness,
the management of a small company will have to concern itself with
questions such as the following:

- What are the markets we want to penetrate?
- What do we offer that is competitively advantageous?
- How do our price, quality, service, terms, and so on compare
  with those of our competitors?
- If we are less than competitive in some areas, are there good
  reasons which require explanation?
- What objections are we likely to get from potential customers
  about switching to us? How can we convert these objections
  into selling arguments?
- Is there a psychologically sound sequence in which our selling
  points should be presented?
- Can demonstration, sample, or multimedia tools be used to help
  salesmen?

To the experienced sales or marketing manager, these questions
are routine, and he knows how to develop practical answers. However,
few small businesses control the ways salesmen operate. Only results count, and, if sales are increasing, top management is happy to
let each salesman operate as he chooses. What this laissez-faire approach misses is the opportunity to maximize the company's marketing
uniqueness and to present a uniform marketing approach which can
be built into a powerful selling tool.

EXAMPLE:

A small, technologically oriented company competed head to
head with one of the world's largest companies. Its problem was not
only to find and keep a unique niche in the market but to present a
uniform and consistent approach without destroying the initiative of
its salesmen. The successful solution to the related problems was
through the development of a formal sales presentation kit. It used
appealing graphics and was carefully planned so that the competitive
advantages of lower price and special services were woven throughout

the printed panels. Marketing analysis had revealed that these two points were the only weak spots in the customers' picture of the large company, which they respected for its strength, reliability, and innovation. But it would have been unwise for the small company to let individual salesmen take advantage of these two points in such a way as to cast aspersions on the big competitor. The formal sales presentation kit acted as a restraint on salesmen, but gave them professionally prepared, solid selling tools.

Further, all prospects were approached on the same selling basis. Backed by advertising and direct mail couched in language that would appeal to the decision maker in the prospective customer's organization, the point-of-purchase kit fit into a complete market plan. Finally, it worked.

In a small firm the top man usually handles the big bread-and-butter sales. This is inherently dangerous because deals can be made with the boss. When a salesman weakens and lets himself be talked into a deal, it is always possible and often beneficial to turn down the order because of price differential, extended terms, or softness in credit requirements. But when the boss himself makes a deal he is stuck with it. Furthermore, if the owner-president undercuts his own sales force to bring home the order he destroys the morale of his sales people.

The owner who acts as sales manager needs above all to have strong self-discipline: the ability to walk away from an order. The best role he can play is in developing a personal relationship, building trust in himself and his company by putting his personality and character on display as representing his company, and then letting his sales force handle the actual selling and order-closing.

Buyers are very much aware of this Achilles' heel of small business and may turn away salesmen, saying "We don't pay an in-between brokerage; we buy direct." This is sheer arrogance. They know better than to say this to a representative of Procter & Gamble who is selling Pampers.

One cardinal error of small firms is to let themselves be manipulated by buyers. A clear price policy instituted with each new account pays handsome dividends. Once a buyer knows that the quoted price is negotiable, the seller will never again be able to consummate a deal without bargaining. The buyer, in turn, never knows whether he has reached bottom, making each sale a painful struggle between economic adversaries.

The problem is that the selling price of small firms for equal products often is determined by the competition. The small business-man must continuously discover and promote the special bundle that makes his product, his service, and his company different and pre-ferred by his customers. Selling price struggles must be last on this list; they always become destructive and eat into profit.

In evaluating pricing strategy, small firms should give careful consideration to the advisability of training salesmen to walk away from zero-profit sales. This is one of the hardest things for them to do unless their commissions are based on gross profit, not sales volume alone. When customers realize that you won't take all orders, you will avoid getting into an auction with zero-profit competitors.

7

MAKING WORK
SATISFYING

THOUGH THE SMALL FIRM should of course strive to achieve lean costs, it should not do so at the expense of manpower. Dependence upon manpower will usually be higher in a small business than a large one, which means that small firms should usually pay as much attention to making work satisfying as large ones do.

Put in another way, small firms should care for the tools of accomplishment no less than any other firm. Since small firms customarily are more labor-intensive than large firms, they should generally devote a higher share of their efforts to improving the conditions under which employees produce at all levels. In our view, improving productivity can be achieved primarily by improving the conditions of the work environment.

Personnel problems in small businesses are distinctive for the following general reasons, among others.

1. Small firms lay heavier burdens upon supervisory personnel than do large firms. The small firm must deal with most of the functions handled in large organizations but it has a much smaller range of competence from which to draw. Smaller volume is not accompanied by proportionate shrinkage in the variety of activities.

2. Small firms are more easily and therefore more often dominated by extraordinary people. Most small companies have at least one such person, whose net effect is to reduce the scale of business perspective and decision making.

3. Small firms offer less emotional security. Dominated by single

figures as they tend to be, and managed in the light of the top man's shortcomings, small firms offer personnel less opportunity to build self-respect on the basis of initiative and contribution.

4. Small firms have less experience in and less time for training and management development. They usually invest much less of their monetary and intellectual resources on expanding their employees' competences.

5. Small firms have a wider gap between the skills available and those utilized. Furthermore, they tend to have a sense of competitive inferiority and, consciously or otherwise, under-recruit.

6. Small firms have comparatively low managerial turnover. Tenure in small companies in most cases is significantly longer than in large companies.

Item 1 causes special problems in small companies because it is rare to have even one full-time manager for each major function. Small businesses usually cannot afford or do not know how to use staff specialists. So they demand a wider range of active skills and abilities of their managers than do larger companies. The manager in a small firm needs to have some understanding, knowledge, and skill in a broad range of techniques, such as production, finance, communication, planning, control, personnel management, advertising, sales promotion, and sales management. He should understand economic conditions and should know what the firm's responsibilities are to employees, customers, and the public and how to discharge them. In short, he has to know something about a lot of subjects, whereas the manager in a large firm has to know a lot about a few subjects.

Such an orientation in small firms is not without its penalties. For one thing, few men can operate consistently across a broad range of activities; for another thing, managers in small firms deal with such a variety of problems every day that they have little time to develop expertise in any specific area.

In that characteristic lies one of the great dangers to small business. If it fails to recognize its knowledge weaknesses or to fill its knowledge needs by the best means available (some of which are outside the firm) it will drift with the tide. The poor layout, production methods, financial controls, and marketing practices so commonly met in small companies testify to the failure to recognize and fill gaps in managerial expertise.

To complement its own management, small business now has at its disposal a wide range of specialized services not greatly different from those available to larger companies. Among these services are business systems, accounting, merchandising and marketing, distribution, engineering, laboratory, advertising, packaging. Using such services has become one of the principal opportunities for improving the performance of small businesses.

Point 2 in our list of small business problems touches on the fact that small companies are often the embodiment, the lengthened shadow, of one or two gifted men. In many cases the founder of the firm is the chief executive and the prime molder of its success. Where the firm has outlived the founder for any length of time, it is often because his place was taken by someone equally exceptional.

The presence of extraordinary talent is a major source of problems unique to small firms. The man who stands head and shoulders over his colleagues in natural or assumed authority can create hazards as well as benefits for his company. The success of the company often hangs on his powers. Equally, however, his skills can be repressive in that the company's organization and operating mode are tailor-made around him and are thereby resistant to the introduction of new and different methods and skills.

That brings us to item 3, the matter of emotional security. Certainly, being able to look upon oneself objectively and with approval is difficult under any circumstances. But satisfaction in work and therefore the possibility of high performance depend on self-approval. The presence of a dominant figure greatly increases the difficulty in building favorable self-images. When the dominance is expressed in irrationality and inconsistency, it can produce in subordinates both frustration and a dwindling sense of worth. This is particularly hard to handle because most of us have a distorted sense of our strengths and weaknesses, especially with regard to the decisiveness and judgment that characterize good managers. The single dominant figure in the small company is unlikely to welcome suggestions from subordinates that he is lacking in these qualities.

As to item 4, few small firms do much to amplify the human resources they command, especially the talents within their reach. Small businesses have little knowledge of formal training because they hire too few people to justify formal training costs, and their preoccupation with daily affairs causes them to adopt sink-or-swim methods. The two methods most often used—assigning new employees to experienced workers and having them attend outside functions—are not conducive to optimal learning. Techniques such as planned job rotation and corporate visitation are seldom used. The result is an inbred environment where prevailing ideas are likely to remain prevalent.

Small firms have special difficulty in developing and amplifying management skills. The small company that seeks to train managers by customary methods faces major questions of relevance and use of the knowledge instilled. Most of the principles and practices embodied in the commonly accepted discipline of management derive from the experience of large companies. There are no cheap and easy ways for the small company to transfer the complicated skills of management.

One remedy available in training lower-echelon staff is to allow them to make operating decisions within prescribed limits, thereby preparing them for increasing authority. The risks can be controlled, and the broadening of decision-making responsibility can foster continuing growth of the company and its management.

Another remedy that has distinct advantages is in-house training conducted by outside specialists. Conferences and seminars held on the outside usually are permeated by big company thinking. Sessions held within the small company by outside professionals who have taken the trouble to learn the special needs of the firm have the advantage of being close to the problems of the company.

The consequences of the fifth shortcoming—the gap between skills available and those utilized—are amplified because most small firms recruit at lower levels than they need to. This skills gap materially affects questions of personnel administration in the small company. Among other things, under-recruiting causes small firms to suffer in the face of the growing professionalization of management. Recruitment is discussed more fully in a later section.

As to item 6, small businesses have lower turnover in management positions than large companies. This creates special problems in skill development and hampers the recruiting and developing of future management personnel. Such promising young persons as a small company may be fortunate enough to recruit are likely to become dissatisfied and leave because they cannot see any prospects of promotion within a period of time acceptable to them. Such losses are unfortunate; but the economic consequences of excessive tenure are probably even greater. Whereas the president of a large company typically serves for 10 years, it is not unusual for small company presidents to hold their positions for 20 to 40 years. Large companies choose older men as presidents, partially for the wisdom and judgment they bring to strategic planning, partially to insure that they do not hold the chief executive's position long enough to stifle the ambition of younger men. But, since the small company president owns the stock and dominates the board of directors, who is to unseat him while his health permits him to continue?

RECRUITMENT

Hiring is a commitment activity. The existing and potential quality of the people it brings in has a large hand in determining what the company becomes or, at the very least, the costs of realizing its potential destiny.

Most small firms employ lesser skills than are available to them. Given a choice between a $15,000 and $20,000 controller (no other data supplied), 90 percent of the managers in small firms will choose the lower-salaried candidate. However, given the choice between a $15,000 and $20,000 truck, the same managers will hesitate. They have learned that variations in the price of machines may be caused by qualities that justify the difference. Obviously, most managers in small firms have learned their lessons about things better than they have about people. Hence, recruitment should be of particular interest to the small company that seeks to become a superior performer.

Managers are more cynical about salary differences than about other kinds of differences involving money because their conditioning, more than is generally acknowledged, is thing-oriented. Keeping salaries down wins more stripes in the typical small enterprise than using compensation as a tool of motivation. Consequently, the typical manager learns early to regard people as expenses to be paid for with the smallest outlay possible, not assets to be valued (as trucks would be) for what they can contribute to the business.

The $20,000 controller might be the preferable choice should the hiring manager take a cost-effective approach; that is, should his approach with people be similar to the one he takes with machines or finances. If the orientation of the hiring manager could be shifted from costs to benefits, from the salary considered alone to the salary measured against what the man can do, the ratio of selections is almost certain to tilt in the direction of higher-priced candidates. When people are viewed as assets rather than expenses, much can be discovered about their potential contribution that would otherwise be left out.

This is not to suggest that money is the only factor in the reluctance of small business managers to invest in effective managerial talent; another factor, less often acknowledged, is an unwillingness to give up authority.

The economic advantages of hiring superior people extend to a wide range of activities: quality of sales efforts (obtaining new and retaining growing customers); quality of work turned out daily (reliability, productivity, dependability of product or service); initiative (ability to react positively to new situations); cooperation (skill in working in and between groups). These intangible assets all contribute directly to long-term profitability and all depend on the interest, skill, and personal qualities of individuals. This is the economic justification for investing in the recruitment of superior employees.

Small firms have been at a real disadvantage in attracting people with specialized training and abilities, such as research scientists, market researchers, and sales promotion specialists. And, because of this, many managers think their small businesses are inherently unattractive. Not so.

Small companies must compete for good managers with large organizations, which are still commonly assumed to be better employers. There is evidence that small firms can considerably improve their competitive positions as employers, in proportion to the time and effort invested in hiring. There is also evidence that the small company, in this day of corporate giantism, is increasingly attractive to competent men who fear becoming robots in the large corporation.

That men can be captivated by the idea of working in a small, tightly knit operation is borne out by the growing resistance to conformity that is evident in young people and by their desire to do their own thing. This has made the small firm more attractive to the business school graduate who wants nothing to do with the apparently monolithic structure and bureaucracy of large corporations. Reports from the leading business schools describe a marked shift in the attitudes of their graduates. The percentage who want to work in small companies has risen sharply in recent years. Many small businessmen do not understand the appeal that small firms hold for this group of highly trained people.

The starting place for the small company recruiter who is looking for superior talent is to recognize that there are advantages in being small. The recruiter for small businesses should sell from strength; that is, place emphasis on what a small company can offer to people with high potential. The idea goes something like this: a small business, because it is small, can offer greater challenge, make use of higher skills, grant more authority, and yield faster rewards than can be found in initial employment in a large firm. No matter how the benefits of small business careers are extolled, recruiters should always emphasize the variety of experience and early opportunity to contribute significantly.

Typical of the opportunities that small businesses can offer people with high potential are the following.

1. *Better chances of becoming the top man.* In a small company the odds in favor of a man's becoming the top executive are far better than in a large company; this is simply a factor of there being fewer people to compete with.

2. *Quicker assumption of power.* Competent men want authority and want it soon. Men in large companies often are satisfied with their salaries but not with the power they exercise. The economics of small businesses, with their few executives, assures the early assumption of significant authority.

3. *Accelerated experience.* Small companies cannot afford large-scale training programs; they develop executives primarily by example and by testing them on the job. Thus the scope of work performed by each manager is usually far wider and more varied than that handled by a person with comparable experience in a large company.

4. *Faster pace of recognition and reward for good performance.* A small business offers faster performance feedback and better measures of one's value and contribution. Views of one's worth are not so much muffled by systems, procedures, and policies designed to assure fairness of performance appraisal and compensation. Further, the small business can compensate its people with greater virtuosity. For example, the man who wants a few extra days for vacation or a summer job for one of his children can be accommodated more readily in a small firm.

5. *Far richer personal contacts.* Relationships between employees and with customers and markets are a good deal closer in small firms. Managers are closer to the action. Relations with the chief executive are more likely to be face-to-face than indirect. In contrast, the man in a large organization usually sees only a small part of the total picture and has little chance of altering the scheme of things.

6. *More relaxed human relations.* The informality of small firms is attractive to many people. It goes beyond the relative absence of organizational differentiation and procedures, extending to dress, flexibility of working hours, and general atmosphere. The human side of small companies is warmer and more fun than that of big companies.

7. *Job security at least as good as in big companies.* The 1969–

1970 recession showed that the successful small company offers employment security at least equal to its large competitors. The reduction in executive staff arising from the recession was disproportionately high in large firms. Being more cost-conscious and less likely to overstaff, small businesses can offer an executive job security at least equal to that of large companies.

8. *Minimized demands on personal and family life.* A small company gives a man a better chance to establish community roots. He does not need to move as often, travel as much, and be away for as protracted periods as his large firm counterpart.

To recruit successfully and at costs in keeping with its size, the small company must observe several precautions. The first of these is that it ought to develop and keep at hand a body of clear-cut recruiting and hiring policies. In doing so it will be confronted with the necessity to recognize and, where possible, reconcile standards, biases, and myths that vitally affect recruitment. One example is the almost universal tendency to search for hirables on the basis of tenure; small company managers tend to search for employees who can be expected to remain with the company for a long time. This prejudice should be junked; people should be hired because they are needed and can produce the results desired, not because they are likely to stay forever. Tenure itself has little inherent value.

EXAMPLE 1:

One small business in need of a controller hired a 58-year-old man who had been turned down by large companies because of his age. He worked for the firm six years, drew on his 35 years of experience in solving problems, and left the firm's financial affairs and systems in solid shape for his young successor.

EXAMPLE 2:

A professional organization drifted into a new area of service which required expertise unavailable within the firm. To get started in the right direction and without embarrassment, establish legitimate credentials to perform the work already in house, and train staff, the firm hired a 69-year-old retired executive with unquestioned experience. He spent two years doing all that was expected and relished every minute of feeling useful. He then returned to his retirement, leaving the firm headed straight along the right path.

These stories have two lessons. One is that neither age nor tenure should be a deterrent to getting a job done efficiently and professionally. Hire the person for the job, not for life. The second lesson is also important: It is often faster, cheaper, and safer to hire someone with the missing expertise than to experiment with developing a home-grown expert.

Small firms must be prepared to lose people but, in fact, generally are not. Their reluctance to let long-time employees go reduces turn-over, limits the openings at higher levels, and makes it difficult to at-tract competent managers or potential managers who are too am-bitious to put up with a lack of movement in the executive ranks.

We have mentioned several problems in hiring practices that small firms might try to avoid. A positive program is even more valuable. Like any other planning function, recruiting requires answers to the standard questions: Where are we? Where do we want to go? How are we going to get there? Who will do the work? When? At what cost?

In addition to the standard attractions that it can offer a prospec-tive employee, each small firm should try to pick out its unique selling points. Creating an identification that spotlights the firm has two ad-vantages: (1) It permits the firm to stand out from all other firms; (2) it selects from the applicants those who are most likely to fit into the firm's style and plans. Uniqueness can be described in any meaningful area: product, plant location, profit-sharing or equity participation plans, technological or service initiative, customer list, growth, social or community responsibility.

The manpower needs of small firms are hard to forecast. Rather than commit a company to an unrealistic number of potential man-agers, it would be wiser to find external sources of trained, experi-enced people who can be called on when needed with less risk and less loss of time. Among the sources are local large companies, retired executives available for temporary assignments, employment offices of graduate schools of business administration, trade association execu-tives who know of management changes, and ex-employees who have risen to management levels in other companies.

Regular sources of applicants to fill job openings include the following.

1. *Current employees.* Before going outside the company for managerial or submanagerial personnel, consider listing the openings and the skills or experience needed so that interested employees can apply.

2. *Referrals from employees.* One level of screening has taken place when an applicant is referred to the firm by an employee: the

applicant has had a solid, frank introduction to the firm's working environment. When job openings are listed, employees can be asked to suggest qualified friends.

3. *Ex-employees.* Some small firms keep in touch with former employees through a bulletin heavily spiced with news of ex-employees or through an alumni association, which is best when handled entirely by alumni. To keep the communication channels open for the possible rehiring of ex-employees requires a change from a commonly held policy never to hire anyone who has left. This restriction not only is invalid but hurts the firm more than the ex-employees.

4. *Advertising.* To bring in applicants through newspapers or trade and professional association publications requires three things: a carefully written advertisement that will attract good candidates and eliminate obviously unqualified ones; time to sift the applications and sort them into good, questionable, and no good categories; and time to interview and check references of the good applications.

5. *Employment agencies.* Agencies vary so in their pre-screening and reference-checking that it is worth the effort, for a small company that will be hiring regularly, to establish personal relations with an individual in several of the biggest local agencies. One firm found it helpful to invite six local employment agency executives to an annual lunch where the firm's unique aspects were described and its hiring plans and philosophy were discussed. The result was a disproportionate share of good applicants directed to the firm's attention. Remember to make clear that the firm will pay the agency fee.

6. *Applicants who were once turned down for reasons that do not make them ineligible.* Starting with the premise that the human organization is an asset, some forward-thinking small firms keep track of the applicants they have interviewed but were unable to hire. This list serves as an inventory. When a new need arises, the list can be reviewed, former applicants called, and, perhaps, a few good people brought in from this little-used source.

Few small firms have the time to become expert at interviewing. More often they adhere to the golden finger fallacy; some top executive thinks he knows how to pick people and, after a single interview, points the finger at the ones he likes. Interviewing is a technique that grows with study and experience. Here are a few basic suggestions.

1. Since most good applicants are working when they apply, small firm managers should fit the interviewing schedule to the availability of the candidates. This probably means holding interviews at night and on weekends.

2. Aim high; spend the time necessary to interview all potential candidates thoroughly so as to get the best one. The investment in the person will be long-term, and the time required to select from among the candidates will be well spent.

3. The normal ratio of interviewing to hiring is nine to one. Remember all those interviewed whom you do *not* hire; if they have been treated with consideration and leave with a positive feeling about the company, they can be ambassadors of good will among other applicants and even future customers.

4. Follow up when a candidate to whom you have made an offer turns you down. Some firms send a letter asking for a frank opinion, others phone, others have someone ask the person to lunch. No matter how the information is collected, it provides a useful view of the firm's competitive position as an employer.

5. Observe standard interviewing techniques: (a) Ask open-ended questions. What has the applicant done best? What would he like to do? Why? How can he help your company? (b) Spend two-thirds of the interview time in listening. This means you must structure the interview so that you say what you want to say but don't ramble on, because you will learn little while talking. (c) Look for patterns of behavior. Since people tend to be consistent, find out what the applicant has found satisfying or challenging in schools, work, hobbies. Test the answers against the interests or skills that will fit into your company and permit him to succeed in the job.

When reference-checking is more than a perfunctory authentication of employment facts (When did he work or study? What were his starting and ending salaries? What did he do? Why did he leave?) it can be one of the most valuable recruitment tools. A telephone call or, even better, a personal visit will produce meaningful information. Written references are generally so carefully phrased that they say nothing.

These are some of the questions you might ask: If this man hadn't left, would you have retained him? Why? How far would he have gone in your company in three years? What were the best things he did for you? On a scale of 10, how would you rate him in the last job he held? How could his performance have been improved?

Remember that people's skills, strengths, interests, ability to deal with others, initiative, sense of responsibility, and thoroughness do not change dramatically from one job to another. You will win more bets than you lose if you predict the behavior of a new employee in your company on the behavioral patterns he has shown in the past.

In selecting management-level applicants directly out of college or graduate schools, the small firm recruiter has additional problems. The applicant comes with no history of comparable or related work experience. He may be judged on the basis of grades, appearance, or interview personality. But good grades indicate little about ability to do good work; appearances have been known to deceive; and since the interview is an artificial situation even when sensitively conducted, the personality displayed is not closely related to job success. A few suggestions may help:

1. Get to know a professor or two at a few, local universities whose graduates are likely to apply to your company. Let them know why your company would be a good place for graduates with specified knowledge as well as specific work and social habits. A professor can influence likely candidates to apply and will have known them for years rather than for the hour or two of an interview.

2. Hire with the expectation that a probationary period of one to three years will be needed before final placement or assignment can be made. This policy eliminates the need to be precise when hiring and gives the firm and the applicant an opportunity to test each other. The selection, training, and judgment-producing experience come later.

3. When you hire a college or graduate school potential manager, be prepared to pay high starting salaries, to meet resistance from long-term noncollege employees, and to absorb mistakes. Developing young managers in a small firm is like growing a plant; you can provide the environment and opportunity for growth, but you cannot force it to grow, nor can you make it into something which it inherently is not.

By giving challenging assignments, expecting errors, and providing feedback the small firm can attract and retain superior personnel at all levels. Not by chance or intuition will this happen, but by conscientious planning and consistent hard work. The results are worth the effort.

Applicants may be sensitive to another characteristic of the company: Is it open, innovative, progressive, or is it closed, static, moribund? The best prospects for key positions won't even go for an interview if the company is static. One of the heaviest prices of being in a rut lies in having to take the leavings of companies that have new things in the works. Men who want to do things and be where the action is normally can't get their hands on the handles and levers early enough in large companies. The small company that attends to its change needs offers a shorter, faster route to the main events. Hence, the small company that wishes to become staffed with exceptional people should attend to its renewal and development work (and the public relations to promote it) before fishing for exceptional employees.

In talking with potential employees whose experience has been exclusively in large companies, the small company recruiter should remember that an executive moving from a large company to a small one is likely to find it hard to make the transition. Top performers in a firm of one size do not always do well in another. Men from big companies, for example, usually are more accustomed to regular hours than their counterparts in a small business. An executive moving to a small firm may have to put in longer days to turn out the same amount of work because he will not have the staff services that were available in the big company. Furthermore, the informal and less structured climate of a small company and the severely restricted choices for socializing can become stultifying.

Though the small firm has more warmth, a man from a large company may be confounded by the whimsical, intuitive management. Accordingly, the small company recruiter should be sensitive to the adaptability of a candidate from a large company. If he does not appear to be fairly flexible, he should not be hired.

The problem of moving to a company of a different size was expressed by one executive in this way: "We had a brilliant controller—technically and personally capable, with a large company background—who couldn't take this atmosphere. He was unwilling to sell his ideas. He was used to putting things in motion bureaucratically. Small business does not work that way. As a result, we had to part company."

Another point to keep in mind relates to allocated powers. The executive who does not intend to delegate specific responsibility almost immediately should not promise it. If the small businessman is really willing to delegate, employment in his company can be almost irresistible to the man with high potential. If responsibility is not delegated, such a man will not stay long enough to repay the costs of finding him and breaking him in.

Small companies should focus on upgrading staff rather than on retaining them. Recruitment is one of the best opportunities for upgrading. The only financial risk lies in recovery of the cost of finding and hiring the man. If you bring a man in and he stays for only a year, did you recover your costs during the year? Most people contribute most of what they have to give within a short time; thereafter they generally do the same thing again and again. Mobility in the executive staff is a manpower strategy that small firms should use more.

In addition to hiring older workers and making use of their considerable knowledge and experience, small firms should seek out women and minority executives as relatively untapped resources. Small business firms should be alert to the changing trends in the labor market. Competent women in increasing numbers are becoming available as managers.

KNOWLEDGE OF THE RESOURCE

One unusual way out of some of the small company's personnel problems is for it to build adequate knowledge about human behavior in general and its own people in particular. Small companies suffer from knowing far less about the capability and potential of their own people than they should. In companies that pride themselves on knowing everything about their machines, ignorance of their employees is inexcusable and wasteful. The assignment of personnel to the tasks for which they are best suited should not be accidental. Correct manning is a function of adequate knowledge of the jobs to be filled and the people available to fill them.

An inventory of skills provides useful information. Personnel records should be kept with long-term uses in mind and not merely for annual or semiannual salary adjustments and performance reviews. A small business manager about to sign a ten-year lease understands the need to plan his space requirements. Similarly, buying machinery often entails long-term capital commitments and thus raises the question of long-term use and payback. But space and machinery are useless without the right people at the right time. The job of people-planning requires not only a guess as to how many people will be needed and with what skills, but an even wilder guess as to the development of the individuals now on board.

A tough-minded evaluation of the potential of present and projected management and supervisory people is one of the best ways of insuring survival in the small business. It may lead to the hiring of a few good people, the retiring or termination of some weak ones, and the opening up of opportunities to younger staff members who are eager to prove themselves—all positive steps. An inventory of interests available and needed provides an even rarer kind of information. To obtain it, a questionnaire should be filled out by every present and potential manager listing skills and interests and willingness to study or to be exposed to experiences which will increase his value to the company. A responsible person must be assigned to implement the program.

The fact that a small business manager knows the names of many of his employees often makes him confident that he also knows how his employees feel about their work, that he has a finger on the pulse of morale. If the organization is small, if the manager is in close touch with operations, and if he is a good listener, he probably has some sense of employee attitudes. But when he is separated from the working group by at least one level of foremen or supervisors, he is probably basing his opinion on past experience or a halo effect untouched by reality.

EXAMPLE:

In reviewing a long-established overtime policy, a group of supervisors in a professional service organization with a staff of 150 people suggested that the staff be given the choice of compensatory time off or money for overtime. The manager took a straw poll among ten principals of the firm, asking what choice the staff would make between time off and money. Nine of the ten principals (average age 45) believed the staff would choose money. But when 20 members of the staff (average age 23) who would be directly affected by the policy were asked the same question, 18 said they would choose time off. The final decision was to offer a choice, with time off available at the company's discretion.

The message was clear: The older men were projecting their memories of their own desire for more money to the younger generation. If they had decided on the basis of experience rather than evidence, they would have made a poor decision, even though their motives in this case were selfless.

How does a manager find out what his employees feel and what they need for increased satisfaction on the job? He can ask directly in a nonjudgmental and nondefensive manner, or, if that approach does not work, he can use indirect means. He can, for example, distribute an attitude survey, conceived along the lines of the one in the Appendix. Attitude surveys are most valuable when used regularly, so that comparisons will show the changing patterns of employee feelings and perceptions and the effects of organizational decisions.

If the prospect of designing and interpreting an attitude survey is forbidding, the small firm manager should call in an expert in this field. Like all other aspects of personnel work which cannot be economically justified as full-time services, an attitude survey is an example of specialization which can be brought in only when needed. Experts who develop a continuing relationship with a small firm are especially helpful because of the intimate knowledge they accumulate of the firm's unique qualities.

MANAGEMENT DEVELOPMENT

The risks of sinking are too great to allow sink-or-swim methods in developing managers to operate effectively in the small business environment. Aside from the personal damage inflicted on a potential manager by failure, the typical small company's need for qualified managers is such that it cannot tolerate their development under conditions of least control and the lowest order of predictability. Leaving their development to chance is a branch of the sink-or-swim school. Just as the maintenance of technical knowledge in the volume and quality needed is too important to be left solely to the judgment of individuals and is best assured when included in organizational planning, so also does management development benefit when accorded organizational recognition.

To most small business managers, the idea of a management development plan that goes beyond seeing that a member of the family is being brought along (but not too fast) smacks of academic theorizing. Sons and sons-in-law (or their female counterparts) may not be available, interested, or competent. More important, even if they are available and have the other two qualities, they also require managerial nurturing. Following are ways of setting up management development to suit the purposes of small firms.

The first step is to determine what the purposes of the program are to be. Is the program to teach concepts or practicalities, to provide greater variety or greater depth of experience, to develop judgment through limited risk decisions, to create an atmosphere in which the intellectual content of management is raised to the level of a corporate performance measure, to prepare managers for change without concentrating on specific knowledge, or, in some degree, all of these? Some of these ideas are compatible, but require priority ranking so that the program to be developed starts with the most important needs of the organization. The developer of a management development program therefore must first ascertain what a company wants to be and what skills and knowledge are needed to make it move in the chosen direction.

Second, the status of present managers' knowledge, interests, and experience should be listed. To know where we are going, we have to start with where we are. To complete the list requires two tough judgments: (1) What is each manager's potential to grow? (2) In what areas in which the company needs strengthening can each individual make a contribution, considering his performance and experience to date, our evaluation of his potential, and the company's future needs? Some of these judgments should be part of a regular annual performance review, shared with the individual. For top-level owner-managers who have the strength to face an honest outside evaluation, an advisory committee or a management consultant engaged specifically for this assignment can provide the required objectivity.

The next step is to plan the development program for each person: courses, books, seminars, regular journal reading, work experiences within the company. Because the training resources of most small companies are limited to on-the-job experience and committee participation, the facilities of trade or professional associations and local universities as well as formal reading programs can be beneficial.

With some effort and luck, small companies can find an outsider to organize and run a management development program. Sources include a faculty member of a local university, whose understanding of the needs of the company should be tested before entrusting the program to him; a successful retired manager, preferably from a larger company; and an organization such as American Management Associations which is experienced in providing turnkey in-house management development programs based on its broad experience in the field of management education. A budget is a necessity so that cost can be measured against performance.

It takes courage to follow up the implementation, to keep the program going when business turns down, to change it as needs and experience change, and to question its value. Now, some specifics.

• Consider a broad basic program of the management seminar type for all supervisory staff, with attendance on a voluntary basis. The purposes are to flush out potential managers and to create a common understanding of the company's goals, needs, and management philosophy. A schedule of two hours a week for ten weeks has worked.

• After listing individual interests and needs, pick someone to develop a magazine list and routing list and assign the reading of articles. The point should be made that articles are to be read and the magazines routed to the next name within a few days. A monthly conference to discuss the articles will encourage compliance and make the program effective.

• Cassettes are available on a wide range of subjects. They can be used in cars and at home if inexpensive machines are lent or given to the managers in the program. Again, summary discussions will increase both the number of listeners and the quality of their retention.

• Use your professionals, customers, and vendors to present relevant material. They will all be flattered, know their subject, and probably provide a qualified speaker at no cost.

• One person should be responsible for the program and should report to the president, if the president does not handle the job personally.

The most important dividends of a management development program are its effect on attitudes toward change and the emphasis it places on the need for continued learning.

FINANCIAL INCENTIVES

Few small company managers see the possession of competitively compensated technical and management skills as a business advantage. The others have held to the view, arising out of the first struggles of a newly formed and thinly financed company, that all things—including personnel—should be bought as cheaply as possible.

Such a view is neither necessary nor economically justified. In the long run it forces the firm to rely on second-rate employees and overlook problems such as low productivity, employee indifference, and inability to grow, which are symptoms of an inadequate organization. The evidence bearing on manpower strongly supports the view that small firms will profit from spending money for good people at every level and treating people as an inherently rich resource.

Small firm managers are no different from their big business colleagues in the way they look at salary review sessions. They are generally content to provide increments which will keep the peace and base their decisions on how little they can give an employee to keep him quiet. Because institutional security, a decent pension plan, or a sinecure earned by doing nothing wrong for years is less likely to be available in the small company, and because individual performance is more visible, salary administration can be positive. Raises and fringes can be tailored to personal needs and be sensitive to changes in performance. Although routinely scheduled, performance and salary reviews can be made dramatically more effective by special changes in salary or status.

More important, does the small company have a plan to permit nonfamily executives to participate in the future growth of the firm through ownership or some kind of profit sharing without financial investment?

The most straightforward approach is to offer stock in the company to managers whose contribution is significant and who will remain with the organization only if they have an equity interest. The problem is that what is a fair price to the family sellers is usually beyond the financial capabilities of a young manager. Take a company with a $1 million net worth, earning a 15 percent return after taxes. The minimum such a company is worth is about $1 million; the maximum (depending on the industry and the current price-earnings multiple) is probably about $3 million. The price of a 5 percent interest is therefore $50,000 to $150,000, an astronomic amount to a 25- or 35-year-old-manager earning $25,000 to $35,000 and probably living slightly above his income.

A recapitalization of the company is one answer. By freezing all or a substantial portion of the company's present net worth in a preferred stock with a fixed value, the company will be able to offer participation in its future growth by selling part of its common shares to the managers it wants to attract.

EXAMPLE:

A manufacturing company with a net worth of $500,000 was run by its 57-year-old president (who, with his wife and 17-year-old son, owned all the stock) and two managers, one 42, the other 35. Moved by a sense of fairness as well as a personal wish to provide for management succession, the president sought outside help in working out a program that would permit him to retain control as long as he wanted, would allow his son to come into the business if he chose, and would let the two managers participate in future equity growth in a digestible way.

Here is what was worked out: The company's $500,000 net worth was recapitalized into $490,000 in voting preferred stock (7 percent noncumulative) and $10,000 in voting common stock. The president sold 20 percent of the common stock to the 42-year-old manager for $2,000 and 10 percent to the other manager for $1,000, prices they could obviously afford. The result was to give them an interest in the future growth of the company without having paid for the net worth that was used to produce earnings. The president chose not to declare dividends on the preferred stock as long as he was active. Included in his salary was some consideration for the use of his capital. Because the range of his salary was within reasonable limits by Internal Revenue Code standards, there were no tax problems.

A buy-sell agreement, which had been drawn up at the time of the stock sale, provided for redemption at book value, by the company, of any shares held by a departing or deceased stockholder. Payment was over five years.

Three years after the recapitalization, the company was worth $700,000. The investment of one manager had gone from $2,000 to $40,000 and the $1,000 investment was now worth $20,000. The two men not only felt they had a piece of the action; they really did. Their efforts to increase profitability resulted in direct benefits—increased corporate net worth—in which they shared. This program was independent of an annual salary review program and a bonus based on profits above 25 percent pre-tax return on beginning-of-the-year net worth.

The formulas available for recapitalization must be designed specifically for each company, taking into consideration the number of managers to whom an equity interest is likely to be offered, the price and terms of the minority interests, age and prospects of the original owners, control, and the possibility that the recapitalization may be only the first step in a program of management succession and estate planning.

All plans to sell stock to employees should provide for a way out, a formula to buy back the stock of a departing or deceased employee stockholder at a price and terms set at the time the stock is sold. Even if these provisions are amended, the company and the new stockholder must agree on when, for how much, and over how long a period his shares will be redeemed. Certainly most agreements require him to offer his shares and obligate the company to buy them when he leaves the company.

EXAMPLE:

After a recapitalization creating 15,000 shares of common stock, valued at $2 each, and two classes of preferred with a total value of $1 million, five middle-aged managers who were not members of the controlling family each bought 1,000 shares at the $2 price. When the last one retired, his shares were worth $300,000, a tremendous return from his original investment over a period of 15 years. To make the cash drain on the company less onerous, all redemptions were over five or ten years, at the option of the company.

Sometimes an equity interest cannot be arranged for nonfamily members because of owner unwillingness to share or because of legal or operational problems. For example, ownership may be in the hands of a trust or estate; there may be a fight between family members; sale to a larger company may be an imminent possibility; or there may be a danger of creating control problems by selling a few shares to outsiders. Whatever the case, when an equity interest cannot be sold, phantom or shadow stock can be issued. Under this procedure, the manager is given credit in a memo account for a negotiated number of theoretical or phantom shares. The amount paid to him upon his departure—or to his estate in the event of his death—is usually the difference between the value of the shares at the time they were originally credited to him and the value when he leaves.

EXAMPLE:

Two brothers-in-law, both in their 60s, each owned a half interest in a successful brokerage business. They did not trust or like each other and could not agree on an equitable division of the company's assets (which would have resulted in an uneconomic split), but did agree that with retirement near, new management was needed. Neither man had children interested in coming into the firm, and neither could accept any plan which would change the 50-50 control or deadlock situation. In other words, they could not permit the issuance of stock to a third party whose vote, combined with that of either brother-in-law, would have put the other in an intolerable minority position.

The solution was to find an executive acceptable to the two men and keep his economic interest warm by offering him a share of the future profits in a form other than voting capital stock. A second-class nonvoting stock was not feasible for tax reasons. Shadow stock was the answer.

The net worth of $1.2 million was the base from which the plan started. The new executive was to be credited with 10 percent of the increase in net worth over $1.2 million, payable over ten years as ordinary income when he left the business. In this case the younger executive found the acrimony between the two owners an impossible obstacle to substantive organizational change and stayed only five years. When he left, the firm's net worth had risen to $2.4 million, largely due to his efforts, and he received $12,000 a year for the next ten years (10 percent of the difference between $2,400,000 and $1,200,000 = $120,000; spread over 10 years = $12,000 a year).

Shadow stock is different from a profit-sharing or pension plan in several ways: It is not tied to retirement benefits; the company pays nothing into a trust for investment purposes and receives an income tax deduction only when a disbursement is made to the recipient; owner-managers, who are by design usually the largest beneficiaries of profit-sharing and pension plans, rarely participate in a phantom stock plan; no Internal Revenue Service approval is required; the phantom stock plan can be offered to individual managers at different times with different prices and terms; and it can be as broad or discriminatory as the owner-managers wish.

Incentives for personnel below the executive–supervisory level are also worthy of the attention of small business managers.

EXAMPLE:

In an electronics manufacturing plant owned by two men who employed 120 factory workers, largely women, pre-tax profits were divided into two parts, with 20 percent of the net worth at the beginning of the year set aside for the owners as a return for the use and risk of their capital. All pre-tax profits in excess of 20 percent were distributed to everyone in the company in proportion to their salaries. Semiannual distributions were based on the computations of the company's auditors, which were disseminated to everyone. Because the profit distributions were 10 to 30 percent of base salaries (which were competitive) and therefore significant, the concern for profits, cost savings, and efficiency was universal. Group pressure to produce was strong. The company was eventually sold to a large international electronics firm at a high price. The new owners changed the formula only to the extent of making the 20 percent a minimum and adjusting it upward when the average overall corporate return on investment exceeded 20 percent.

EVALUATION

Experience in many performance evaluation sessions with subordinates convinced a group of small firm managers that there was something vaguely wrong and disappointing with a process that sounded good, was effective in many cases, but ran into trouble when the employee and the manager differed over salary. The problem simply was that performance evaluation tied to salary discussions deals with two often contradictory approaches. One concerns future *performance:* How can the employee do better in the future? What has he done in the period under review which will cause the plan to be revised? The other aspect deals with *evaluation* of the past and is often tinged with criticism to justify the salary. Evaluation is also necessary to provide information for advancement and other organizational changes.

Many an employee has left a meeting with his supervisor feeling that his frankness in discussing problems was used against him. The problems become the excuse for a reduced salary, rather than the basis for a discussion on how to do better. One such discussion and frankness disappears. Yet the managerial dilemma remains: Future performance and past evaluation must be discussed, and salaries must be adjusted in line with both.

The answer is to separate the evaluation of performance and the salary discussion, if possible by several months. Better yet, have different people handle the two functions. Salary should be tied to performance and an administrative procedure which sets wage levels. Normally, the salary discussion should be considerably shorter than the one on performance.

The problem is not size-related, but for the small firm it is especially difficult because of the paucity of competent, sensitive managers who can handle one kind of employee interview, let alone two. Unless the small firm manager is aware of the inherent conflict, he will follow the lead of other managers in dropping performance evaluations except as they relate to salaries. If he can train supervisors to handle the performance sessions and assign salary conversations to someone who has the personnel staff responsibility, he will have eliminated a problem. Only the people reporting directly to the top executive will have to discuss performance and salary with the same person. In those cases two carefully and openly differentiated meetings at different times should work.

THE ASSUMPTION OF SOCIAL RESPONSIBILITY

One way to increase satisfaction in work is to give it greater importance. A good way to accomplish this is to broaden its connection with wider issues. Such issues are mounting in importance and are bearing ever more strongly on corporate affairs. The small firm need not wait until the relevance to its affairs is forced on it. It can benefit from anticipating small changes and build a broader basis for work importance.

With consumerism, sensitivity to ecological problems, the long-suppressed demands of minorities, and the increase in social-minded managers, social accounting and responsibilities to society are of growing interest and concern. Publicity on the programs tried and the successes and failures achieved has been focused largely on giant companies. Although the small company manager is less frequently subjected to attack for failing to live up to some as yet undefined standard of corporate responsibility, he cannot escape involvement. His time, his resources, his opportunity to make a significant change in society are all limited. Assuming he wants to do something, what should he do?

Aside from whatever financial support he gives to organizations that interest him, the manager of the small firm should concentrate his acts of social responsibility in a few areas; for example, initiating pollution control in his own business, training and employing the underprivileged in his firm, or responding positively to consumer education or safety as it affects his products. The small business manager can have a direct and immediate result in socially sensitive areas that will be productive and satisfying. In all cases we are of course referring to activities that go beyond those required by law.

Social involvement can broaden the interests of an executive and expand the areas in which he will become sensitive to stimuli that may affect his business. Education and cross-fertilization of ideas continue for life. They are particularly valuable when new issues are interrelated, as they are in social activities. In sum, the way to succeed is to concentrate in the area of social action as in all other significant areas.

MANAGEMENT BY OBJECTIVES

Among the management techniques of big firms that can be useful to smaller firms is management by objectives, or MBO, whereby an executive and his superior jointly set performance goals that tie in with organizational plans.

Only recently has much attention been paid to the effects on productivity and profitability when the organizational climate and goals frustrate or go contrary to the personal goals of managers. These conflicts seem to be more readily reconciled in smaller companies. For one thing, the management group is smaller and there can be a higher rate of agreement on corporate goals than in the larger, more diverse, more dispersed company. For another thing, size affects our feelings toward the institution we work for. It is hard not to feel insignificant in a $100 million company; the organization's size dominates. The $5 million company and its proportionately smaller organization permits a sense of identification; it does not overwhelm.

Though management by objectives can greatly benefit the small firm, few have reaped the benefits. In most cases, the obstacle is informality. The informal structure of most small firms makes it difficult to be explicit about two MBO essentials: responsibilities and performance standards. Informal personal relationships, which contribute greatly to the organizational effectiveness of small firms, make it difficult to impose formalization and measurement of progress against individual plans. The psychology of the small firm is against the adoption of MBO.

How does the president of a small company (especially one in which family members are working) initiate a program requiring his key people to put down on paper what they expect to accomplish in the coming year and how their accomplishments will be measured (with some effect on their compensation)? How can he change his relationship from that of a friend and colleague to that of a counselor and evaluator? It is not an easy problem but has to be solved if the individuals involved are to grow or be identified as incapable of growth. MBO offers a solution.

A short definition of MBO is in order. MBO is both a form of integrated planning and an application of motivation theory. It is a structured way to force a firm to establish practicable goals and objectives and break them down so that each person has his own piece, his own subobjectives.* In the process of having each man share in setting his part of the total goal and allowing him to challenge corporate plans, a review of the firm's master goals is forced before they become fixed.

After seeing that overall objectives have been set, the soundest way to start an MBO program in a small company is for the president to prepare a plan for himself and have it challenged and reviewed by an outside person or group: consultant, board of directors, or advisory committee. No other example can be more convincing evidence of his interest. He should then get the people who report to him to set down what they expect to achieve and how it will be measured. Although the program can be extended well down the organizational line, most small companies will find it prudent to stop at the first tier

* John W. Humble, *How to Manage by Objectives*, AMACOM, 1973.

of executives below the owner-managers. It will take several years, sprinkled with frustration, open opposition, quiet sabotage, and the diversion of management effort, before this start will take hold.

The ingredients of a successful MBO program are honest participation in forming goals by the person responsible for their achievement, counseling/advisory relationships between the manager and his boss, frequent feedback on actual achievement, and support of the top man. Tough enough! But interestingly, the goals most managers set for themselves are higher than the boss at first feels can be met. Review of the goals is the next crucial step to reconcile the expectations of superior and subordinate. It is also at this point that discrepancies between past predictions and actual performance are analyzed. The fear of failure and the overcoming of an atmosphere of accepting routine performance require close thinking by both parties.

Let us consider a hypothetical case. What are the specific objectives a small firm manager might list as his own? Like corporate plans and budgets for the smaller organization, an MBO program should rarely stretch beyond three years in the broadest outline. It should be specific for one year; the objectives should be material items only (the immaterial ones should be disposed of by direct action without dignifying them by listing) and should number no more than five or six. Measuring points should be set as closely as possible; once a month for a one-year program is ideal, once a quarter the least frequent.

Table 2 gives some examples. Notice that specific plans for the achievement of goals have *not* been listed. That is not an oversight. One of the main attractions of MBO is that it leaves the implementation to the manager whose objectives they are. He will use his creativeness and knowledge of the changing world to do what he thinks best.

MANPOWER UTILIZATION

Human resources are poorly used in most firms. The typical small company bias is to undervalue or underutilize the resources, or both. As a result, many small companies can materially improve their performance by acquiring exceptional management and technical people and having them work to the limits of their competence.

The value added to a product or the provision of a service is heavily labor-dependent in the small company. The reasons have to do with the markets served and the niches filled by small companies, which tend to focus on individual and specialized service. The large

Table 2

Position	Goals for the Year	Measures
Sales manager	Increase sales of product in regions 2 and 3 by 10%	Sales statistics
	Introduce two new products in the education market, each to generate $200,000 in sales	Sales statistics
	Hire and train 3 new salesmen	Commissions earned should equal draw by four months after hiring
	Review salesmen's travel allowance program	Report by June 1 for president's approval
Vice-president, manufacturing	Reduce down time on screw machines by 10%	Machine hour usage reports
	Reduce scrap from 10% to 7%	Scrap; production reports
	Train five new foremen	
	Shorten production cycle by three days	Production reports
	Complete plans for new warehouse	For president's approval by July 1
	Improve two-way communication between management and workers	Attitude survey, informal conferences

company can or must become more routinized, mechanized, and therefore dehumanized.

All organizations wrestle with the problems of providing job satisfactions to motivate workers whose jobs are not inherently challenging. Few people look forward to a lifetime of dull, repetitive, fragmented tasks removed from the final product or user. A further complication is the effect of union membership, which alienates workers from management by developing a we-and-they attitude.

How do you keep an employee content during 35 years of doing the same work? Perhaps the answer is to build closer identification with the company by listening to him and recognizing and rewarding his contribution in unusual ways. That should not be manipulative. Although the typical small firm may have limited opportunities to satisfy employee needs on an individual basis, its managers can be more personal because they know more about each employee and can attack each problem with sensitivity and knowledge.

The many organizational levels in large companies keep the workers far removed from the decision makers, and personal contacts are largely with peers and immediate supervisors. Thus there is tenuous identification between the individual and the firm.

Smaller companies can exploit their own advantages in this regard in several ways. A variety of individualized products fits the market plans of the smaller company, and the variety and changing nature of the work provide greater job satisfaction. Job enrichment and job rotation are more than current buzz words *; they seem to make sense. With smaller production runs, more frequent style changes, more specialized jobs, and custom servicing, the smaller company offers workers a chance to see and be responsible for larger and more meaningful pieces of work rather than doing a single piece of work until the repetition becomes onerous. These elements of job design give managers of small firms an opportunity to make work more satisfying.

The implications of the *need* for job enrichment should not be ignored by the small business manager. If job enrichment is a possible solution to an emerging problem which is facing larger companies (where most of the research and applications have taken place), then the variety of work, changing products, and changing job requirements natural to the smaller company can provide workers with enriched motivating job experiences.

Without being phony (workers are extraordinarily sensitive to this quality in management), small firm managers can develop a personal identification with many of their workers that sheer numbers make it impossible for the large company to duplicate. People want to know their bosses and to feel that their bosses want to know them. The boss who attends the annual office party, makes a show of fraternizing with a few older workers and secretaries, and then either leaves early or

* See Robert N. Ford, *Motivation Through the Work Itself*, AMA, 1969.

spends his time with pals does not convince anyone of management's concern for the individual.

What the small firm manager can do is meet with small groups of his workers to give them a chance to talk and ask questions. If his firm is small enough, he can run an annual meeting of all employees. He can write a personal note in a company publication or let employees know what is happening by means of an occasional payroll envelope insert. He can personally present the 25-year awards and provide a warm sendoff when staff members retire. He can get out of his office and walk into the factory or warehouse; or he can visit with salesmen, ask questions, and listen to the answers to prove his interest in the work as well as in the problems of the people doing the work. In this way he will come to understand the conditions under which people work and, by his actions, provide identification with the organization and recognition.

EXAMPLE:

The head of a $15 million a year manufacturing company spent two hours twice a week in his factory, listening. The president of a giant airline tried to create the same feeling by visiting every installation once a year and addressing every employee in the smallest groups that could be fitted into his schedule. His attempt to personalize the giant institution had mixed reactions. Some employees appreciated the effort because he listened; others felt it was tokenism since he had been so late to a meeting that there had been no time for anything except a canned speech.

Worker identification with the heads of the two companies was obviously different. In the smaller company, the employees held a party for the president when he retired and sent him off with a truckload of gifts; in the big company, presidential changes were considered the result of board politics and meant nothing to the worker.

In effect we have been saying that an organization's concern for the individual is symbolized by the actions of its president, that the head of a company sets the tone, and that the impact of his personal quality usually is greatest in the small company. This is not an argument for one-man management and paternalism, however enlightened; both are limits on growth. It is an argument for small firm managers to exploit their advantage in satisfying the universal desire to be recognized and to feel a sense of identification with an organization.

Another aspect of personnel problems in small firms that should receive attention is the two-sided question of providing for the future and keeping good people. This is a difficult task in the small company because it has comparatively few key positions, and not many competent people can be found who are willing to stand in the wings waiting to fill them. Replacing a key executive is difficult in any firm, but large size gives advantages which smaller companies do not have in dealing with the problem. Succession is complicated for the typical small firm because it does not have many organizational layers that can act as waiting stages for men on the rise.

Small firms can use three approaches in solving this problem: (1) Have an active program to identify and put to work underutilized talent. (2) Offer all employees assistance in developing their skills further. (3) Increase the responsibilities of every employee as his competence is demonstrated without hindrance from established procedures, salary questions, or prerogatives. These steps will not solve the retention and replacement difficulties of the small firm, but they will go a long way toward alleviating the problem of breaking in new employees and forestalling the departure of skilled employees who may be tempted to seek more responsible work elsewhere.

Small firms need to focus on the utilization rather than the development of individuality. One of the prevailing myths is that small businesses make better use of individuals whereas large companies have a minimum tolerance for individuality. We need to rephrase this and say that because a small business tends to be dominated by one person or group, it does not utilize the individual competences, the offbeat capacity of others in the firm. In a small firm, we often find we need to be concerned more with the generation of individualism, to sponsor differences and contrasts of opinion, to balance the unilateral management of one-, two-, or three-person control.

Small firms should be much more concerned with involvement than with acquiescence. Involvement requires acceptance by the top managers that they do not have all the answers, that information should be shared, and that decision making should be distributed as widely as possible.

The informality of most small organizations is the cause of one of the most disturbing problems in personnel relations: the job that is undefined, unmeasured, without priorities, and doomed to failure because of a lack of communication.

EXAMPLE:

A growing metals fabricator owned by two strong principals hired a plant manager who had 15 years' experience with one of the international giants in the industry. He started work as the two owner-managers were still struggling with a new plant, equipment which was not yet debugged, and a large backlog of undelivered late orders. Three months later one of the principals was ready to fire the plant manager. He showed no understanding of small business flexible practicalities, his systems had made the backorder problem worse, production was one-third less than the owners had looked for, and cash was tight because of those late shipments.

Investigation revealed that the plant manager had been unable to get anyone to say what problems he should tackle first except that a specific amount of production should go out daily. It took him four months after he had started (two weeks after the principal had suggested he be fired) to get production up to the expected level. Working with a consultant, the plant manager and the owners developed a procedure to deal with the problem. Subject to a review by the owners, the plant manager prepared a job description listing the tasks and results he was to accomplish, how they were to be measured, and the priorities he would apply. To keep the arrangement sensitive to changes, the three men arranged to meet for lunch once a week, as a start, to discuss progress and problems.

In the enthusiasm of hiring specialists, small business managers are often guilty of the white-knight delusion: Get the new man on board fast and don't bother with job details; just turn him loose and he will solve all our problems. Instead, the new employee should be told the tasks he is to perform, the results expected, the standards for measuring performance, the order of priorities, the review and communication procedures, the person he reports to, the employees who report to him, and the kinds of money and personnel decisions he can make without approval.

EXAMPLE:

One controller, hired primarily to prepare timely financial statements but also to act as office manager, was told that he was to be a member of the newly formed executive team. Since his office manager's duties were not spelled out, nor was he told his spot on the executive team, he got into irretrievable trouble when he tried to develop standard priorities as to hours worked, absenteeism, and sick leave. The head of the company had previously dispensed individual benefits with regard to time off in accordance with his mood at the time of the request. Long-term employees knew how to read his moods and felt that a standard policy would deprive them of special favors. The controller had no clear-cut authority from the president, who had oversold the position without defining the specifics.

Men coming to a small company from a large one or directly from a major graduate school of business administration have a difficult adjustment to make. They are particularly upset by the lack of formal organization structure, the focus on the present and past to the almost total exclusion of the future (absence of planning), the difficulty in determining what they and other executives are supposed to do first, and the basis for evaluating their performance.

The M.B.A., fresh from successful analyses of case studies, faces two problems that he and his small firm employer should be aware of so as to reduce his integration time and his frustration at finding business and business school so different. The first point is that each business is unique, particularly in its human organization. No amount of case study analysis can prepare a new executive for the power structure, the whims, and the informal communication of a particular organization. The unwritten laws of corporate behavior are more idiosyncratic in the small firm than in the impersonal large one. Until the young man becomes sensitized to the individual style of his organization, he will find the classic approaches of the business school unworkable, and he will not know why.

Style—a personal style of management—is a factor in the second problem the M.B.A. faces in fitting into a small company. Fresh from rational solutions to business problems, the new employee has not formed his own style of managing because he has not yet done any managing in the real world. How he reacts, deals with problems, makes decisions, and handles ambiguity are unique to him. Until he has developed the confidence or at least the consistency that experience brings, his managerial behavior is likely to be inconsistent and hard for his employer, colleagues, or subordinates to follow.

In the small firm there should be more concern for understanding than for morale. Small firms tend to have problems of morale that are inherent in their financial, production, and other conditions. Morale is attendant upon their way of doing business, upon the spirit of administration, and they are more or less stuck with it. Yet there is great concern for employee feelings and little concern for understanding. Legitimately, large firms have to be more concerned about morale because employee attitudes are more concealed and can cause very real problems.

The personnel function must be handled in some way by all organizations. Aside from the routine, administrative tasks—payroll taxes, payroll preparation and recordkeeping, fringe benefit paperwork, hirings and firings—the essence of the function is for management to know the interests and needs of the individual employees and provide the structure to permit them to be satisfied consistent with the goals of the firm.

Because small firm managers *can* get to know their employees, if they are aware of the need for and the payoff from doing so sensitively and consistently, they should set aside managerial time—a company resource—to see that it is done. Without such a strategy as a start, the company's personnel procedures will suffer from crisis reaction: good people leaving, unionization, shortage of management-level personnel.

The individuality of employees can be respected in setting hours and schedules. Not all work need be started and ended at the same time; not all employees need work at their desks (much can be done at home); some jobs can be part-time, others seasonal; vacations can be fitted in with family plans. One small firm gives two weeks' vacation after one year's employment, three weeks after five years, four weeks after fifteen years—not unusual. But it also permits accumulation of unused vacation time in excess of two weeks (for internal control and health reasons, the firm insists that everyone take off at least two weeks) so that employees can get away for six or eight weeks for special trips or projects.

SABBATICALS

Managers should have sabbaticals. Instituting sabbaticals in small business firms is admittedly difficult because of managerial shortages, but the problem can be overcome.

Requiring a manager to get away for three to six months every six years or so can bear fruit in work satisfaction, relief from routine, fresh ideas and experiences. The company can benefit (and the program may be more acceptable) by requiring that the sabbatical have some work orientation—a course at a graduate school of business administration; volunteer work for the related trade association; a stint with a governmental agency; visits to noncompeting firms in the same industry; writing an article or a book. In time the small company may accept a sabbatical that serves no purpose other than recreation, renewal, or reflection on life goals. Aside from helping to preserve a company's most valuable asset, its management, the unusualness of sabbaticals makes them a good recruiting device in attracting competent young managers.

8

ATTAINING LEAN COSTS

IN ADDITION to providing wanted products and making work satisfying, the third paramount objective that the small business manager should seek to achieve is lean costs.

As is true in other sections of the book, our discussion of lean costs is not intended to be a complete treatment of cost reduction or cost-saving methods. Our concern here is more limited: to point out a few special opportunities for small business managers.

For the most part, big firms prosper by making products more cheaply than small firms can. Sometimes small firms can make things that large firms cannot afford to make at all, but this changes with technology and market size. Where small firms shine is in the provision of a product or service to fill a niche, and for this a knowledge of costs is essential.

If a small company expects to stay in business, it must have a strong cost accounting system, cost-sensitive controls, and systematic attention to indirect costs. Given the operational orientation of the average small company, those are not easily created or kept going once they are installed.

One of the distinct advantages of being small is that the firm can resist the snowballing of costs better than a large concern can. Some large-scale inefficiencies are inevitable in big organizations and are tolerable because they are offset by large-scale efficiencies. The procedures of large companies are often cumbersome and costly, even when soundly conceived and implemented, but without them large
156

companies cannot work. Yet they would soon destroy the small firm.

The small company has none of the advantages of large scale; it prospers by finding tasks it can perform more cheaply than big business. And maintaining some form of cost differential is critical to the small firm's survival. Small firms are the most likely to suffer when big ones discover how to lower their costs through elaborate technology or production consolidations. Since it is almost impossible for the small business manager to anticipate or keep up with such developments, the best insurance for the small firm is to exercise tough cost control. In progressive firms that need will be recognized in the objectives stage of planning. Specific programs can then be planned for cost-effectiveness.

The next step in a program of effective cost control is taken when the manager finds ways of spending the same amount to create more value or of spending less to create the same value. Though product or procedural stagnation is commonly associated with large companies, reflection will show that small companies are also guilty of this fault.

The most common benefit of increased production volume is lower cost per unit of output, and this is at the heart of the vulnerability of small companies. By the very nature of the markets they serve and the products or services they provide, small companies are labor-intensive. And the costs of labor are not as easily manipulated as other components of cost. Labor therefore represents a significant cost area which should be closely watched and controlled so that it can be kept as low as possible.

Small firms have special difficulties in balancing income and outgo. Nor can they often achieve the unit costs of their big competitors because they can seldom purchase equipment, materials, or supplies as cheaply. Costs associated with developing, launching, and marketing salable products are also a problem.

The small firm cannot conduct product or market research over a broad front, as it can usually afford little research and development; it cannot put money into swiftly executed assaults on the market and systematic selling efforts because the funds are usually more urgently needed for other things. Because the markets to which small firms sell are less dense and their selling is more personal, the available money usually has to be used to keep salesmen on the road. Yet small companies have little margin for error, and they need market research even more than the large companies that routinely use it for new product introduction.

In big firms more costs are for selling, less for cost of goods sold. In small firms the reverse holds true; more costs are for cost of goods sold and less for selling. In one respect this works against product differentiation and the idea that small firms must work in the interstices of markets. The small firm's protection lies in the size of the markets which will not support high-volume economies.

In a small firm each transaction is a much greater percentage of the whole than in a large firm. The cost of a pound of, say, stainless steel, no matter how much it may decline with increased volume, nevertheless constitutes a large part of the total transactions of the small firm. As that amount increases, so do the consequences of each decision.

COST INFORMATION

The information provided by a strong cost accounting system is crucial to the quality of decisions. The lack of such information probably is one of the leading reasons behind the high turnover among small firms.

Effective cost accounting systems are not easily created in small companies. The ability of the managers to put their fingers on almost every activity and their experience of running things directly, particularly in the early years, generally make them reluctant to spend money on cost systems. Because the typical small business manager had to watch dollars in the early days, he dislikes giving up personal control to a system. Yet resistance to a cost accounting system can be very costly, as the following example shows.

EXAMPLE:

The president-owner of a successful specialty manufacturing company for years resisted all attempts by a younger executive and the accounting firm to install a simple cost system. He said he knew his costs, and, more important, a cost system would inhibit his remarkably profitable pricing skill. Then he fell ill, and while he was hospitalized, new items had to be priced to complete a line. The resultant chaos in the pricing decisions made him accede. The clinching argument was that a cost system would do no more than provide information (which he could use or not as he saw fit), but that less creative and more methodical people would use the data as a floor or as part of a formula in pricing new items. Not only did the cost system become crucial to pricing by permitting more rational decisions, but it disclosed wide variations in profitability (including the identification of no-profit items) and became the basis for worker performance measurements and compensation.

The information developed was simple: Material amounts were estimated, and semiannually actual units produced were compared to estimates and scrap records. Daily labor records provided target labor measurements. Overhead (largely fixed) was applied on the historical relation to direct labor and adjusted annually.

When he can, the small business manager should compare his costs with industry averages. When his figures are out of line, he will have identified areas to investigate.

The effective manager looks for trends. Each period's sales, expenses, profits, and balance sheet items should be presented so that significant variations are highlighted. Also useful are statistics on budgeted costs per unit (which can be more meaningful than dollar figures alone) compared with actual results for the current and previous periods. Graphs displaying these comparative figures and trends may be justified.

Accurate cost information is also a useful selling tool. It permits custom pricing for custom products or services; it strengthens the backbone of the salesman who has to handle pressure from customers for lower prices; and it provides the information for a decision on any large-volume, off-season, or off-line order.

CONTINGENCY PLANS

Lean costs cannot be consistently maintained by planning only for stable conditions (another name, usually, for favorable conditions). Since favorable economic states change, to achieve and keep tight control over costs demands that firms plan for unstable (that is, unfavorable) conditions as well.

Many small businesses went broke because they could not pare their losses quickly enough during the 1969–1970 recession. The main reason for their failure was that they did not anticipate the downturn, and they could not respond quickly enough because they did not have plans covering the contingency. By the time these firms were anywhere near ready to make the needed adjustments, they were economically dead.

Every small firm should consider what-if plans that cover three alternatives: one outlining the way business is expected to go, a second to be used if sales should fall wide of the mark, and a third to be used in the event of disaster. This approach forces advance consideration of what people you'd have to let go if your business were to flounder, how you should rechannel capital into more productive lines, what lines or customers could be dropped. That kind of planning requires toughness of mind and an understanding that no price within the law is too high to be paid for business survival.

TURNOVER OF ASSETS

Since inventories are assets, not costs (until sold), it may seem inappropriate to discuss inventories in relation to lean costs. The truth is that costs are related almost directly to size or quantity of assets and inversely to asset turnover; the greater the investment in assets (receivables, inventories, plant and equipment), the greater the costs of maintenance and operations. In contrast, the greater the turnover of assets in relation to sales, the smaller (leaner) the costs are in proportion to sales. That relationship is rarely understood or used in cost control, yet it can be used with considerable benefit.

Except when extraordinary investment in receivables, inventory, or plant has been made for strategic reasons, it is worthy of top management involvement to keep funds in these areas to a minimum. Beyond the obvious advantages of freeing cash and improving liquidity, the policy reduces costs.

Let us start with receivables. Lower receivable balances almost always mean fewer bad debt losses, less need for credit insurance, and fewer employees required to pass on credit, make collections, or follow up on delinquencies. There is a direct relationship between the age of receivables and their collectability. Since the total receivables balance and the proportion that is in older accounts are also usually related (bigger receivables imply older receivables, assuming similar volume), lower receivables generally go hand in hand with more current receivables.

The annual cost of holding inventories averages 20 to 25 percent of their dollar value. The same logic should apply to cutting costs by monitoring investment in and turnover of inventories. Improving the turnover ratio (average inventory divided into cost of sales) has long been a financial and operational goal, generally touted for its potential as a source of cash. A reduction of inventory from $500,000 to $400,000 (assuming the same volume and therefore an increase in asset usage as measured by turnover) should produce a saving of $20,000 to $25,000 through reduction in the cost of money (to carry the inventories, either direct or imputed), space (if use is flexible or alternate uses are created), insurance (with a reporting policy), handling, obsolescence, damage, and embezzlement.

The final example deals with plant and equipment. Among the financial or efficiency ratios used by all managers, turnover of receivables, inventories, and total or net assets is common. Applying turnover to plant and equipment is generally restricted to organizations that are capital-intensive such as utilities, transportation, and real estate firms whose assets are more directly concentrated in plant and equipment than in working capital. For the small business manager the concept has value, as can be seen in the effect of a change in the relationship of his fixed assets to sales. For example, a $500,000 (depreciated cost) factory turns over six times in relation to a $3 million sales volume. The effect on factory costs of increasing the volume to $4 million (assuming the increase is digestible by the financial and operational structure) is obviously to spread the $500,000 over more sales dollars and reduce certain fixed factory-related costs in proportion to sales.

In addition to showing a leaner use of depreciation, insurance, property taxes, basic supervisory salaries, and minimum electric power (all of which will change little on a change in volume from $3 million to $4 million), there is a more subtle contribution to reduced cost brought on by higher asset turnover—the increase in labor efficiency that takes place when assets are more heavily used. The productivity of workers is not a straight line on a graph of rising sales or production. It moves up faster over a basic level. This observation is particularly valuable to organizations that are small enough for workers to feel a sense of participation, even excitement, when business turns up and customer demand creates pressure. With a solid backlog on one side and sales pressure on the other, worker productivity usually increases in manufacturing and service industries.

The word "turnover" (of receivables or inventories) implies a dynamic, changing situation. However, a comparison of the levels of receivables and inventories over several years will show that there is a *fixed* element to these current assets which is unchanging as long as volume remains at some minimum level. The manager of a retail chain with $8 million in annual sales made the observation that, if his business did not decrease, he considered his $6 million investment in receivables and inventories more fixed than the $500,000 he had in fixtures and equipment. The latter had decreased through depreciation charges, disposals, and an acceleration in leasing rather than buying cash registers, trucks, and store equipment. The individual items making up receivables and inventories might turn into cash within a year and thus satisfy the accounting principle of current assets, but the company's overall dollar investment in the two assets was as fixed as if they were pieces of land.

Aside from the novelty of his approach, the manager found that his way of looking at receivables and inventories as an investment placed a high priority on their size and turnover. He thus justified devoting a major part of his own cost-saving efforts to controlling the size of the receivables and inventories. To institutionalize his interest, he included inventory aging and turnover, bad debt write-offs, and aging of receivables as factors in the bonus paid to store and merchandising managers.

INDIRECT COSTS

The search for cost-trimming opportunities should not be limited to the manufacturing process; the small company must also control indirect costs. Overhead costs may appear low in the small firm because it has few layers of supervision. This is probably illusory, because overhead is spread over fewer dollars of sales or production than in the large firm. Cost control should also be exercised in connection with seemingly cost-free elements or aspects of the business such as sales territory distribution and organization structure. Selling costs are vitally influenced by the former, decision-making costs by the latter. The informal ways of a small firm may seem to favor effective exploitation of its markets and low-cost decision making. In actuality, few small companies have either.

Lean costs imply efficient management of sales opportunities. Long-term arrangements with salesmen or sales representatives are hard to change, especially when they are tangled with personal relationships. Thus the small business manager may be slow to question and change uneconomic sales territory allocations or distribution methods. Population movements may be overlooked because of the informality of the original market plan and the inability or unwillingness to develop a continuing objective information system that alerts management to significant external changes.

EXAMPLE:

In a move to reduce selling costs, one manufacturer reversed the usual suggestion that costs be "unfixed." Disturbed by the absolute amount of salesmen's annual earnings, he examined the total commission costs for the five preceding years. The average earnings of the 15 salesmen had risen from $25,000 to $55,000. More dramatically, each of the three top salesmen had earned more than $100,000 in the previous year. Analysis revealed that the same commission rate had been in effect for the whole period; the increased earnings had come from increased sales, disproportionately higher in the three territories because of population movements and high acceptance of new product lines. The manufacturer (not the salesmen) had created the new lines, advertised directly to the public, made the product institutional, and in effect changed the function of the salesmen from that of opening doors to servicing existing customers. The answer was a compensation package that reflected these changes. It started with a salary (for the service aspect of the salesmen's function) based on 50 percent of the average of the last five years' commissions, and then a commission at less than one-half the prior rate. The reduction in the salesmen's current earnings was offset by the security of a salary and some additional fringe benefits. The company was willing to commit itself to a fixed payment for the salary portion of the salesmen's compensation in exchange for immediate reduced cost and a lower rate for future commission cost.

We deal with barriers to small firm decision making elsewhere. Let us point out now that in addition to its central place in the priority of managerial activities and purposes, making decisions has its own cost. This is another cost not reported in the normal financial report because its elements are hard to assign to traditional accounts. Poor decision making not only wastes the time of executives and others but prevents the firm from taking advantage of opportunities. Symptoms of these costs of missed opportunities include abortive stabs at growth, constant redoing of past decisions, and finger-pointing at apparent mistakes rather than analysis to improve performance.

EXAMPLE:

In an organization that was taken over by a new group of managers, it took only a few months of poor decision making to make several top people decide to quit and to leave the employees confused and then apathetic. The income statement effect of these changes was to decrease payroll costs in the periods immediately following the resignations. When the remaining employees' apathy and discontent caused quality and customer service to decline, there was a loss of business, and the firm's growth stopped.

Until more precise evaluations are found, the economic results of good and bad decision making will probably not surface for 6 to 18 months after the fact and will even then be hard to trace.

Compensation, mentioned in connection with the provision of satisfying work, is not used as often as it might be in the small company as a cost control tool. Small companies should therefore look for ways to reward quality work by offering raises and bonuses as incentives for higher productivity, lowered unit costs, reduced absenteeism, and so forth.

Another cost area deserving of special scrutiny in the small company is that of customer or product service. Service policies should be measured against product pricing and service costs. Because the costs are rarely accumulated in one account, many small companies do not treat service as a controllable, assignable cost item. The result is that prices are inadequate to support suitable and consistent levels of customer service.

As yet another cost control element, small firms should be especially careful about trying to sustain growth that is due primarily to expansion in the economy. Boom years should be exploited to the full, of course, but should add to the basic scale of the enterprise only after careful study. A well-run business will naturally experience a pickup in sales during peak periods, even though the growth in sales did not result from organized effort, and will act vigorously to derive financial benefit from the added sales. But it will be cautious in adding to fixed costs such as its production capacity. The reason so many small firms are so hard hit during slumps is that they have made decisions which prevent early cutbacks when losses appear. By fattening overhead and increasing inventories, they have raised their breakeven point. Surgery is usually required to survive.

OUTSIDE ASSISTANCE

In analyzing their managerial problems, small businessmen need to use more fully the sources of assistance available to them. Small companies have restricted staff services and in-house skills and could derive as much benefit from outside assistance as large companies do. Further, many of the problems most frequently mentioned by small businessmen (for example, planning and financing) can be better handled with outside help.

New sources of information are constantly opening up, and tapping them not only can spell the difference between successful and mediocre performance but in small companies may spell the difference between continuing in and going out of business.

In striving to improve the data base from which it operates, small business can draw on many outside sources especially geared to fill its needs, including banks and other financial institutions, university business service centers, trade associations, research laboratories, consulting firms, specialized service companies, federal and state agencies, and other government sources.

Suppliers and customers are also important sources of information. To an increasing extent large companies are realizing that it is good business to help their small distributors, suppliers, and customers in solving operating, merchandising, recordkeeping, training, and similar problems. Many large suppliers now provide a wide range of management services, and access to technical information is free or at nominal cost. Large customers have offered quality-control, design, and engineering help. They have also used their buying power to provide access to raw materials needed by their small firm suppliers.

Service firms now offer small business techniques and equipment previously available only to large companies. Many companies, themselves small, offer scientific management services—such as computerized bookkeeping, inventory control, and personnel finding, testing, and placing—to a wide range of customers.

When only one service is utilized, it is most likely to come from an independent public accounting firm that performs auditing and tax work; when two outside firms are regularly employed, the second usually is a law firm. But outside consulting assistance is being used more and more. Few small firms use no outside services, and these are usually the smallest firms of all.

An alert trade association can be a rich source of help. It should have information about the industry that would be helpful in anticipating problems. Most good associations are alert to legislative changes under consideration which will affect the industry, and many employ lobbyists to plead the industry's cause. We have referred to the accumulation of industry operating statistics which individual managers should compare with their own performance. Other trade associations have full- or part-time experts or conduct seminars in management areas which are generally troublesome: training salesmen, finance and accounting, compensation methods, insurance, inventory control, buy-sell agreements.

To make an association responsive to the needs of its members usually requires the active interest of some members. Too many associations are run by and for a cadre of attorneys or professionals who call members together only to present a common front in labor negotiations. Information that members need, education programs that touch on their problems, industry stands on significant public or legal issues—these are the responsibility of an active membership which can then direct association professionals to carry out the programs chosen.

The successful small business manager realizes that his meatiest problems do not arise out of current operations but are future-oriented and opportunity-oriented, and solving these often entails using outside services. The successful manager tends to use outside services for problem-finding activities and not merely for emergencies. The most valuable contribution that outside specialists can make probably is assistance in unearthing and dealing with hidden or potential problems.

Making the attainment of lean costs a corporate goal obligates a firm to focus on knowledge of the costs of its operations, pricing, and purchasing. Full-time experts in almost every field are a luxury beyond the capacity of most small companies. Yet their need for specialized knowledge is just as insistent, and the consequences of *not* applying sophisticated expert skills can be wasteful or even dangerous.

Expert skills are readily available to small companies in most areas: telephone costs; freight rates; utility charges; personnel finding, testing, and training; data processing, feasibility studies, and facilities management; insurance claim settlement; fringe benefits; warehousing; and materials handling. Most organizations have continuing relations with law, accounting, and insurance firms and know of the services that advertising agencies provide. The other services are available on an as-needed, variable-cost basis. Not only can experts in these fields save money or increase efficiency, they can provide a sense of organizational well-being much like that of a physical examination which discloses no illness.

Freight, telephone, and utility rate experts are often compensated in whole or in part out of the savings generated by their audit of paid invoices. The complicated regulations and the techniques of appealing for refunds are routine for these consultants but not worth the effort of the small business manager. The classified pages of the telephone directory are an excellent source of names for these experts. Companies far from large cities can ship or mail paid invoices to a firm of rate consultants for audit, wherever their office is.

Because judging the services of outside experts is difficult, the choice of consultants requires the same type of investigation that a manager should conduct in picking an attorney or an accountant. References from clients and other professionals are usually the best source of information.

Most important, the small firm manager should not shrink from calling on a variety of experts out of fear that his size limits their interest in him or limits his right to call on their specialized skills.

USING BIG BUSINESS TECHNIQUES

We have pointed out that one of the common mistakes made by small firms seeking to improve performance is their uncritical adoption of big firm management techniques. Such emulation produces errors of the following kind:

- Detailed inventory control systems whose costs greatly exceed benefits.
- Management information systems that demand more from individual managers than they give.
- Computers with power and costs far in excess of business needs.
- Plans stretching further into the future than it is possible to see in the firm's markets.

Common as the errors are, they should not deter managers in small firms from searching among big business techniques for some that are relevant and practical.

EXAMPLE 1:

One company whose performance was below expectations adopted the following procedure common to large companies.

After taking steps to see that workers knew their jobs (thus ascertaining that training was not the missing ingredient), management provided fast feedback by having the workers keep records of their activities on the job.

Both managers and workers thought a desired standard was being maintained 90 percent of the time; measurement showed that actual performance was less than 50 percent. When workers were instructed to keep track of their daily performances, the result was a dramatic improvement, bringing performance close to the 90 percent the workers had thought they were reaching. What's more, the jump was not temporary but was maintained at the higher level thereafter.

EXAMPLE 2:

An international airline with 80 locations kept track of the time spent in preparing planes for departure at each location. Since adherence to schedule was a factor in passenger satisfaction and the airline's profit strongly correlated with the percentage of time its planes were in the air, all ground personnel were pressed to do their work within the limits that had been set by engineered standards. But one airport manager was not content merely to enforce the standards. After making sure that the standards were known and understood, he had the people who cleaned the planes, loaded the fuel and food, and handled the freight keep track of the time they actually spent and compare the time with the standards. The result? In three months the station moved from fortieth to first. No other change was made beyond providing immediate feedback to people who knew what they were supposed to do so they could correct deviations from standards on their own.

The message should be clear: Size is not a factor in the use of tools such as these. Small firm managers should, for example, establish reasonable performance standards for the number of salesmen's calls made, the number of invoice lines picked in a warehouse, the number of orders typed and wrapped in a billing and shipping department, or the number of confirmations prepared or checked in an internal audit department or accounting firm. They should take steps to be sure that employees know their jobs and accept the standards. And they should provide fast, simple, dependable feedback, preferably created by the workers. But they should never do these things simply because big firms do them. Nor should they fail to do these things because big firms do them. They should always keep an eye on the other side of the fence to see what their larger neighbors are doing and adopt the procedures that can work for them.

9

MANAGING THE SMALL BUSINESS

IF MANAGING is viewed as a linkage of decisions, some short-term, others long-term, it then follows that any improvement in decision making will help a firm reduce the risk of failure and increase its growth potential. Managers are not always conscious of the survival and growth factors in their decision making, though these are always present. In certain decisions the effects upon survival and growth override other considerations. Therefore, a decision that endangers survival should rarely be taken, regardless of its attractiveness for profit or growth.

Certain exceptions are worth mentioning. The small firm properly takes risks that could result in disaster if the alternative—*not* taking the risks—is even more likely to result in disaster. This do-or-die choice is faced when the leading product becomes obsolete, when irreplaceable personnel leave, or when a unique method of manufacture or distribution loses its advantages.

These changes happen usually when the firm is unprepared for them. But often there is adequate warning.

EXAMPLE:

A company had a patent on an item which gave it a near monopoly in its small market. There was no secret as to the day and hour when the patent would expire. Blinded by the long-time success of the product and the assumed but unproved lack of public interest in competing products, the company's management was shocked when a shipload of a duplicate item (at one-third the price) arrived from

Japan several hours after the patent expired. It took a two-year battle before the company made a profit again.

In this case, the company did not anticipate changes that common sense showed were bound to come. Because the changes were related to survival, the company almost folded because it did nothing to prepare for them.

Most decisions are not a matter of life or death, but are often concerned with growth. Growth is rarely considered in the context of survival and most commonly is identified solely with sales. Managers in small firms should realize that growth involves risks which are worth taking but may be fatal and, further, that sales growth is only one aspect of organizational movement.

Consider the effect on a company's balance sheet of a substantial increase in sales volume, achieved by seeking out marginal customers with slower-than-average payment histories. The increase in inventories and accounts receivable will predictably be greater than the increase in accounts payable, resulting in a cash gap. Not until sales reach a plateau will the company's cash needs be satisfied internally, assuming that operations are profitable in the first place. Factoring, accounts receivable and inventory financing, and short-term borrowing are other common sources of financing growth. However, the additional liability must be weighed against the return on the borrowed funds.

The point is simple: The factors that must be in balance to maintain a firm's financial health are so closely related that any single change, regardless of how appealing it is or how persuasive the argument for sales growth, should be coldly questioned if its implementation endangers survival. There is a homely expression that gets to the heart of the matter: You can increase sales until they choke you.

EXAMPLE:

A contractor with $100,000 net worth was operating at a $3 million annual sales volume, up in one year from $2 million. Since he was turning over his capital 30 times a year ($3 million sales divided by $100,000 net worth), he had to maintain a delicate balance between financial and operating factors. The move from $2 million to $3 million had not been digested—receivables were overdue and back charges for poor or incomplete work were high because of inadequate supervision—and the contractor needed time to organize. He was advised to limit the rate of future growth and the size of individual contracts, and not to bid on any single contract over $300,000 since an error or loss of 10 percent would represent 30 percent his capital. He did not listen. He took on additional marginal contracts of $500,000, $700,000, and $800,000, which brought his annual volume to $4 million, and went bankrupt.

In addition to recognizing that sales growth cannot be a universal element in business strategy, small firms must be aware of the dangers to survival of fixed asset acquisitions and unwieldy debt when assumed under the banner of growth rather than for specific risk-reducing purposes.

LEASE-OR-PURCHASE, MAKE-OR-BUY DECISIONS

Technological obsolescence and cash drain are both excellent arguments for leasing rather than buying or buying rather than making. A few small firms owe their success to rigorous adherence to the concept of incurring a minimum of fixed costs and a maximum of variable costs.

EXAMPLE:

The manager of a specialty materials handling manufacturing firm inferred from the irregular timing of the receipt and delivery of orders and the costs of freight that he should have no in-house fabricating facilities but should subcontract the manufacture of his products to several regional companies. He focused the efforts of his 20-man headquarters staff on design, application, and marketing activities and on helping the international network of manufacturers' representatives and licensees to close sales and keep informed of new uses and markets for the product. He also chose not to have full-time salesmen because the fixed financial commitment was more than he wanted to risk.

In this instance the variable costs were not only for manufacturing facilities but for selling as well. The real reason for avoiding the fixed costs was that the risk entailed in investing in either a manufacturing plant or a dedicated selling organization was greater than the possible increase in profitability. The value of avoiding fixed costs extends beyond physical assets. When the 1969–1970 crunch hit, large companies dropped many executives who had been hired in better times, but who contributed little or nothing to making decisions better. Fortunately, small companies are less likely to acquire that kind of corporate fat. Nepotism aside, most executives in small firms are more heavily laden with work, more visible, and more active than in large firms.

The expertise of some specialists, though useful in small businesses, is needed only occasionally. The moral: Don't hire the occasionally needed skill. Commitments for people are usually long-term but are decided as though they were only weekly payroll items. Hiring a $20,000-a-year man is usually a $40,000 decision because it may take two years to decide whether he has made the grade. When an expert is needed it is usually cheaper and wiser to hire a consultant. In the course of a year he will receive less money than the full-time expert and, even more important, will bring a variety of experiences and an outsider's objectivity.

Compare a consultant who charges $60 an hour with a full-time specialist who is paid $25,000 a year. Add $5,000 for normal fringe benefits and we have a cost of $30,000 for the full-time employee. It would be rare to use any consultant 500 hours a year (one-third to one-quarter of his time). Regular service might require two or three days a month or approximately $12,500 a year. Not only is this cheaper, but it is likely to produce results equal to those of a full-time expert, and often a good deal faster.

To expand on the concept of growth and its relation to survival, let us consider the place of liquidity. If we agree that no decision should endanger survival, including any growth-inducing decision, how does a decision affecting liquidity fit? It is second only to survival and a giant step above growth and profitability, two other corporate goals often placed high.

Consider the two histories of sales growth and profitability shown in Figure 2. Company A has had no profits, minor losses for five years, and small sales growth. Company B has had big sales growth and big profits; substantial debt, fixed assets, accounts receivable, and inventories; little cash; and losses and bankruptcy in five years.

Company A has gone nowhere; its sales have kept up neither with the growth of the market nor with the pace of inflation. Its return on investment is hardly worth a look. Yet it is alive, and it has the potential of moving from a financial base that is still viable.

Company B is dead. Its sales growth was spectacular, its profits were above average, its return on investment was dramatic. Yet it went out of business because it put liquidity—the ability to pay its bills and exploit its opportunities—second to sales growth and immediate profits.

Working capital ratios and dollars are not good indicators of survival. The components of working capital are more significant. Heavy proportions of receivables and inventories in high working capital

Figure 2

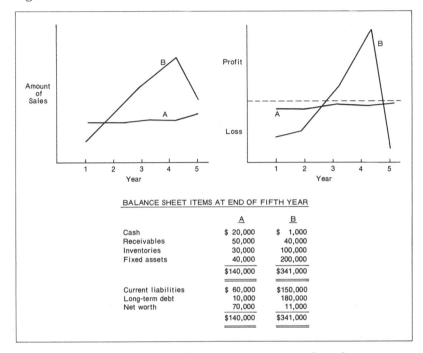

BALANCE SHEET ITEMS AT END OF FIFTH YEAR

	A	B
Cash	$ 20,000	$ 1,000
Receivables	50,000	40,000
Inventories	30,000	100,000
Fixed assets	40,000	200,000
	$140,000	$341,000
Current liabilities	$ 60,000	$150,000
Long-term debt	10,000	180,000
Net worth	70,000	11,000
	$140,000	$341,000

ratios mask the company's inability to retain enough cash to survive.

Consider the two companies in Table 3, which are in the same industry. It is obvious that Company A is in trouble, even though its working capital in dollars and its working capital ratio are exactly the same as Company B's. Without benefit of additional data, we can assume that Company A has stocked inventory for future sales which have not yet materialized (note the disproportion of receivables to inventories) and that no plans have been made for paying the current debt.

The message: All companies, but small ones especially, because they rarely use cash controls, should place liquidity or cash flow high in making any corporate decision.

Growth, as we have already said, is not merely a linear forward progression in sales volume. It can even be a reduction in sales. The small firm grows when the quality of its earnings improves through an increase in asset turnover or elimination of low or unprofitable sales, or when liquidity increases without corresponding decreases elsewhere. In one industry of small contractors, for example, where the

Table 3

	Company A	Company B
Cash	$ 1,000	$ 50,000
Receivables	29,000	30,000
Inventories	70,000	20,000
Total current assets	$100,000	$100,000
Current liabilities (all trade debt)	$ 50,000	$ 50,000
Working capital	$ 50,000	$ 50,000
Working capital ratio (current assets/current liabilities)	2 to 1	2 to 1

profitable companies had lower average sales than the unprofitable ones, it was widely held that the unprofitable firms had higher sales because they reached for sales volume without consideration of profitability.

EXAMPLE:

In a service organization, profitability picked up when a group of small customers, several of whom had traded with the firm for years, were dropped. The moans and cries of traditionalists died down when the income statement for the first year after change showed less gross income than the previous year, but substantially improved profits. Thus the company "grew" by reducing its sales.

Sometimes, growth in smaller firms may not be immediately measurable. Moving into a new market and dropping a dying one represent steps toward growth or survival. Because the provocations for such changes emanate from the society and the environment, small firms may not see the changes as quickly as they should.

EXAMPLE:

A business forms company became aware, through its experience with its own CPA, that many accountants were not interested in servicing the simple system needs of small clients because they were busy with increasingly technical tax, consultancy, and other more challenging and remunerative services. After a few days of checking with CPAs, the company concluded that there was a market for a service that worked exclusively through CPAs in offering design and installation of business systems for their clients. The concept was sound and the company today is highly successful. Growth in this case came from identifying and filling needs unseen by competitors.

The subjects of research and development, choice of product, and development of innovative products are of general concern and deserve more extensive treatment than they usually get. In terms of small firm growth, for a time sales growth or profits may be negatively affected because of investment in new products. But a company that does not use its current assets in the hope of long-term payoffs is existing in the past or present, not in the future.

The small firm needs to have sound answers to the what-if questions that touch on areas of survival. We are not referring to the strategy or opportunity-finding questions such as what business a company is in, or what 20 percent of its customers, products, or salesmen represent 80 percent of its sales. Rather, the company should ask, What would happen if our top salesmen or representatives quit or became disabled tomorrow? What one thing could make our plant or warehouse inoperable?

EXAMPLE:

When the executives of a metal fabricating company were asked what could make their plant inoperable, the answer came back: "An old loading dock, which requires almost weekly repairs and is the focus of all shipping and receiving." Because the dock was in use six days a week, there was never time for more than temporary repairs. Yet if the dock were to give way, the company would be unable to receive or ship for several weeks, seriously endangering its fast-service reputation and its good relations with customers. The solution was to schedule a two-week vacation shutdown for the whole plant in July (one month from the date when the problem was discussed), set plans in motion for permanent repair of the dock, and pray nothing happened in the interim.

Another what-if question: What would happen if our market grew enough to attract a large company as a new competitor? Do we know what we would have to do to survive?

EXAMPLE:

One company manufactured a specialty item that was also made by several large firms. It had developed a number of unique wrinkles that made the item salable in a small special market (total annual volume $5 million nationally) and required different distribution channels. The firm's strategy was to keep the market small and use low-key, low-visibility promotion (small advertisements in women's magazines) to discourage large competitors from feeling that the market was worth entering. The firm has succeeded for 20 years in keeping big firms out and has maintained a stable sales volume over which it has retained a limiting control.

A third what-if question: What would happen if our major supplier went out of business? If it raised prices X percent? If it went into competition with us?

EXAMPLE:

A specialty electronics firm with $1 million in annual sales volume started in business doing only design, engineering, and assembly work and subcontracted all manufacturing. When its managers were asked what would happen if their major supplier went out of business, they analyzed their purchases, found two items to be critical (they were obtainable only from one company), and immediately took steps to produce these items. The decision proved timely because the supplier went bankrupt during one of the downward cycles in its industry in the 1960s.

A fourth what-if question: What elements in the environment, among competitors, or overseas are likely to affect us?

EXAMPLE:

A builder of individual vacation homes in New England was negotiating with an insurance company for a long-term loan which would have permitted him to expand his business over the next five to ten years. The loan officer asked whether the builder was aware of the effect of ecological legislation which was to be introduced into two state legislatures. It would restrict the building of homes to plot sizes ten times greater than the builder had been using and would obviously change the character of the market to which he had been appealing. Without a drastic change in strategy caused by the proposed legislation (which eventually was written into law), the builder could have been totally off the mark. He developed a townhouse condominium plan which was acceptable under the new legislation.

MAKING GOOD USE OF TIME

Making the best use of time is a problem for every manager; for managers in smaller firms it is greatly aggravated. Given the limited scale of operations and no staff of technical experts, the small firm manager has to cope with a never-ending stream of problems, among them some that require skills he may lack altogether. Suggesting to such a manager that he devote time to keeping in touch with the business and social environments so that he can plan for the future will elicit no more than a numb assent, expressing the conviction that there is barely enough time for survival, much less for speculative investment.

Yet there are ways for the small firm manager to analyze, control, and focus his time. First, he must be aware of the practical rather than the metaphysical aspects of time. His days, like everyone else's, are limited to 24 hours each. Success as a manager depends on three elements: selflessness, individualism, meticulousness. The first assures objectivity in the form of company-oriented decision making; the second assures advantages to the firm in the form of decisions that others lack the foresight or courage to make; the third consists in painstaking, detailed follow-through. Although these appear to be personal characteristics, all three elements can be strengthened or exploited when sufficient time is devoted to them. Since time is limited, each manager must learn to treat it as a finite resource, an asset whose proper use is often the key differentiating factor in managing.

The techniques for successful utilization of time are not esoteric. Note that we refer to utilization of time, not saving it. For time is to be used; it cannot be saved. We can choose not to do something (weed the lawn) and do something else (sleep, play golf, write a book). But when we do this we are merely making a conscious or unconscious choice as to what we want to do with our time; we are not saving it.

To use time wisely demands self-knowledge, an awareness that we can change our ways of using time, and an understanding of the individual style, history, and flavor of our own organization.

Both the uses of managerial time and the uniqueness of individual firms are demonstrated in the understanding of the return on investment concept brought to a seminar in accounting for nonfinancial executives by two executives, each from a technologically sophisticated company. One had been weaned on the ROI concept; the other, of equal status, had no idea what it meant or how to use it. Each of these managers had spent his time differently and would continue to do so because of the differing corporate emphasis on what was important.

Before any manager can organize his time for more effective use, he must have a starting point from which to measure progress. That means he must know what he is *now* doing. Until he makes a formal analysis he can have no more than a hazy picture of how he spends his time. Although managers are forever being told that their functions require them to spend time on planning, organizing, delegating, controlling, and evaluating, small business executives find that *their* days rarely fit this pattern. They have little control over their time and are so busy with customers, suppliers, employees, and peers as well as with family, community, and social responsibilities that they tend to react to rather than initiate most of the things on which they spend time. Communications inundate them: reading, phone calls, meetings, people dropping in—most of this without warning or filtering, all of it hard to turn off. And to top it off, the maelstrom is psychologically seductive. Though most small business managers aver they would relish the chance to plan, organize, delegate, and so on, they really believe that being busy proves that they are effective.

Activity analysis is the first step in organizing time; in other words, a two-week listing in 15-minute pieces of what is done. The analysis should indicate who was spoken to, what was read, why each meeting took place. It should show which communications were initiated outside (reading, phone calls received, unexpected visitors) and which were initiated by the manager (letters, memos he wrote, phone calls he made, meetings he called). The record must be kept current; otherwise the idealized image of what we think we did will distort the facts.

Completed, the analysis becomes the basis for some tough questions: Must *I* do all the things I do? What would happen if somebody else did them—or if nobody did? Can I bunch similar tasks? How much time was spent with subordinates because they didn't know what they were supposed to do?

The analysis will probably reveal or hint at our individual time patterns, the kinds of decisions we make, and the number of decisions we make. Each has potential to improve performance.

Some of us are morning people; some are night people. Some of us are impossible to deal with before meals. Many of us procrastinate over tough decisions. It is important that we know our own cycles and patterns of behavior so that we can allocate our most efficient time to our toughest problems. Some of us work best during the early hours of the morning and then again in the evening; others have a steady level of effectiveness from morning to midafternoon and then fade for the rest of the day. Although work does have to be done at times when we are not operating at peak efficiency, the wise manager tries to leave his own best hours free for the challenging problems.

Decision making represents a rich area for improved time use.

Good managers do not boast of the number of decisions they make because they make relatively few. Who makes more decisions on a baseball team, the catcher who gives the pitcher a signal for every pitch or the manager who decides what man will be the starting pitcher and when or whether he should be removed? The more conceptual the manager's work and the longer the effect of his decisions on the organization, the fewer decisions he should make.

Thus if a small business manager is making many decisions (which should be revealed by his time analysis) he should consider delegating some of his decision making, setting limits until the subordinate has been tested so as to insure that the organization will not be endangered.

The kinds of decisions a manager makes may provide a clue to their disposition. Perhaps what is needed is simply a policy to cover the common repetitive situations. Consider the time saved when individual decisions are not required in granting credits, allowances, and personal time off with or without pay. Only exceptional situations should require managerial decision making.

EXAMPLE:

The controller of a manufacturing company with 225 factory employees used to spend an hour every week going over the slips turned in for reimbursement by the three cashiers who handled petty cash. He cut the time to half an hour per month by looking at only ten or a dozen items each week and asking a question or two. Results: The cashiers knew that checks continued to be made, the dollars in total were reviewed, and the controller freed time for more valuable work.

We all have the tendency to develop habits in time use and then retain them long after their purpose is gone. The time analysis will help to pinpoint these habits and question their continued validity.

EXAMPLE 1:

One of the rituals in a family manufacturing business run by two brothers in their sixties and the son of one of them was to be in the office every Saturday morning. The plant was closed and no office or sales employees were asked to show up. Ostensibly the brothers had been coming to the office on Saturdays to open the mail and prepare work for Monday morning. When the young man joined the firm he dutifully went along with the custom for a few months. Then he asked, "What are we doing here? Nothing in the Saturday mail is any different from any other day's mail, and what the factory produces and ships is based on what came in on the previous day." When he realized that the Saturday morning session was entirely social, he

told his uncle and father he had other things to do and stopped joining them.

EXAMPLE 2:

The administrative partner of a service organization had opened
all mail addressed to the firm, even as the volume grew. When he retired the firm was receiving two sacks of mail daily, and opening and
distributing it took about 45 minutes. His successor asked the key time-
saving question: "Why, and why *me?*" Then he instructed his secretary
to open and distribute the mail herself, on the assumption that any
significant problems would be brought to his attention as needed. In
12 years all such problems have come to his desk and he has saved
thousands of hours.

The small business manager must use his time to manage, not
merely to do more as the business grows. This means he must spend
his time on providing needed products and services, maintaining lean
costs, and creating an environment in which people can find satisfaction in their work. Activities which do not contribute to these three
basics are at best housekeeping. To provide the time for the three managerial imperatives, deal with some of the universal time wasters:
telephone calls, meetings, reading, and conversations with subordinates.

Telephone calls should be screened. A secretary or operator can
usually divert half of all calls to other people qualified to deal with
them. Bunching outgoing phone calls can also save time, particularly
if the manager first prepares himself for each call. And no calls should
be permitted during meetings or planning, personnel evaluation, or
other periods when concentration or courtesy make the telephone an
intruder.

Meetings in small firms are generally poorly planned and infor-
mally conducted, rarely analyzed for content, results, or process, and
frustratingly wasteful of time. We propose the following minimum
standards for a proper time-sensitive meeting.

Informality should not be an excuse for sloppiness in holding
meetings. The person who calls a meeting should record what he
wants to accomplish, who should attend, and—except for sessions on
basic strategy, which should be open-ended as to time—when the
meeting will start and stop. Relevant material should be distributed
with the agenda before the meeting so that everyone can digest the
background information in advance. Just as no one should call a meeting without first deciding on its purpose and distributing an agenda,
no one should attend a meeting, politics aside, unless he has received
the agenda and is convinced his attendance is necessary. Meetings

should start on time and end when planned. Calling them before lunch or at the end of the day will insure that they are brief and to the point. Notes should be taken and distributed without delay to everyone concerned, with follow-up assignments specifying who is to do what by what date.

Finally, since meetings are so much a part of organizational life, a few minutes spent analyzing each meeting will improve your meeting technique. Was it necessary? Was it productive? Could you have saved time with more preparation? Did the right people attend? How did it go—as a social process? Was there enough participation?

Reading should be delegated for two reasons: to save your time and to give a subordinate a chance to learn something new. Organizing the information flow to stay in touch with the external and organizational world is a subject covered elsewhere in these pages. We are concerned here only with the need to monitor the flood of printed material so as to save time. Experienced managers admit that there is little new in their professional reading, but they continue to scan almost everything that crosses their desks in the hope of finding the exceptional idea. By assigning reading to subordinates and requesting that a short report (perhaps merely underlining useful portions) be submitted, the manager expands the horizon of a subordinate at little risk to the organization's ability to keep up to date.

Questions from subordinates can be insidious time wasters since flattery is more often involved than the need to know. Time-sensitive managers learn to suppress the natural tendency to provide answers and instead ask: "What do you suggest?" The head of a small retail chain became so convinced of the value of this technique as a way to save time and develop subordinates that he made it a rule that all questions be put in writing. The number of interruptions by subordinates dropped 90 percent and the good people grew by being forced to make their own decisions.

Two activities that justify uninterrupted managerial time are people decisions and strategic decisions. What business should we be in? Where do we want to be in three years? What are our people resources and needs? How do we spread decision making, and to whom? What's happening in the world that is likely to affect us? Should we promote Harry or Bill? To deal with these decisions properly requires time without pressure. Corporate strategy questions are best handled in one- to three-day meetings away from the office, giving them the dignity and serious attention they deserve.

People decisions almost always involve long-term commitments.

They also demonstrate to the whole organization the kind of performance that is recognized; in other words, promotions create the corporate tone and environment. They are usually difficult decisions, since most are based on judgment rather than objective measures. Our advice is to make no significant personnel decisions without sleeping on the question at least one night.

To return to time-saving techniques, the individual manager should plan his goals for a year, a month, each day, leaving half his day free for the inevitable outside interruptions. Two points about the daily time plan: Before starting each day, list the things to be done in order of priority, so that at least the most important things will be done; and provide some time in the daily plan for long-range activities. Unless some time is set aside daily for planning your company's strategy, people development, organization structure, and new products, these planning activities will tend to be submerged by today's and yesterday's problems.

EXAMPLES:

One small firm manager stays home one morning a week to wrestle with tough long-range questions. His employees have recovered from the shock of realizing he is not loafing but planning and thinking, and both he and the organization are better off for the use he makes of these uninterrupted hours. In another successful small firm, the hour from 8:30 to 9:30 each morning is set aside as a "quiet hour" for all executives. The individual executives work behind closed doors on matters that require high concentration. Except for long-distance calls, no telephone interruptions are permitted. There are no visits and no meetings. The president attributes a substantial part of the company's success to the products of this daily quiet hour.

Finally, by being aware that time is precious and by using it with respect, the small business manager creates a sense of urgency that is characteristic of a healthy organization. He does this not only by saving time in the ways we have discussed but by planning his hours, being on time for meetings, and respecting the time of others so that they can do their own work more effectively.

10

FINANCIAL MANAGEMENT

LET US PLACE ACCOUNTING in a reasonable perspective in terms of survival and growth. Great accounting rarely makes a company superior, but inadequate accounting will certainly prevent it from achieving superior results and may cause disaster by failing to provide timely information on problems and trends or the controls required to preserve a firm's assets. Good accounting is necessary but does not itself contribute greatly to outstanding success; it helps link the muscles, blood vessels, and brains of the organizational body and helps, much as the nervous system does, to keep the parts in touch with each other. Other resources (not on the balance sheet) such as the proper uses of time and people are more significant in determining profitability and growth.

MEASUREMENT THROUGH ACCOUNTING

Most small business managers know that net income at the end of the year is not the whole measure of the operations of the business any more than the book value shown on the balance sheet indicates its true worth. Yet managers are enveloped by the din in the financial press emphasizing earnings per share and price-earnings multipliers. Both are based on a single figure: earnings or net income. This figure may significantly influence stock market prices (irrelevant to most small business managers) and is an important factor in analyzing performance or establishing net worth.

Accounting policies are as revealing of management philosophy as cold figures are of results. Tax consequences weigh heavily in the accounting decisions of small business managers, particularly in periods of growth or fixed asset acquisition when tax dollars saved have an immediate payoff. Since taxing authorities must have a specific amount on which to base taxes, ambivalence often develops between taxable income and income used for accounting or management purposes. Earnings in any one year are unlikely to be more than 80 percent accurate (with the clarity of hindsight) and are a poor indication of future profitability or basis for determining a firm's worth for buy-sell or acquisition purposes. Economic earnings are masked by estimations in accounting decisions and the perfect balance of the double-entry system. For example, rarely are inventories sold and receivables collected for the amounts shown, nor are assets depreciated within the years originally set up.

Thus the limitations of accounting in general and earnings in particular must be dealt with and supplemented by other measurement tools, some of which are uncomfortably less precise. But measuring the right thing with less than perfect accuracy may be more useful than measuring the wrong thing perfectly.*

SHORT-TERM VS. LONG-TERM FUNDS

Maintaining a balanced financial position is a fine art. Overcoming the deficiencies in cash that result when a sales increase causes receivables and inventory to grow more rapidly than payables is an absolute necessity. Although the rule of thumb that short-term needs should be met by short-term funds and long-term needs should be satisfied by long-term funds (maturity of more than five years) is applicable to all firms, small firms have the greatest difficulty in meeting their needs for funds.

Small firms generally have less trouble finding short-term money (although the rates are higher than for large firms). Lenders are wary about long-term loans because of size-related factors that affect borrowing:

1. Small firms have less depth in management and, statistically speaking, less chance of continuity than large firms.

* See Martin J. Whitman and Martin Shubik, Technical Report No. 63, Yale University, New Haven, December 1972.

2. Insurance and estate tax plans in small firms are often inadequate, exposing the lender to problems he would not be concerned with in dealing with large companies.

3. A strong financial man who inspires confidence that inventories, receivables, and cash management are well controlled is a rarity in small companies.

4. Rarely do projections and budgets imply that planning and control concepts are known and used. Small firm managers wait to develop their first comprehensive projections until they make their first application for long-term financing. They are then met by the request of experienced lenders for the projections that were used two or three years earlier to see how they compare with results.

5. Small business accounting strategy has often been oriented more toward tax savings than toward proper and consistent disclosure. Unaudited financial statements are therefore regarded with suspicion by lenders, and whispered explanations of what "the true figures" are do not diminish these suspicions. Obviously, if the statements of the past years do not stand on their own, lenders have a right to expect that future statements will also be less than reliable. It is economically and managerially sound to have statements audited as early in your business history as possible. The cost of the audit and the nondeferral of taxes are a modest price to pay for the additional financial options created through having acceptable financial statements.

The steps that can be taken to mitigate or reduce the concerns of lenders are implied in the preceding list of small firm borrowing problems: Develop a management team; provide sufficient key man and stockholder-manager insurance; prepare an estate tax plan which will be digestible to the company; hire a competent financial man who understands how to apply basic financial tools; and maintain your accounts so that you can have an auditor's clean opinion.

Short-term funds are available on an unsecured basis from banks and vendors. When receivables, inventories, leases, and fixed assets are offered as collateral, funds are available on a secured and longer basis from banks, factors, and secondary finance sources. Although receivables and inventories are classified as current assets because the individual items are normally convertible into cash within one year, the total of receivables and inventories, as well as accounts payable, usually remains fairly fixed and, except in the event of more profitable or reduced operations, may not become a source of cash. The relationship of asset turnover to costs is discussed in the chapter on lean costs.

Let us consider cash resources from three viewpoints: internal, external, and strategic.

ACCOUNTS RECEIVABLE

Receivables require constant attention if they are not to soak up cash. The small firm should have policies on granting credit, following up on delinquencies, and limiting credit risks to avoid putting its own future in jeopardy. If a small firm finds its sales concentrated among a few large customers, it should investigate the cost of credit insurance on the major accounts receivable. This protection is available with different levels of deductibles; the greater the deductible, the smaller the premium. A company policy on credit granting is helpful as a time saver. Not every situation is worth executive attention, but without a procedure to insure consistency of treatment and fast response, executive attention is mandatory if customer relations are not to sag.

EXAMPLE:

As a method of keeping the problem in check, one wholesaling company puts a $5 handling charge on every order under $25, which covers physical handling, paperwork, and the risk of not checking credit. The owner-manager is given a weekly list of receivables that are slow to be paid and have been followed up unsuccessfully at least once by a clerk. An annual analysis of gross profit produced by each customer, reduced by variable costs of commissions and shipping returns and allowances, is compared with average receivables balances. Customers in the bottom 15 percent of the list, in terms of return on receivables tied up, are reviewed to determine whether increased sales (and gross profit dollars) or better collection efforts would result in a higher return. Those considered hopeless are dropped as graciously as possible. The results: a higher than industry average receivables turnover and minimum executive attention. The latter item, while less often the subject of analysis and certainly not to be found among the key ratios, may be the bigger cost saver of the two.

Along the same lines, an analysis of slow payers over several years will show many repetitions of the same names. If the normal effort applied to delinquent receivables has not changed the status of the slow payers, dropping them may make for faster turnover with less effort.

INVENTORY MANAGEMENT AND CONTROL

Inventories are harder to control than receivables and require more attention in almost every company. Cutting the cash investment in inventories involves control of buying, stratification of inventories into different values, physical security, and balancing stock levels and service to customers. Let's take a look at a few key items that relate to inventories as a source of cash in small firms.

The first among these items is information—the need to know, but only what is worth knowing. This is not economic mumbo-jumbo but an attempt to highlight the ratio between the cost of accumulating and reporting information and the value of using it.

EXAMPLE:

A retailer set up a system to develop sales information on the several thousand items he sold. The first month's report was so voluminous that the merchandise managers and store managers who were expected to use it were overwhelmed by the detail and set the report aside. Analysis of inventory values showed that 200 items out of 2,800 represented about 75 percent of inventory investment and sales volume.

A revised report containing information limited to the 200 best-selling items was favorably received and used. One of the results was a reduction of $100,000 in inventories with no change in sales and a substantial reduction in the costs of maintaining inventory.

Open-to-buy, a system which helps to control purchases, is used in all but the smallest retail businesses. Controlling disbursements for inventories (or any other item) *before* liability is incurred is many times simpler than correcting purchase abuses or sloppiness. For most small firms the key lies in an analysis of the major items in inventory. What are the economic order quantities for purchases? What is the lead time for delivery? What is the projected rate of usage? The traditional economic order quantity formula takes into consideration the cost of placing an order. In almost all small businesses, this is irrelevant and should be disregarded for the simple reason that the cost of ordering tends to be small and fixed.

Physical security for readily salable inventory items is a simple precaution which may violate the informal atmosphere of small firms. But temptation is not a size-related factor and should be recognized in formal efforts to control it.

EXAMPLE:

Two managers in a family-controlled firm manufacturing a common household item that was sold through department stores, discount chains, and some specialty retailers were troubled. Reported profit rates did not jibe with the increased sales volume; the profits were significantly too low. Members of the family were closely involved in daily management (each plant was run by a relative) and had always resisted suggestions from their auditing firm that unit records be kept of at least the high-value, high-turnover components and finished products.

At the suggestion of the two managers the auditors were called in to investigate the low profit rates. After taking a physical inventory they analyzed the raw materials purchased less goods shipped and found a $150,000 discrepancy in the final inventory value. Management engaged an undercover investigating firm that pinpointed the problem in two weeks: The plant superintendent, an employee who had worked for the company for more than 20 years, had been shipping out finished merchandise on trucks he rented, using part-time shipping labor which he changed frequently and did not put to work until after the plant was officially closed for the day. In effect, he was a "midnight salesman," disposing of part of the company's production at 40 to 50 percent off list prices without cost to himself except for shipping. The superintendent was convicted and served several years in prison.

The simplest independently maintained unit controls of physical movement of goods in and out of the factory would have prevented the theft. The company now has adequate controls, but the cost of the lesson was high indeed. The cash drain to the company was not only the $150,000 stolen during the year when the theft was discovered (plus an estimated $250,000 previously stolen), but the sales and customers lost when management attention was diverted by the theft, combined with the loss in factory efficiency because of the investigation.

Small business managers who are imbued with the goal of paring inventories to the leanest so that cash can be freed up must keep in mind the balance of inventory needed to service customers properly.

EXAMPLE:

A distributor with an accounting background returned from a management seminar presented by his trade association convinced that progress and profits were to be found in a profit center responsibility accounting plan. He set up such a plan with several departmental managers, including the two men in charge of parts and service. The formula was a standard one: Each manager was assigned—and accepted—responsibility for the gross profit and controllable costs under his direction, and each was promised a substantial part of any increase in the marginal income over a budgeted figure. Only one thing was missing from the formula: the level of stock-outs (goods not available), a nonfinancial measure, which was acceptable to customers.

The two managers reacted differently. The service manager took as a personal affront any instance when he could not satisfy a request for customer service. He increased the inventories of all the items under his control so that, although he reduced the possibility of being out of anything a customer might request, he added $75,000 worth of goods to the inventory.

On the other hand, the parts manager was aware of the total cost of holding inventory, and he decided to cut back the inventory under his control from $750,000 to $600,000. The effect on his costs was positive. In the first year of the new plan there were no major customer service problems while he was liquidating inventory. But when inventories reached the low level, customer relationships also tumbled into the basement because stock-outs rose from 5 to 20 percent. Unfortunately, the parts manager had trimmed inventory across the board instead of selectively.

Leasing instead of buying new fixed assets, or selling and leasing back existing assets, can be used to free up cash. There will usually be an interest cost (explicit or included) for the long-term payout, and this should be compared to the present value of the funds available for use within the company so as to ascertain the opportunity cost. If velocity of asset turnover is accepted as a measure of profitability, a strong case can be made for keeping to an absolute minimum the amount of assets used in the company so that the denominator (receivables, inventories, fixed assets) in computing the ratio will be small.

Small firms, which have a limited capacity to borrow, should be extremely careful before making long-term capital investments. Not only may short-term opportunities be impaired, but the probabilities of success in decisions requiring long-term fruition are distinctly lower than those in short-term decisions.

LIQUIDITY

Liquidity is among the last things a firm should risk, one of the last assets it should consider swapping for something else. Liquidity is a measure of a small firm's ability to make a quick decision, seize opportunities, outmaneuver its competitors. In only two circumstances can a firm justify endangering its liquidity position: (1) to save the firm from going under; and (2) to seize an opportunity with a potential gain far in excess of the reduction in liquidity and with a high probability of success. The first point is self-evident; survival takes precedence over all other considerations. And, since it is harder to launch a successful new business than to save an established one, any asset of an existing business is expendable when it comes to helping it survive.

However, the second point—seizing an opportunity—is more valuable for operational purposes. We are not operations research men, but it seems to us that survival studies of small firms would show an inverse relationship between reduction in liquidity and degree of risk. Small companies are more likely to have survival problems as they reduce liquidity and consequently incur increased risks. Even minor reductions in liquidity should be incurred only for results that have a high probability of success. The time factors for the reduction in liquidity and the payoff from the investment should be related and should be as short as possible.

BALANCE

Used for more than 50 years, the Du Pont model of the financial structure of a firm graphically reveals not only the computation of return on investment, but the manner in which factors in the balance sheet and income statement are affected by change in any single major element of either. Healthy financial management requires that there be a balanced relationship between sales, cost of sales, personnel costs, and warehousing costs, on the one hand, and payables, receivables, and inventories on the other. The relationship will change with changes in volume and the management of the cash–receivables–inventory cycle and will in turn affect both financial position and operating results.

To the small company, this organic relationship puts a constraint on extraordinary growth and exposes the danger of a sudden decline. The structure may not be able to stand dramatic changes such as a doubling of volume or a sales decrease of 40 percent because the components necessary for a smooth mesh would be out of proportion.

CASH CONTROLS

During a time of growth, profits rarely generate the cash needed to support increased inventories and receivables. This creates a cash gap that requires a sophisticated level of financial control. One way to obtain this control is to hire an experienced financial executive. The problem is that small firms place a low priority on accounting and financial skills, in part because they are intangible and the cost of providing them is almost universally considered overhead. Without proper financial controls to maximize the available internal sources of cash, sources will have to be found outside the company, which may result in a dilution of overall control or even of ownership.

One of the controls an experienced financial executive will usually prepare, especially in a period of growth, is a cash projection. But cash forecasts of even experienced financial executives are almost always wrong, and they are almost always wrong in the direction of underestimating cash needs. Control of cash therefore requires that borrowing arrangements or vendor payment promises based on a cash projection include a generous error factor. In other words, always arrange for more money than your plans call for. The occasions when you will not need it will be rare.

Control of cash through provision for error brings up the relationship between money and time. These are opposite sides of a resource available for contingencies. Time usually requires money; money provides time; and the opportunities for and consequences of error are reduced with either time or money. Because money is more subject to planning and control, managers should realize that they have more options for a longer time when cash pressure is reduced.

Managers who suffered through the Great Depression of the 1930s remember how the struggle to survive was aggravated by a shortage of cash and how better decisions, and perhaps a longer business life, would have been possible with a cash reserve.

Several specific techniques can help small firms manage their cash effectively. Following are a few.

Challenge your procedure for handling accounts payable. Delay all payments that offer no cash discounts. If the regular payment date for an invoice falls on a weekend, pay on the following Monday rather than the preceding Friday. If the amount of business you are giving a vendor is important to him and you are in a position to negotiate, see whether you can stretch out payments over a longer period.

Banks are reluctant to credit your account until funds are collected. If customers draw checks on out-of-town banks, especially small town banks, you may have to wait three to ten days before you can write checks against the deposits. Therefore, any cash management techniques which speed up deposits or increase *your* use of the float (the difference between your bank balance as shown on the bank's books and on yours) will strengthen your cash position. Consider direct conversations with your bank manager aimed at speeding up credits for bank deposits. Also consider using local depositories with wired deposits to the main branch.

As for the float, most companies have a fairly consistent pattern. To find yours, prepare a chart or table of the cash balances in your books and on the bank statements. The bank is concerned with the latter.

Finally, deal with your customers' payment habits individually. Some will pay only when they receive statements; others pay on receipt of invoices. Wherever possible, ask them how you can make it easier for them to pay you more promptly.

The purpose of these efforts is to make more cash available so that you can pay necessary invoices and take advantage of discounts and short-term interest-yielding investments. A higher turnover of cash is a valid goal of financial management as well as part of the basic asset management strategy that relates profitability to high asset usage.

Cash is only one point in the working capital cycle. Without consideration for the long-term diversion into fixed assets, the cycle is from cash to work-in-process inventories (salaries for service organizations) to receivables to cash. Because cash is constantly flowing, its control requires careful planning, implementation, and monitoring at all stages of the cycle. Working capital should be scheduled so that the forecasts on source and application of funds are constantly modified in accordance with current results.

Specifically, small business managers should have a four-week or monthly cash projection (if payroll is paid on a weekly basis, the four-week period is more efficient than the monthly); an aging of accounts receivable at least monthly (with weekly follow-up on delinquent accounts); and monthly inventory figures showing turnover of major items or comparing work-in-process plans with job status (job shop, contractor, service organizations such as professional firms, software houses).

Backlog is useful for planning—cash, labor, space, delivery times —and can be maintained daily, at least in total. Labor statistics should include not only hires and fires but overtime incurred daily, to prevent excess. Better yet, a procedure can be set up requiring supervisor approval before any overtime is ordered.

Moving away from the more routine financial controls, let us look at measurements of productivity and value added. If we analyze the unique economic service an organization provides, we will find that in some way it transforms an existing product into something more valuable. The manufacturing process, the most obvious example, converts raw materials into a finished product by the addition of design and the application of labor and machinery.

In retail and wholesale operations, the product is bought as a finished item but has value added because it is brought to the point of sale and its availability is made known. Professional or service organizations provide knowledge to solve problems or expertise to satisfy needs (health, education, recreation). Proper control requires identification of the value-added factor, measurement of its productivity, and high-level skill devoted to its overall management.

The manager of a professional service organization keeps track of operations by budgeting the number of billable hours needed to break even and then devising profit goals and the ratio of billable hours to total hours for each staff person. Staff members are kept informed of the number of budgeted total hours and the billable ratio at different experience levels so they can monitor themselves.

Since the labor applied to a manufactured product is the value added, one job shop operator accrued income for its internal statements on the basis of labor dollars added (independent of billing arrangements). These figures were compared weekly with the estimates prepared for each job at the time of bidding and also with the number of labor dollars calculated to achieve a profit. Knowing the number of labor hours available weekly and the backlog of hours required to complete orders on hand, the firm was able to act more intelligently when it made a bid, promised delivery, and planned manpower changes.

CASH DISCOUNTS

A common reporting procedure is to show cash discounts taken either as an item of other income or as a deduction from purchases. Given a choice between knowing the amount of cash discounts taken and knowing those that were not taken, almost all managers prefer to know the discounts lost. The reason is that if they are armed with information on the cost of missed discounts, they can decide how much they can afford to spend for the funds necessary to take advantage of discounts. Data on discounts taken do not provide information on which to act.

The cost of missing a discount can be significant. When the terms are 2 percent in ten days, net 30 days on a $1,000 invoice, the company that does not take the discount and pays the invoice at the end of the 30 days has had the use of $20 (the discount) for 20 days. The cost is therefore $1 a day, $365 a year, or a 36.5 percent interest cost. Any borrowing arrangement which will enable the company to pay its bills in 10 days at a cost of less than 36.5 percent will prove attractive.

To alert management to discounts lost, invoices should be entered net of the available discount: $980 in the case above. If the discount is taken, no entry is made. If the discount is missed for any reason, $1,000 must be paid and the extra $20 disbursement over the $980 entered will be shown as an action-triggering "discount not taken."

ACQUISITION TECHNIQUE

One of the flag-waving motivations for owning and running a small business is the attraction many a man finds in being independent, running his own show, being able to play golf or to work long hours when he wants to. Perhaps the family background of such a man impels him to prove his independence from a strong parent, or perhaps his years of working for someone else were the driving force. In either case, to such a man the motive of independence runs deeper than mere economic freedom; it is a symbol of everything by which he measures himself, the essence of his self-image.

When the manager of a small business has an opportunity to acquire a business owned by a man whose background is similar to the one described above, he will run into hidden shoals in his negotiations unless he provides a psychologically as well as economically acceptable way for the potential seller to relinquish his independence.

EXAMPLE:

A company that sold a business service through a brokerage arrangement was heavily dependent on its salesmen. Once the salesmen were established with customers, they had the mobility to take the sales volume with them if they moved to another firm. The two principals of a $2 million company were interested in expanding by acquiring the sales and sales talent of individual salesmen who were working independently as well as of smaller companies (usually owned and run by one man). The firm had an attractive package to offer: clerical help, specialization in buying, responsibility for billing and collecting, competent peers to help solve problems and take over during illness or vacations, profit sharing, and other fringe benefits.

One negotiation was with an independent salesman who had been successful on his own for four years, after many years as an employee.

This man would not accept the offer to join the firm. He talked of playing golf when he wanted to without feeling guilty, of making a decent living while working no more than half the time, of the comfort of working out of his own house and not being involved in organizational personnel problems.

Finally, following a negotiating session in which little progress was made, it was suggested to the principals that the loss of independence had a price altogether separate from the economics of the deal. The independent salesman had proved that he could operate successfully on his own. To go back to work as an employee was to go down in status. The price for this change in his self-image was the ingredient missing from the negotiations.

The formula that was finally developed called for a $50,000 payout, $5,000 a year over ten years in a tax-deductible form. The net cost to the firm, using a 10 percent rate for present value considerations and a factor for inflation, was about $1,000 a year. The $50,000 figure was large enough, from the salesman's point of view, to justify his loss of independence. Other deals were consummated once this formula was proved both economically and psychologically.

INTEREST STRATEGY

Although interest paid on borrowed money is one of the lower costs in running a business, small business managers should relate their borrowings to basic financial strategy.

For example, many companies in financial trouble have tried to maximize earnings by borrowing at the lowest rates available in the short-term market, when they should have borrowed for a long period and paid the higher rates. They were caught in the vise of onerous terms for repayment of loan principal and a project that had not produced cash as fast as it was supposed to. A margin for error of 25 to 50 percent in terms of time requirements is simple insurance. The extra interest that may have to be paid for borrowing longer than originally or optimally planned eliminates a lot of sleepless nights.

As part of the same strategy, no long-term project should be financed in the short-term market. Even temporary short-term financing can be dangerous unless the long-term arrangements have been made firm. Speculative real estate ventures, started with short-term construction loans, have been lost when the equity owners were unable to arrange long-term financing in time to pay off the loans.

As an example of the relatively insignificant cost of money, consider a ten-year loan for $500,000 originally offered at 8 percent but now available at 10 percent. The average net after-tax difference each year between the two interest rates is about $2,500. If the success of the project for which the money is to be borrowed hangs on $2,500 a year, it should be dropped; no one can be so accurate in a ten-year projection.

MAXIMIZING LIMITED CAPITAL

Concentration of all resources (people, time, and money) in the area of specialization and market differentiation suggests that all costs be reviewed in the light of their payoff and relevance to the firm's central objective. Put another way, to get the most out of limited resources in achieving a goal requires that traditionally accepted ways of spending money be challenged.

Why do Sears, Safeway, and Woolworth's rarely own the real estate in which they operate? Without being privy to the decisions of their directors, we would surmise that their reasoning goes like this: What they do best and what warrants their capital investment is merchandising. Therefore, they lease their stores and leave the real estate problems to others. The decisions on what operating assets must be controlled through ownership depend on the significance of the value-added factor of each business: the answer to the question, What business are we in?

Space, or real estate, is perhaps the most obvious resource that need not be owned. But there are others. Lease-or-buy alternatives exist for machinery, equipment, trucks, autos, furniture, telephone equipment, computers, and collection facilities. In addition to the choice between leasing and buying a specific asset or service, the decision must also include the opportunity cost of capital use in the total firm.

Aside from the asset or service which is vital to a firm's operations, a generally sound maxim is: Keep costs variable and un-fix the fixed costs. There are strong reasons for this. A downturn in volume or profits is easier to digest because breakeven sales should be lower; executive effort can focus on the main effort because there are fewer diversions (for example, upkeep of a leased building is the landlord's problem); and more resources are available for use in exploiting opportunities because nonessential costs have been eliminated.

A sensitivity to costs not usually shown as separate items on the income statement can produce unexpected profits for the small business manager. These costs are rarely segregated or questioned, some because they are normally viewed not as separate costs but as part of necessary functions, others because they are above questioning.

The most important example of the first group is the cost of control. Since almost every organizational function has some element of control, we tend to consider control inviolate. Because the elements of cost that are concerned with control of any procedure or asset are rarely segregated, they are difficult to identify, measure, and monitor. Let us suggest only a few areas for possible questioning.

The first deals with accuracy. It costs something to insure that accounting, cost, and sales computations are 100 percent correct and that all details balance with controls. Such accuracy is rarely necessary for either asset protection or decision making. Consider the use of pennies in accounting transactions. Cents-less bookkeeping is not precise. By dropping pennies on items of 49 cents and under and rounding up those of 50 cents and more, we create an unbalanced set of accounts, the difference between debits and credits being assigned to a penny-elimination account. Because the average figure in a set of books amounts to hundreds of dollars, pennies should be dropped as early as possible in the bookkeeping process for all items that deal with the company itself (sales, expenses, depreciation). Less clerical time will then be taken up in entering, extending, footing, posting, and checking errors. And executive decisions will of course be no different because financial statements are in whole dollars. Who cares whether monthly sales are $125,121.15, or $125,121?

Double-checking any transaction that deals with outsiders—payroll, customers, vendors—also costs money. Companies that compare the cost of checking with the value of the errors found rarely conclude that they have spent their control money effectively. A better idea is to set budgets or limits of reasonableness, install sensible internal control procedures, see that these controls are observed, and wait for complaints as a symptom that the system is not working.

LONG-TERM FINANCING

Because the institutional status of a lender may awe the potential small firm borrower, incurring a liability that takes 10 to 15 years to liquidate may seem like voluntary financial peonage. And because there are assumed limitations on freedom to operate, many managers do not take advantage of long-term financing with investment bankers and insurance companies.

Investment bankers are usually a first step in going public or selling out. For the most part these bankers are not interested in the income from debt instruments sold to small companies. They are interested in investments with potentially substantial gains. Going public and selling out are two of the techniques generally used to convert an interest in a small company into a profit.

While waiting for the small company to mature in market position or in quality and size of earnings, the investment banker will lend the company money at higher than short-term interest rates. The loan may bear a nominal due date of five to ten years and will almost always be accompanied by options or warrants to buy common shares. Or the debt may take the form of a convertible security, generally a debenture convertible into common shares. In rarer cases the investment banker may at the outset invest all or part of his funds in the firm's common shares.

For the small company that will accept immediate or eventual dilution of equity and can use both the capital and the sophisticated financial advice that goes with it, the investment banker is a source of funds worthy of investigation.

More to the taste of most small firm managers are the terms of long-term funds available from insurance companies through their commercial or industrial loan departments. Following are some of the key characteristics.

1. Loans are unsecured; although secured loans are available with real estate or equipment as collateral, our concern here is not with them but with loans based on corporate signature.

2. No equity dilution is involved; although this provision has been applied irregularly, for the most part insurance companies have not required it.

3. There is no automatic placement of an insurance company executive on the borrowing company's board of directors. Nor is there any participation in the operating management of the company. The lender apparently is interested in placing a loan after careful investigation and then in receiving quarterly and annual audited financial statements to monitor performance. When requested, general management advice is available. It is rarely offered otherwise.

4. Terms are 10 to 15 years, with some penalty for prepayment except when the lender is unwilling to meet a competitive additional financing or refinancing. Interest rates vary with the size of the loan, the

quality of the borrower, and the overall money market. Minimum loans have ranged from $125,000 to $500,000.

5. Other requirements—the maintenance of working capital and restrictions on the sale of assets, on mergers, on salaries and expenses of principals, and on the right to pay dividends or redeem stock—are reasonable. Prudent managers have found these loans not only tolerable but good financial discipline.

The use of the funds provided by long-term loans must be justified in a formal cash projection that spans at least five years. Any sensible business purpose is acceptable: acquisition of another company, a new or updated plant or equipment, increased working capital to support increased sales volume, refinancing of short-term or other debt which would be more economical as long-term debt, or even acquisition of the stock of a retiring or deceased stockholder.

In summary, these sources of long-term funds have been used by small businesses less frequently than they might be. Insurance company loans in particular represent no dilution of equity for money which has an almost permanent character. True, the principal must be repaid; but even a conservative projection of growth, profit, and inflation should make such a loan attractive.

II

THE FAMILY
IN SMALL BUSINESS

INHERENT in the concept of the family-run or family-dominated business is the widely held assumption that family ownership and operation confer great blessings on the firm, fostering tight coordination and simplifying administration. Few notions are so hard to prove or so likely to be wrong.

Family control may serve the purpose of ownership, but that does not mean that survival of the firm necessarily is put first. Family-owned firms face problems common to all businesses as well as several that are unique. And too few family businesses are run to the limit of their potential.

Perhaps the shortcomings of family-run businesses have a simple origin; perhaps they are rooted in the idea that ownership creates or forces superior stewardship. Evidence in support of the idea is hard to find. Even when the owners are members of the same family, parental dominance, competition between branches of the family, sibling rivalry, and other matters usually take priority over administrative needs. Superior intelligence and relationships spanning several generations go for naught when the needs of the business are not recognized as being superior to individual wills. One executive involved in the management of his family's firm observed: "If enough generations are involved in a business, it will inevitably fail because inevitably poor managers come along."

Nepotism, which may be defined as "patronage bestowed or favoritism shown to relatives," is not a neutral word. The effects of nepotism are bad when decisions are motivated by family interests rather than
200

organizational needs. On the other hand, Rothschild, Rockefeller, Mellon, Tishman, Tisch are names of family-dominated enterprises that seem to have derived strength from their family relations.

Another common view is that ownership of a business is sufficient basis for the exercise of authority. But this, too, is more often myth than fact. The more democratic the culture in which authority is exercised, the more broadly based the authority is. In societies such as ours, "single-stringed" authority—authority based solely on the power of ownership—frequently drives away good employees who cherish their independence and creates resentment or indifference among the dependent employees who remain. Unfortunately, most owner-managers cannot see the difference between their own motivation as owner and the motivation of the people they employ.

Another faulty notion is that ownership justifies excessive contrasts in compensation and benefits. Though it is part of the American dream that every man can become a millionaire, too often the dream is achieved at the expense of others and without regard for the firm's survival needs. What an owner thinks he is entitled to may violate current social trends and prevailing ratios. Few men are worth a great many times what others in the same firm are paid. When an owner takes 20 times the salary of an employee, faulty organization or performance appraisal probably exists.

If family ownership is to be effective it must display more self-discipline (placing the needs of the firm above all other needs) than is commonly found in business. No statistics record the lack of self-discipline, but it is probably one of the root causes of mortality among family-owned businesses. The usual absence of outside standards of performance means that the family-owned business must be protected against unreasonable burdens—the principal consequence of being family-owned. And the only agency that can provide that protection is the family itself.

The beginning of self-discipline is to engage in company-oriented planning and impose tough constraints on personal whims or tastes that place undue burdens on the firm's finances and profitability. This is a difficult accomplishment in a firm that has run for any length of time as an enterprise supporting the family, but it is an absolute requirement for survival nevertheless. A positive action is to allow non-family members to exercise decision-making power.

Once the move toward systematic management in the family-owned business has begun, capitalizing on the strengths of family ownership can also begin. What are the potential strengths, the advantages of smaller family-owned companies, over others? Here are a few examples.

• Small family-owned firms have shorter lines of communication, a common mind-set, common values—all those factors that make possible an environment in which powerful motives can be readily energized and set to work. Integration of understanding and activity is simplified because personal standards derive from a common background.

• Small family-controlled firms have greater financial flexibility. It is much easier for them to vary the demands upon company resources than for publicly owned firms. Family members may also have personal resources they are willing to commit in order to meet a need or exploit an opportunity.

• Individual involvement is easier for family firms, which can create a sense of identity between employees and firm. The mere continuity of a family name in management often has value because of the loyalty generated by a small paternalistic organization. Membership in competing subgroups such as unions may be easier to avoid.

• Small firms are less dependent on indirect sources of knowledge such as market research or modeling of one kind or another. They can get more mileage out of the judgment factor and the personal contact of principals with key customers.

• Family firms have a shorter "turnaround" or response time—an existing but vanishing margin.

EXAMPLE:

A family-controlled business serving a small market for specialized equipment reacted with concern when its two competitors of equal size were taken over by large companies. This feeling changed to relief when the firm first experienced the slow reaction time imposed by large company procedures. In one dramatic case, all three companies competed for the U.S. rights to a European manufacturing process. The manager-owners of the family company submitted a proposal in 48 hours. It was two weeks before the headquarters staffs of the other two companies were ready with proposals of their own. By that time, the family company had established such rapport with the European firm that it was awarded the contract.

PATERNALISM AND TURNOVER

The family-controlled business is susceptible to the disease of benevolent paternalism. The disease is characterized by the family retainer syndrome, which requires that length of service and loyalty be given higher priority than competence or contribution to profit.

Although it may strengthen the self-image of the owner-manager to be responsible for employees from start of employment to retirement, such a course is neither necessary nor helpful. In a society offering mobility of employment and characterized by increasing speed of technological obsolescence and a reduced value for past experience, paternalism, however benevolent, should be replaced by a policy of upgrading rather than retaining staff.

EXAMPLE:

In a relatively small service firm the 35-year-old owner-manager who took over from his father inherited five long-time employees who compared poorly with personnel available in the local labor market. The new owner arranged early retirement for two men who were three years away from normal retirement age, gave two others six months to find other jobs (both did), and provided a generous termination payment for one employee who had a long-standing alcoholism problem. None of these decisions was easy, but the organization benefited in two ways: It was no longer burdened with incompetents and it was free to hire qualified people, with a resultant upgrading of staff.

The example shows that experience is often overrated. There is a substantial decline in the incremental value of each year on a job. Except for a position that requires high technical or judgment factors (doctor, musician, top executive), additional years in most organizational positions add little to effectiveness. Twenty years on many jobs can be translated to two years (usually the first two) repeated ten times. Change brings a fresh look at such positions, and in time it may even be appreciated by the long-term incumbent who is terminated, because most people know their inadequacies.

EXAMPLE:

For years a firm had put up with mediocre performance from long-term employees because long-term employment was considered to be a family responsibility. Then a performance evaluation program was undertaken. The first review session resulted in the decision to terminate three men who had been with the company an average of eight years. Within six months, each man returned to thank the manager who had handled the exit interview. They all had found more suitable work and admitted that their inertia about leaving had been overcome by the company's initiative. In the following two years, ten other long-term employees left as a result of past or pending performance reviews. By treating the separations as sensitively as possible, the company kept the goodwill of the ex-employees and did not lower the morale of those who remained with the organization.

THE BUY-SELL AGREEMENT

The owners of a family-controlled or closely held company have special problems in setting a price and arranging for the sale of their shares. If they are unhappy with their holdings or want to convert them into cash, they have no immediate market. The holder of shares in IBM or General Electric who wants to get out or needs cash for any reason (including payment of estate taxes) knows what his shares are worth at all times and can get cash for them in a matter of days. Because both valuation and marketability require agreement among the shareholders and the corporation, a buy-sell contract is a unique and necessary document in the closely held company.

Business history is replete with tales of small firms that were destroyed because a workable buy-sell agreement was not in effect when one of the shareholders got sick, wanted to retire, disagreed with the management philosophy of other shareholders, or died.

EXAMPLE:

Three relatives who each owned one-third of a manufacturing firm refused to sign a proposed buy-sell agreement because it insulted their close personal and social relationship. A year later one of them wanted to sell and move away, and he asked an amount for his shares that the other two shareholders considered outrageous. Six months and $30,000 in legal fees later (and at a cost of permanent family dissension) the departing stockholder's interest was purchased by the corporation—at the price asked in the original proposal.

An article that suggests the areas to be covered in a buy-sell agreement is reprinted in the appendix.

NEPOTISM

As has already been mentioned, a company should exist for its customers, not for its owners. If it exists for its owners it will not have a long future. A firm in which ownership is of primary importance cannot assign primary importance to its product or service.

Because of the close relationship between corporate ownership and the pride and security that go with family control of a business, nepotism is fairly common in family businesses. And it is important that managers deal objectively with the problems and opportunities it creates.

Family ownership provides a haven for relatives who might otherwise be unable to find or keep jobs at the salary and fringe benefit level that membership in the family permits. Some scions of founding families operate production equipment at salaries five or six times what is normally paid to operators of such equipment. There can be no justification for inflicting such burdens on the firm. The use of the business as a family support agency diverts the energies of the competent members, focuses the business on personal rather than corporate ends, and frustrates the development of staff members who are not part of the family.

EXAMPLE:

A small chain of retail stores was owned by a family that had seven members actively involved in the business. Although the most able man was designated president, he could make no significant decisions without the concurrence of the family. Further, status considerations and speculation about the reactions of wives and uncles loomed large in any conversation concerning the business. Family members looked to the company for economic protection and ego security, and the firm's welfare was given short shrift in the conduct of the business. Two divisions were kept going for years after they were uneconomic because the family members who managed them would have been hurt if they had been closed down. An antiquated inventory control system was untouchable because a cousin had personally developed it and fought off all recommendations that it be revamped.

Solution of this common problem—when it is possible at all—requires a toughness of mind and a willingness to separate the needs of the family and the needs of the firm. One technique is to buy out the incompetent family members or have them exchange common stock for preferred stock that pays a dividend but has no voting rights. Another possibility is to sell a viable part of the business to a family member who is unwilling to accept change and thus remove him from decision making. If a family member cannot be found to run the company with proper authority, it may be possible to install someone who is not a relative as the top manager and let him use his objectivity in balancing conflicting family and business pressures. Men of such Solomon-like qualities are rare, and the balancing act may not succeed. By the time a family acknowledges the crisis and puts a nonrelative in power, it may be too late; the firm may already have been mortally wounded in the family battles.

Toughness of mind is required in evaluating the place of the incompetent relative. If he must be taken care of within the firm, he should be put where he can be used to best advantage or can cause the least damage. He cannot be allowed to push his weight around with other employees or affect significant decisions. If these conditions are met, he may even develop into a useful employee. A firm needs many kinds of people and can accommodate almost any kind as long as it is not excessively burdened in the process.

Planned nepotism is a delicate and happy compromise to the problem of keeping family control while strengthening managerial competence. Assuming that family members will have a basic loyalty to and pride in the family enterprise, two generations of family members can jointly structure gradually increasing responsibility, decision making, and remuneration for the younger members. Planned nepotism requires planned retirement or loosening of the control mechanism to avoid a generation clash.

If younger family members are to be tested and rewarded while older members are available to counsel and evaluate them, there must be an open, preferably written definition of successful performance and a reasonable timetable for achieving it. The informality and emotional relationships between family members in business together make planned nepotism rare, but it is effective when tried.

Family members usually stay with the firm for their full working life. One consequence of this low family member turnover is that competent employees see little chance to move up in management or acquire an equity ownership position, and they do not stay long.

One way to overcome the stultifying effect of nepotism is to call in an independent consultant who is respected by all family managers. As second- and third-generation ownership dilutes control, family members may want substantially different things from the business. Older, inactive shareholders want steady income; younger members of the family want leverage and are willing to take risks to get it. If the board of directors cannot agree on fundamental policies, and if its decisions are often complicated by family disagreements and questions of status, the firm would probably do well to turn to an outsider who understands both the income needs of one group and the growth desires of the other. Admittedly, this is a poor solution, but it may be the only one available. When the board becomes divided into opposing camps, neither side is likely to yield to the arguments of the other. And, when a policy is finally chosen, whoever implements it has to contend with a group of disappointed family members. The independent consultant is an alternative to inaction or conflict which could otherwise threaten corporate survival.

ONE-MAN RULE

A more insidious problem is the gradual closing of mental doors that is inevitable as the same faces appear around the management table year after year and no new ones are brought in. The condition can be called ownership elitism; it arises when an owner-manager's philosophy is: "I own the company; I run it and I know what's best for it." Ideas originating outside the ownership circle in such a firm are of little or no interest, particularly when they come from employees who are not part of the family.

EXAMPLE:

A manufacturer developed a mobile repair shop which proved so useful that it was sold widely during World War II. After the war, sales were limited to oil exploration companies and a few worldwide construction firms. The second in command had no stock in the company and therefore no clout; he was turned down when he suggested that the firm exploit its excellent reputation and accept subcontract work from the many companies whose employees remembered the mobile shops from wartime and had learned to respect their design and quality. The president considered it his company's mission to make only what he designed, and he refused to consider subcontract work. Instead, he tinkered in his shop and waited for an inspiration. But inspiration eluded him, and the company failed. The lesson? Every organization must be open to ideas from all sources and must be run so that its survival is not endangered through elitism.

Following are some suggestions that have proved successful in overcoming the problems of one-man administrative rule and the difficulties in persuading an owner-manager to change.

1. Someone who has influence with the manager—his lawyer, accountant, friend, wife, long-time employee, or advisory committee member—should tell him that he is wasting his time on petty decisions. He should be advised to free himself for the few key decisions which require large blocks of time and have the greatest impact. Further, letting his subordinates make minor decisions will build their skill and confidence and test their judgment while he is still around to see that they make only limited errors.

2. He should be encouraged to take long vacations, or to begin

taking vacations if he has never permitted the business to run without him, and leave specific parameters for subordinate decision making. When he finds that the business has not collapsed in his absence he will begin to develop some trust in his subordinates. Further, there will usually be some unanticipated problem to test subordinates' ingenuity.

3. If illness were to keep the one-man manager away from his desk and phone, who would fill the management vacuum? Such a question is likely to be disconcerting enough to make the manager go along with the suggestion that he develop a plan indicating who is to do what and how regular transactions are to be handled in his absence. If he procrastinates about preparing written directives, perhaps he can be cajoled into recording what he does and why, so that when he is not there the organization will be run as he wants it run. This is an effective technique since almost all one-man managers share a sense of mortality.

PUTTING COMPANY INTERESTS FIRST

We have emphasized that the small business should be managed in such a way that its own needs come before the personal or family interests of the owner-manager. When faced with the issue, many small firm managers reply along these lines: "Why not run the company to serve my interests? If I don't want to perpetuate the business beyond leaving it to my children, and if I don't want it to grow bigger for the sake of bigness, why should I take steps to put the company first or to make it grow? Such a course would cramp my style, cut into the salaries and expenses for my family and myself, and change the informal decision making that has worked for us and that we feel comfortable with. The business supports us and our employees, the work gives us personal satisfaction, and we're obviously providing a service the world wants or we couldn't stay in business. What more should we want? Besides, is there really a difference between running the business for our sake as stockholder-managers and managing it for its own sake?"

We think there is a real difference, and managing the business objectively will benefit the family's interest, not harm it.

The limitations of putting owners' interests before those of the company are simply stated: Short-term considerations begin to take priority; the firm's ability to react and plan is reduced; unilateral decision making and a closed door to the executive suite discourage the interest and commitment of nonfamily members; secrecy and fear of disclosure go hand in hand with disproportionate salaries and expenses and other questionable accounting practices; and dependence on the family for new blood and management succession may not only restrict the business but be unfair to family members who do not want the responsibility or are not up to it. Of course, succession is of decreasing significance as more sons adopt the philosophy of doing their own thing and fewer feel an obligation to follow their fathers into the family business.

Unless there is concern for the business, even the selfish interests that the family has sought to protect will ultimately suffer. Who will provide for the continuity of the business and supply cash for the family to live on when the owner-manager dies or is told by his doctor that he has to retire? How will the family maintain its status if changes in society, customer needs, or competition are not recognized in time? What happens to family security and satisfaction when arbitrary, uninformed decision making leads the company into loss activities or even bankruptcy?

These are not wild fantasies. Each situation has occurred because personal or family considerations were put above those of the business. The 42-year-old younger brother in a $2 million a year manufacturing company summarized the problem clearly: "When my older brother retires or dies, I don't want the responsibility of taking care of his family and of our three sisters, who don't work in the business but depend on it for their livelihood. None of our kids is interested and we have no managers in the company aside from my brother and me. It's also harder getting business; the old techniques don't seem to work as well. All these years we've run the firm for our own personal needs. Now what do we do?"

In this case, as in most others, it was not too late. Organizations have the capacity for self-renewal provided that the people responsible for them accept the condition as worthy of attention and are willing to change their priorities, their behavior, and perhaps their status and function. There is value in the respectful objective treatment of the firm. In the long run, and perhaps in the short run, this approach serves stockholder interests as well as the interests of the business.

ATTITUDE SURVEY

1. How do you feel when you tell people what firm you work for?
(1) Proud _____ (2) Good _____ (3) Just a place to work _____

2. Do you think the firm offers you the chance to have the kind of job that you will want five years from now?
(1) Yes _____ (2) No _____ (3) Not sure _____

3. To what extent are you made to feel that you are really a part of the firm?
(1) Not at all _____ (2) To a small degree _____ (3) To a large degree _____ (4) In every possible way _____

4. Do you feel that favoritism (e.g., in making assignments, giving promotions) is shown in the firm?
(1) None _____ (2) Very little _____ (3) Some _____ (4) Much _____

5. To what extent do you understand just what work you are supposed to do and what your duties are?
(1) Very poor understanding _____ (2) Fairly good understanding _____ (3) Clear understanding _____

6. Are the performance reviews of your work adequate and helpful?
(1) Always _____ (2) Usually _____ (3) Seldom _____

7. How do you feel about the closeness of supervision of your work?
(1) Generally too close _____ (2) Sometimes too close _____ (3) About right _____ (4) Sometimes not close enough _____ (5) Generally not close enough _____

8. Do your supervisors on the job set a good example in their own work habits?
(1) All of them do _____ (2) Most of them do _____ (3) Some of them do _____ (4) None of them do _____

9. When you want information or help on a difficult problem, how likely are you to get the help you need? I get
(1) very little help _____ (2) fairly good help _____ (3) all the help I need _____

10. When changes are made in the work you have done, how often are you told the reason for the change?
(1) Rarely _____ (2) Sometimes _____ (3) Usually _____ (4) Always _____

11. When you are corrected or when your work is being criticized, how often is this done in a way helpful to you?
(1) Sometimes _____ (2) Usually _____ (3) Always _____

12. Do you find the work assigned to you challenging and interesting?
(1) Sometimes _____ (2) Usually _____ (3) Always _____

13. Are you encouraged to offer ideas and suggestions for new or better ways of doing things?
(1) All the time _____ (2) Often _____ (3) Sometimes _____ (4) Rarely _____ (5) Not at all _____

14. What progress have you made with the firm?
(1) Excellent progress _____ (2) Satisfactory progress _____ (3) Some progress _____ (4) Little progress _____ (5) No progress _____

15. In general, how well do you like your present position?
(1) I like it very much _____ (2) I am satisfied with it _____ (3) I neither like nor dislike it _____ (4) I dislike it _____

16. How do you believe you are compensated relative to your worth to the firm?
(1) Very fairly _____ (2) Adequately _____ (3) Unfairly _____

17. How do you believe you are compensated relative to others in the firm?
(1) Very fairly _____ (2) Adequately _____ (3) Unfairly _____

18. In general, how do you feel about the workload expected of you by the firm?
(1) I should like to have more work to do _____
(2) The amount of work expected is reasonable _____
(3) The amount of work expected is somewhat too great _____
(4) The amount of work expected is unreasonable _____

19. How do you feel about the appearance of the firm's office?
(1) Proud _____ (2) Satisfied _____ (3) Neutral _____ (4) Somewhat dissatisfied _____ (5) Embarrassed _____

20. How do you rate the firm's policies on vacation, holidays, and other payments for time not worked?
(1) Excellent _____ (2) Good _____ (3) Fair _____ (4) Poor _____

21. How do you rate the firm's policies on group medical insurance, life insurance, and similar benefits?
(1) Excellent _____ (2) Good _____ (3) Fair _____ (4) Poor _____

22. Do you think your personal problems will be given adequate attention if you bring them to the firm's attention?
(1) Substantial attention _____ (2) Some attention _____ (3) Not much attention _____

23. Do you think there is sufficient opportunity for advancement in the firm?

(1) Much opportunity _____ (2) Some opportunity _____ (3) Little opportunity _____ (4) No opportunity

24. When you were interviewed for employment, did the people who talked with you about the firm and the opportunities within it describe them fairly and honestly?
(1) Not as good as described _____
(2) Fairly and honestly described _____
(3) Somewhat better than described _____
(4) Much better than described _____

25. When you are given new duties and responsibilities, how well are they explained?
(1) Well explained _____ (2) Adequately explained _____ (3) Partially explained _____ (4) Not satisfactorily explained _____

26. How do you feel about the firm's training program?
(1) Highly beneficial _____ (2) Of considerable value _____ (3) Of some value _____ (4) Of little value _____ (5) There is no program _____

27. When you started to work for the firm, did you get enough training and help to learn the work properly and quickly?
(1) More than I needed _____ (2) All I needed _____ (3) Almost all I needed _____ (4) Less than I needed _____ (5) Very little _____

28. Does the firm keep you informed about its activities and plans?
(1) Always _____ (2) Usually _____ (3) Sometimes _____ (4) Seldom _____ (5) Never _____

29. When you were hired, how well were the firm's professional and personnel policies explained to you?
(1) Very well _____ (2) Adequately _____ (3) Not altogether adequately _____ (4) Inadequately _____

30. How would you rate the value to society of your work?
(1) Of great value _____ (2) Of some value _____ (3) Of little value _____

31. How do you feel when you tell people what profession or business you are working in?
(1) Proud _____ (2) Good _____ (3) So-so _____

32. Considering the opportunities which were available to you, do you now feel that you chose the right career?
(1) I prefer this career to any other _____
(2) I like this career better than most others _____
(3) I sometimes wish I had chosen some other career _____
(4) I definitely wish I had chosen some other career _____

33. If you were to start again, do you feel you would go to work with our firm?
    (1) Yes _____ (2) No _____ (3) Don't know _____

34. What do you think of this opinion poll?
    (1) I like it _____ (2) Probably all right _____ (3) I don't like it _____

35. Please tell us any ways in which we can improve the firm.

PERSONAL AND BUSINESS ASPECTS OF STOCKHOLDER AGREEMENTS

Martin J. Milston and Theodore Cohn

How would you handle the following situation?

After 20 years of working together in a contracting business in which they had succeeded their fathers, two cousins found that their long-range life aims differed. One, a bachelor, wanted to leave the business within two years and devote himself to his hobby, the restoration of antique cars—a hobby which had some commercial possibilities. The other, along with an unrelated executive who had a small interest in the company, wanted to expand the business.

The relations among all the parties were warm, friendly, and sympathetic. Problems posed:

- How should the bachelor cousin's shareholding be disposed of?
- What should be the price, terms, limitations on future activities of the departing stockholder?
- What should happen to the shares in the company held by the withdrawing stockholder's old, sick father?

The answers to these questions were highly individual and involved a knowledge of the personal needs of the principals and the business considerations of the firm. Only with such knowledge could a viable stockholders' agreement be worked out with counsel. . . .

Stockholders' agreements generally include the following provisions:

1. A definite price or some kind of formula to establish price
2. A method of pay-out including terms and interest rate on the outstanding balance
3. Limitations on lifetime disposition of the stock
4. A determination of the disposition of the decedent shareholder's shares
5. Funding stock purchase through insurance or other means

6. Salary continuation and severance terms for a disabled stockholder/ officer

7. The machinery for settlement in the event of dispute.

Separation of stockholder interest during lifetime because of retirement, disagreement, or change in personal status requires that the same basic terms be covered.

The best time for the CPA to suggest an agreement is when all the parties are talking to each other. The stockholders may find it hard to see the need when everyone is healthy and on good terms, but this is the time to urge that an agreement be drafted.

PRICE

In the family-held corporation or those with a limited number of stockholders, the price at which shares should be redeemed at death or during lifetime is crucial. Several basic methods have been used.

1. Annually, the stockholders agree on a certificate of value for their shares. In some cases where the business is highly volatile, this valuation can be made quarterly. Provision should also be made that, in the event the shareholders fail to agree for any reason on an annual or quarterly valuation, a formula adjustment can apply. The formulas listed below are useful in this regard:

(a) The previously agreed-upon valuation will be adjusted by increase or decrease in book value from the date of the last agreed-upon valuation. Assume that book value was $400,000, agreed valuation was $500,000 on December 31, 1965, but no adjustment had been made for the agreed valuation in the forthcoming year. The book value, however, has gone from $400,000 to $600,000 on December 31, 1966. In this situation the shareholders' valuation would be $700,000.

(b) Submit an unagreed-upon valuation to arbitration. This method is not recommended because of additional problems created by an imposed value which satisfies no one.

(c) Disregard the certificate entirely and use a formula based upon book value, earnings, or a combination of both.

2. The book value method is most applicable where the assets of the corporation rather than the individual abilities of management are the prime source of revenues. In using book value, in the absence of special considerations, the time for valuation for death purposes should be prior to the date of death so that the face values of any insurance are omitted from the valuation.

The weakness of the method is its disregard for earnings. In the early years of a new business, however, book value is often the only valid valuation, as a new company has no reliable history of earnings. Book value should be defined and questions such as subsidiaries' equities and intangibles should be clarified to the satisfaction of all parties involved.

3. Valuations of business in mergers and acquisitions are generally based on earnings as the major factor. In stockholder agreements where earnings are the truest measure of a company's worth, an earnings formula is often the fairest method of valuation.

The problem, of course, is what formula to use. If trade association or industry statistics are available, they may offer a guideline. The individual company's earnings must be adjusted for excess salaries, expenses, liberal profit sharing, pension plans, etc. In our experience, a multiplier of 5 to 15 times the average of the last three to five years' earnings is fair. The choice of the multiplier should include consideration for the price-earnings ratio on publicly held companies in the same industry, the history of earnings, and the significance of assets as compared to individual management in the contribution to profits.

We must consider the effect of the death or retirement of a major income producer in deciding on the multiplier. Further, greater consideration should be given to the more recent years in determining the average earnings in an expanding business. If we are using the three years' average, the most recent year's earnings might be multiplied by three, the prior year's earnings by two, and the year before that by one (see Example 1).

EXAMPLE 1

Year	Net Income	Multiplying Factor	
1	$150	1	$ 150
2	300	2	600
3 (most recent year)	350	3	1,050
Totals		6	$1,800
Divided by 6 =			$ 300 (weighted average)

The average earnings would then be multiplied by whatever the shareholders' agreement calls for. Thus, if the multiplier were ten, the net worth for shareholders' agreement purposes would be $3,000.

4. In our firm, we have successfully used a formula which takes both book value and an earnings multiplier into consideration. One-third of the total valuation is attributed to book value and two-thirds is computed through an earnings formula (see Example 2). The minimum, however, should not be less than book value.

5. Real estate and investment companies are more properly valued on the basis of current independent market appraisals. Some real estate companies obtain independent appraisals periodically (e.g., every three years) and provide for depreciation adjustments based on the most recent appraisal to date of sale or death.

6. A practical price in small companies may be the maximum insurance

EXAMPLE 2

Book value at valuation date	$2,400	
⅓ used		$ 800
Earnings valuation—		
10 (agreed-upon multiplier) times		
weighted average earnings of $300	3,000	
⅔ used		2,000
Total		$2,800

the stockholders want to leave their families, balanced against the amount the firm can afford to pay in premiums.

7. We have seen agreements which provide for a redemption price at death which differs (generally higher) from that used in lifetime. The reasons for a difference are: an agreement to penalize lifetime redemption and the absence of insurance proceeds.

TERMS

Our firm was called in to solve a problem for a business in whose shareholders' agreement we had not participated. This client had an agreement in which the widow was to be paid the book value of the company. The agreement was specific as to price. Unfortunately, no provision had been made for the term of payment so that a few days after the funeral the widow went to the remaining stockholder with whom her deceased husband had been in business for 40 years and asked him for the $500,000 due the estate. Negotiations which severely tested personal relations were required to permit the company to pay out the $500,000 over several years.

The pay-out terms should be based upon ability to pay, taking into consideration the effect on earnings of the death or retirement of the departing stockholder and on credit standing with banks and other lending institutions.

If an older person leaves the business, it is conceivable that his salary can be the basis of the annual pay-out to his estate or to himself if he retires.

If the salary does not bear a relationship to the value of the shareholder's interest, the earnings of the company will then have to be the basis of the annual pay-out. Our firm has successfully recommended use of the greater of a percentage of the net income after taxes and a fixed minimum. Protection for the departing stockholder usually includes some limitation on salaries, dividends, and disposition of assets. This is the province of the attorney.

When shareholders are insurable, it is generally advantageous for the company to take out coverage in order to insure the down payment or, if possible, the total amount required for a pay-out. Cash values of insurance policies are not as useful for this specific purpose as either term policies renewable to an advanced age or minimum deposit policies, even with their tax limitations.

If insurance is too expensive or cannot be obtained and a total buy-out over a period of years is uneconomical, it may be necessary to have the shares *not* wholly repurchased but to leave some in the hands of the deceased stockholder's estate, probably as preferred stock.

OPTIONS

When a minority stockholder invests in a business or when a company is organized with no one stockholder owning more than 50 per cent of the voting shares, a situation of possible inequity exists.

We have generally recommended that a minority stockholder be given an option to sell his shares to the company or to the other stockholders when he wishes to sell, under the following terms.

If he offers the shares, the company must agree to accept them or liquidate within a certain period (such as six months). The purpose of the alternative is to prevent one minority shareholder from taking advantage of first knowledge of a change in business fortune (such as loss of a major customer or a fire) and, through his offer to sell, get an unfair edge on the other shareholders. The price and the terms must be set in advance through one of the methods described above. This type of option which permits a minority stockholder to sell out is not only fair but it may eliminate some of the many problems that minority stockholders create in a company. One common limitation on the offer is to prohibit it in the early formative years of a new corporation when all the capital is required for operations.

There may be a situation in which a shareholder offers his stock to the corporation for redemption and the price (either certificate or formula) is in excess of the liquidating value. The remaining shareholder(s) may decide that it is cheaper to liquidate the company (and continue its operations subsequent to liquidation) than to buy out the stockholder who took the initiative in offering his shares. This liquidation would obviate the intent of the agreement. We have seen recommendations that in such a case the shareholder(s) who choose to liquidate the corporation may not go into the same business for a period of at least six months.

Some agreements require that the corporation or stockholders be given the right of first refusal to match a bona fide offer from an outsider to purchase any stockholder's shares.

DISABILITY

If a stockholder employee becomes disabled, a human problem arises concerning the continuation of his salary, the assumption of his responsibilities by other employees, and the disposition of his shares. We have suggested that the company continue to pay an officer/stockholder's salary in full for six months and at the rate of one-half his annual salary for an additional six months. The payment may be reduced by the disability proceeds received from disability policies whose premiums were paid by the employer.

If at the end of the year an independent medical opinion is obtained suggesting that the employee is unable to return to work, we recommend that his shares then must be offered and the company must buy them at the agreed-upon price and terms.

One technique that can be used in a disability buy-out where a company is unable to finance a complete purchase is a recapitalization into common and dividend-paying preferred shares, followed by a redemption of the disabled shareholder's common as quickly as possible. Upon the death of the disabled shareholder, proceeds from insurance (obviously taken out before disability) would be used to redeem the preferred stock.

This program has the advantages of limiting or eliminating the disabled stockholder's participation in future earnings while providing him a return on his continuing investment in the company.

POST-REDEMPTION EVENTS, EMPLOYMENT

Since it is difficult to determine the price at which shares should be redeemed, regardless of the validity of formulas, post-redemption events may be used to adjust the redemption price. Objectively, if a business is sold to a complete stranger or if a merger is accomplished in a true arm's-length arrangement, the fair market value of the company is most accurately established.

Thus, the agreement might provide that, in the event a sale of the business is made within one or two years from the date that the shares of one of the stockholders are redeemed, a price adjustment be made to give effect to the sale when the price exceeds the value at which the redemption took place. In most cases, adjustment would not be made in the event the selling price of the business is lower, since that would be the responsibility of the remaining stockholders. The operative period of a post-redemption clause is substantially related to the type of business, and the participation of the ex-stockholder should be reduced as time passes. Perhaps as a rule of thumb we may say that the greater the proportion of fixed assets, the longer the period should be.

It is common to include basic employment terms in a shareholders' agreement in which the shareholders are all employees of the corporation. Provisions concerning salaries, vacations, and a covenant not to compete upon termination are usual. Limits on offers, pledges, and disposition of the stock are not included in this article as they are fairly standard and are the province of attorneys.

A RESOLUTION

How was the situation described at the beginning of this article finally resolved? Following are the major points which were included in the agreement.

1. The trade association of the industry in which the client operated published annual statistics on return on net worth. The formula to determine price was to apply the industry's average rate of return on net worth for the last three years to the company's average net worth; the average excess earnings, if any, were to be multiplied by six and added to the book value. This formula seemed fair as it gave positive but limited credit for excess earnings.

2. Pay-out was to be the greater of 20% of the price or 25% of the net income with interest at 4% on the unpaid balance. The five-year term was chosen, as a shorter period would have seriously affected the company's credit standing and a longer period seemed unfair to the departing or deceased shareholder.

3. Disposition of the stock during life was limited to the corporation and other shareholders.

4. A decedent's shares had to be willed to a male family member active in the business or be offered to the corporation within six months after death.

5. Funds for repurchase were not provided, as the period of the pay-out made the annual payments feasible.

6. Disability provisions were the same as those mentioned above.

7. The shares of the withdrawing stockholder's father were to be purchased by the corporation at the older man's death, with payment for these shares to the departing son (the designated heir) to start after the son's own shares had been paid for. There was no assessment for prepayment penalties.

8. Finally, a withdrawing shareholder was prevented from working in the same industry within a radius of 50 miles of the corporate office for two years.

The reader will probably see other solutions, even with the limited data provided. The one described grew out of a series of compromises by all parties to the final agreement.

INDEX